WHEN CHOICE BECOMES GOD

F. LaGARD SMITH

HARVEST HOUSE PUBLISHERS
Eugene, Oregon 97402

WHEN CHOICE BECOMES GOD

Copyright © 1990 by Harvest House Publishers
Eugene, Oregon 97402

Library of Congress Cataloging-in-Publication Data

Smith, F. LaGard (Frank LaGard), 1944-
    When choice becomes God / LaGard Smith.
    ISBN 0-89081-828-2
        1. Pro-choice movement—United States.   2. Abortion—Religious
    aspects.   I. Title.
HQ767.5.u5s732   1990
363.4'6'0973—dc20   90-35979
                                                                            CIP

Printed in the United States of America.

To my nieces and nephews
who as part of a pro-choice generation
face an increasingly complex moral world.

With Appreciation

Catherine Françoise McCarney, for her knowledge, insight, encouragement, and commitment to the cause.

James M. McGoldrick, Jr., and Robert F. Cochran, Jr., for their scholarly acumen and collegial advice.

Dorothy Patterson, Mark Lanier, Trish Bigelow, Bill Henegar, Dawn Solheim, and Daniel Martin for their valuable contributions to research and editing.

Woody Allen, for Crimes and Misdemeanors *and his generous permission for use of the script.*

Mead Data Corporation, for its research assistance through LEXIS/ NEXIS data retrieval.

CONTENTS

Part One
THE PRO-CHOICE GENERATION

1. Choosing The Unthinkable 9
2. The Birth Of A Pro-Choice Generation 21
3. Any Choice But God 39
4. Separating Church And Choice 49
5. Through The Eyes Of Radical Feminists 67
6. Whales, Furs And Human Life 81
7. Creation, Evolution And The Right To Choose 95

Part Two
THE BATTLE OVER ABORTION

8. If Wombs Had Windows 111
9. Phantom Choices 133
10. Defective Babies, Defective Choices 147
11. Choice On A Slippery Slope 163
12. Hard Cases And Easy Outs 181
13. The Hypocrisy Of Choice 197
14. Sacrificing Life For Lifestyle 219

Part Three
RESOLVING OUR NATIONAL DILEMMA

15. Deciding Who Decides 233
16. The Way Forward 247
    Epilogue
    Notes

PART 1

The Pro-Choice Generation

ONE

Choosing The Unthinkable

We are all faced throughout our lives with agonizing decisions—moral choices. Some are on a grand scale; most of these choices are on lesser points. But we define ourselves by the choices we have made. We are, in fact, the sum total of our choices.

—Professor Louis Levy in
Crimes and Misdemeanors

"**N**OW WE ARE ENGAGED IN A GREAT CIVIL WAR, testing whether that nation, or any nation, so conceived and so dedicated, can long endure. We are met on a great battlefield of that war." With those words Abraham Lincoln not only dedicated the cemetery at Gettysburg, but captured the nobility of the great national struggle over slavery which threatened to divide the nation. Never in the intervening century have we faced so grave a moral crisis as the one about which we in our generation have become deeply divided: the battle over abortion.

Yet our current civil war is not specifically about abortion—at least not in the long run. Certainly, as at Gettysburg, there are countless victims who, though unseen, hallow the ground upon which we tread. But on a broader canvas the issue of abortion is, like Gettysburg, merely a great battlefield in a larger struggle. The real battle is about *the right to choose*, and whether there *is* such a right.

9

Ours is a pro-choice generation. In just one generation America has radically changed the way it thinks. In just one generation we have moved from intolerance of homosexuality to giving special recognition to "gay rights"; from the social stigma of divorce to recognizing broken marriages as being a permanent fixture in society; from censorship of suggestive movie ads to slick pornography on the front shelves at the local convenience store; from hush-hush back-alley abortions to widely accepted legal abortions.

> *&* **All choices are now thought to possess equal value or at least to merit equal recognition under the canopy of being socially acceptable "alternative lifestyles."**

And at the core of the revolution is *choice:* The right for us to decide for ourselves, and the right of others to decide for themselves. Being nonjudgmental about others seems to be our only guarantee of their being nonjudgmental about us. In order to maintain our own right of choice, we have become willing to honor all the choices of others. Hence the language of a pro-choice generation:

"I am not a homosexual, and would hope that my children were not, but if a person happens to be gay, it's none of my business."

"I don't believe in divorce for myself, but if two people can't get along with each other, who am I to say that they must keep living together?"

"Let's legalize drugs and stop all the violence. After all, if a person can choose whether or not to drink alcohol, why can't he choose to use drugs?"

"As long as it doesn't harm anyone else, a person can live and act any way he or she wants. To each his own."

But the pro-choice language of the 60's, 70's, and 80's is only a whimper compared with the roar of the crowd in the 1990's.

Today the language of pro-choice is the battle cry in an escalating civil war over abortion: "I personally do not believe in abortion," say most Americans, "but a woman ought to have the right to decide for herself whether to terminate a pregnancy."

With the widespread acceptance of this popular sentiment in support of abortion choices, personal moral choice in virtually every area of human concern is poised to replace the social norms previously invoked by a broader moral consensus. All choices are now thought to possess equal value or at least to merit equal recognition under the canopy of being socially acceptable "alternative lifestyles."

Ours is not only a pro-choice generation but a *tolerant* generation. As long as it's "live and let live," we thrive on pluralism—with the idea that you scratch my moral back and I'll scratch yours. The scriptural injunction "Judge not lest you also be judged" has been twisted to become the latest Constitutional precept, couched in the all-American language of "right to privacy."

The "right to privacy" now covers a multitude of acts which in past generations would have been unthinkable. As for the acts themselves, that which 50 years ago would have been denounced from the nation's pulpits—including divorce, homosexuality, and abortion—has become today, in the words of many church leaders, "the loving thing to do." With even the liberal church on the side of choice, that which 50 years ago would have been "gross immorality" has gradually won both judicial and legislative backing. It's official now: Choice has both the imprimatur of the upmarket church and the credibility of legal sanction.

Of Crimes and Misdemeanors

Considering the revolutionary phenomenon of our pro-choice generation, Woody Allen ought to be given a special Oscar for the most thought-provoking film of the year. His *Crimes and Misdemeanors* is vintage "Woody"—filled with all the New York Jewish angst and edged humor we've come to expect. But *Crimes and Misdemeanors* moves one step beyond. Its story of a successful family man deciding to kill his mistress raises crucial moral questions which, if we let them, manage to work their way into the backroads of our own consciences. All the right questions are raised for a pro-choice generation.

On what basis, for example, do we make the moral choices with which we are faced each day? Do we take into consideration the interests of other people, or do we make our decisions with an eye toward satisfying only our own self-interests? Woody's central character—a successful, well-respected ophthalmologist named Judah Rosenthal—appears to make his decisions solely out of self-satisfaction (in first having an extramarital affair), then self-protection (when he pays to have his mistress killed).

His justification for eventually taking his lover's life is that she is ruining his life by interfering with his marriage and career. He shows little concern for how he has managed to interfere with *her* life by toying with her feelings over a two-year period of clandestine lovemaking laced with hints about a possible future marriage.

We get a good picture of his selfish motivations when Judah confronts Dolores, his mistress, about her letter to Judah's wife (a letter which he intercepts) that exposes their affair. "Do you wanna destroy my life... and my family?" Judah demands angrily. Put heavy emphasis here on the words *"my life."* Despite his gratuitous reference to *"my family,"* you can bet that his own welfare is his only real interest. Having allowed himself to become involved with another woman, it is obvious that Judah has shown little previous regard for either his wife or his family.

Interesting, isn't it, how we manage to exploit the interests of others when we wish to justify cleaning up the messes we ourselves have gotten them into by our own poor choices? "The children will be hurt if we keep on living together with this tension between us," says the husband in attempting to explain his decision to divorce his wife. "I can't possibly have this child since I'm not in any position to give it a good life," says the teenage girl upon learning that she is pregnant. How much easier our own choices become if we can convince ourselves that they are in the best interests of others, even if those other people end up being victims of these very choices!

Amazing, too, the ease with which we see how other people are ruining *our* lives but rarely have a clue as to how badly we

ruin *their* lives. Judah says to Dolores, for example, "Think . . .
think what you're doing to me, will you? Please!" However,
Judah doesn't stop to consider what it would be like with the
tables turned. For instance, what might we expect Dolores to say
to *him* if she knew he had paid someone to kill her! "Whose life is
being ruined at *that* point?" we would rightfully ask.

Like Judah, we often justify our own wrong choices by
pointing a finger of guilt at the wrong choices of other people—
even in the face of clear moral strictures against what we are
about to do to them. This happens to Judah when he is confronted by his friend Ben, a rabbi, in an imagined conversation.
When Ben reminds him that "without the law, it's all darkness,"
Judah shoots back with impatience, "What good is the law if it
prevents me from receiving justice? Is what she's doing to me
just? Is this what I deserve?"

The self-justifying question "Is this what I deserve?" has
been the driving force behind *many* "crimes and misdemeanors."
Once we convince ourselves that we have been wronged
unfairly, then we can justify almost anything which seems to
put the situation right. After all, we are simply doing whatever
it takes to bring about *justice* where an *injustice* threatens to ruin
our life.

How often we tolerate in ourselves moral "indiscretions"
which, if done by other people, would be anything but mere
indiscretions in our book. When Judah tries to explain to his
brother Jack why Dolores' threat to take him away from his wife
is so devastating, he fudges ever so conveniently in referring to
his own *slight* moral deviations: "Add to that her blabbing about
my financial indiscretions. Not that I stole, but I was indiscreet,
and if they look hard enough, who knows what they'll find?"

Do we not all make moral choices with a blind eye to the
mirror? Do we not all place our decisions in the light most
favorable to ourselves—even if we may be dead wrong? Juggling
funds between money raised for charity and money for his own
personal bank account—a crime by any name—is minimized by
a simple change in terminology: Embezzlement becomes "financial indiscretions," and clearly illegal action is sloughed off as
merely being "indiscreet."

Do we find ourselves playing the same game with terminology about choice? Is it easier to go through with a divorce when
we think of it as "going our separate ways"? Or to be "gay"

rather than homosexual? Or to "terminate a pregnancy" rather than to have an abortion?

Implications for Pro-Choice

Perhaps the lesson here is that we are not always the best judges of the choices we ourselves make. Perhaps being pro-choice puts us at a disadvantage by allowing us the freedom to mask even from ourselves the seriousness of what we are doing, and also to become lesser people than we really want to be. When Judah envisions what Ben would say to him if he knew it was murder he was contemplating, Judah hears Ben asking: "Is that who you really are?" Unfortunately, Judah's short-term *self-interest* outweighs the validation of his longer-term *self-image*, and Ben's question is ignored altogether—until it's too late.

In the big picture, many of our choices are relatively inconsequential, like deciding what we will eat for breakfast. Other choices are monumental, like deciding who we will marry, or whether to get a divorce. Beyond those decisions are choices which usher us to the very threshold of the meaning of life. Sometimes we refer to these as "matters of life and death."

Premeditated murder, as committed by Judah Rosenthal, is one such choice, dealing as it does with the most fundamental of all human rights—the right to life. Abortion is another such choice, because, in the eyes of those who oppose it, we are still dealing with the most fundamental of all human rights—the right to life.

It hardly matters that those who favor abortion (or who are pro-choice, if not actually pro-abortion) do not believe that human life is being taken. As long as pro-life advocates are convinced that innocent human life is at stake, they have no choice but to defend the rights of the unborn. The debate must therefore continue beyond the issue of "choice" until the larger "life and death" issues are resolved.

By its very nature, abortion is a life-and-death issue of consequence that forces us to grapple with all the ultimate questions: Who are we? Why do we exist? At what point do we become a person? What happens to us when we die? What is the source of our human rights? What is the source of our "right to choose"? The "single issue" of abortion is in reality a *cluster* of crucial issues.

As Ben told Judah: "We went from a small infidelity to the meaning of existence." Likewise, in discussing issues such as abortion, we are drawn from relatively "small questions of morality" to the entire compass of human experience. In this regard there is much to be learned from the unusual insight in Judah's response to Ben: "Miriam won't think two years of scheming and dishonesty is a small infidelity." That is true, of course, anytime we attempt to minimize what we have done by shifting the focus elsewhere.

We kid ourselves, for instance, if we think we can reduce current moral issues to the relative simplicity of power politics, Supreme Court decisions, or legislative battles in state capitols. Nor, especially, can the issue of abortion easily be dismissed by bumper stickers or protest placards.

It's all the more reason why Woody Allen deserves a special Oscar for *Crimes and Misdemeanors*. Certainly no movie—no matter how searching in its scope—can provide us with all the answers to such challenging questions. The balance of this book, drawing as it does from a wide range of contemporary and intellectual sources, will demonstrate that resolution of the issues before us is hardly as simplistic as a cleverly crafted piece of Hollywood entertainment. However, in one insightful film, Allen has managed to capture the very essence of moral choice—whatever the issue. Note, for instance, the following conversation between Judah and his brother, when Jack first suggests that Judah pay a "hit man" to kill Dolores.

If we read the dialogue with other moral choices in mind (divorce and abortion, to name just two), we are led into many of the mental gymnastics and rationalizations in which we tend to indulge before making those drastically poor choices we sometimes make:

> Judah: I'm fighting for my life. This woman's gonna destroy everything I've built.
>
> Jack: That's what I'm saying, Judah. If the woman won't listen to reason, then you go on to the next step.
>
> Judah: What? Threats? Violence? What are we talking about here?
>
> Jack: She can be gotten rid of. I mean, I know a lot of people. Money'll buy whatever's necessary.

Judah: I'm not even gonna comment on that. That's mind-boggling. . . . Am I understanding you right? I mean . . . are you suggesting getting rid of her?

Jack: You won't be involved . . . but I'll need some cash.

Judah: What will they do?

Jack: What'll they do? They'll handle it.

Judah: I can't believe I'm talking about a human being. Jack, she's not an . . . an insect. You don't just step on her.

Jack: I know. Playing hardball was never your game. You never liked to get your hands dirty. But apparently this woman is for real . . . and this thing isn't just gonna go away.

Judah: I can't do it. I can't think that way.

In the end, of course, he *can* do it. He *can* bring himself to think that way. As do we. That which at first seems unthinkable becomes that which we do. Somehow we do it! Somehow the unthinkable happens, and sometimes with surprising ease.

When the wedding vows are first made, of course, divorce is the last thing on our minds. So with all the talk of love and commitment "in the presence of God and these witnesses," how do we ever get to the point of divorce? And how have we ever gotten to the point where abortion is so easily put on a par with contraception? Are we doing the unthinkable simply by not thinking? Do we rationalize poor choices by refusing to be honest about the bigger issues involved in moral choice?

Pro-Choice Without a Wake-Up Call?

In a vision of conscience which Judah experiences while struggling about whether to have Dolores killed, he imagines Ben reminding him that God sees what he is doing:

Ben: It's a human life. You don't think God sees?

Judah: God is a luxury I can't afford.

Ben: Now you're talking like your brother Jack.

> Judah: Jack lives in the real world. . . . You live in
> the kingdom of heaven. I managed to keep free of
> that real world, but suddenly it's found me.
>
> Ben: You fool around with her for your pleasure
> and then . . . when you think it's enough you wanna
> sweep her under the rug?

Do we likewise want to sweep under the carpet the "bigger" issues which impact the "smaller" issues? Have we too decided that God is a luxury we cannot afford? Judah later discovers that he has to deal with God whether he likes it or not—not in the religious trappings of a synagogue, but in his own conscience. He meets God on territory very close to home—in the recesses of his mind—from which he cannot easily escape. If there are times when that confrontation can be avoided—even long periods of time—the issue is never completely resolved.

In the vision, Ben knows in advance that Judah will not be able to put the decision behind him, as if it were a mistake of judgment in his professional life or a wrong decision about which house or car to purchase. Life-and-death decisions tend to linger for the duration.

> Judah: There's no other solution but Jack's, Ben. I
> push one button and I can sleep again nights.
>
> Ben: Could you sleep with that?
>
> Judah: No—

No, Judah knows he can't sleep with that decision, but he makes the decision anyway! Actually, that is less surprising than we first might think. Moral choice in a pro-choice generation is all about *immediacy*. As the country-western lyrics put it, "I don't care what's right or wrong . . . Let the devil take tomorrow . . . Help me make it through the night." Of course we know we'll have to pay, but right now we've got no other choice—or so it seems. Either way, we'll have to pay, so we choose to pay at a later day. It's a kind of moral credit system: Choose badly now; pay later. Conscience on layaway.

But demand for payment comes sooner rather than later for Judah Rosenthal. When Jack calls to confirm that Dolores has been killed, Judah can no longer avoid the consequences. Nor can he avoid the God in whom he has earlier professed little belief. At this point he faces head-on the guilt that he had hoped to delay:

> Jack: I just wanted you to know everything came out fine. It's over and done with. No problems. So you can forget about it.
>
> Judah: Oh, my God. Oh, my God. I'm in shock, Jack.
>
> Jack: Judah, I'm telling you, it's like the whole thing never existed. It's a small burglary. Nothing more. Yeah. So go on back to your life and, uh, put it behind you.
>
> Judah: God have mercy on us, Jack.

It doesn't matter how Jack tries to reassure Judah that "it's like the whole thing never existed." In his heart Judah knows better. It *did* exist. *She* did exist. A life had been taken, and no one would be able to undo what had been done. There was no way Judah could just "go on back to his life and put it behind him" as if it had never happened.

We're not talking here simply about buyer's remorse after the mortgage is signed, or even second thoughts about getting a divorce. Nothing less than a life-and-death decision was made, and it was made in favor of death. Not just death of a relationship, but death of a human being. Not a human being who was threatening one's physical life, but a human being who was simply interfering with the way someone wanted to live his life.

❧ Without our ever intending it, moral choice has a way of leading us to roads we never expect to take.

As outrageous as he was to make the decision to kill, Judah is not so foolish as to believe there are not moral consequences of the highest order to be faced. When his wife, Miriam, later asks Judah in an unrelated conversation what he thinks about acupuncture, Judah is lost in a world all his own—a world of moral conflict. His answer is nonresponsive to Miriam, but poignantly responsive to his own thoughts: "What do you think, Judah?" asks Miriam. "I think I've done a terrible thing," says Judah. It wasn't a body being pricked by silver needles that Judah was concerned about, but the inescapable, moment-by-moment pricking of his own conscience. But by then it was too late.

For a man with seemingly no moral insight prior to the killing, Judah quickly acquires a depth of perception that few of us carry around with us from day to day. If the lesson had to be learned in the tragic crucible of moral irresponsibility, nevertheless it was a lesson learned well. Musing aloud to his brother Jack, Judah saw the clear progression from "misdemeanors" to "crimes": "One sin leads to a deeper sin . . . adultery, fornication, lies, killing."

At that point, of course, Judah had plenty of company. We all recognize our potential for moral wrong—*progressive* moral wrong. Without our ever intending it, moral choice has a way of leading us to roads we never expect to take. And the roads leading from *bad* moral choices inevitably lead downhill.

In the Big Picture

It would be disquieting enough if our look-the-other-way attitude toward our own moral choices led us to do the unthinkable. However, that same look-the-other-way attitude toward the moral choices of other people has become a social issue of national importance. "Pro-choice"—a phrase now almost exclusively associated with abortion—has far wider ramifications than whether a woman may choose to terminate her pregnancy.

The questions facing a pro-choice generation are staggering: Have we as a nation lost our sense of moral values? If so, how do we regain the high moral ground? If not, how do we propose to reach a moral consensus on abortion or any other social issue having moral implications? And if individual choice is to prevail, what prevents us from slipping into moral anarchy? What point of reference will be left to guarantee basic human rights— even the right of choice itself?

The battlefront is immense and the issues are colossal. For a nation born from the womb of political and religious freedom, perhaps no challenge since the Civil War has threatened graver consequences—not even two world wars and our humiliating defeat in Vietnam. In war, "God is on our side." In the battle for abortion, the struggle is one of allegiance: Which God shall we choose? By whose rules will we play the game of polity? Is God to be our God, or is Choice to be our God? In the very fact that we must make a decision, Choice has a headstart.

Choice is also the odds-on favorite because of the secular nation that America has become. If once we were a nation "under God," we are rapidly becoming a nation "under Self." No prizes for guessing where that leads: Self obviously relates better to Choice than to God.

At first glance God also loses out in a nation obsessed with individual rights. God appears to be more about *responsibilities* than rights, more about *duties* than privileges—not an exciting prospect when we are accustomed to gorging ourselves on a daily diet of unrestrained liberty-cum-license. Only a closer look will reveal that, without God, our freedom and liberty, as well as our rights, are at risk. Are we willing to take that closer look? Are we willing to risk having to acknowledge that there are some choices about which we can have no personal choice?

In the finest sense of the word, this book is pro-choice. It proceeds on the assumption that informed individual choice is necessary to a healthy society. But it also recognizes that being *pro-choice* in the contemporary sense of the term is not always the *right* choice. With some choices, especially those involving innocent human life, there can be no choice, either for ourselves or for others.

TWO

The Birth
Of A Pro-Choice
Generation

*Men no longer are bound together by ideas, but by interests;
and it would seem as if human opinions were reduced to a sort of
intellectual dust, scattered on every side, unable to collect,
unable to cohere.*

—Alexis de Tocqueville

PRO-CHOICE. IT SOUNDS SO AMERICAN. After all,
ours is a generation of choice. In what other time and place
could a person choose between Coke, Diet Coke, Caffeine-Free
Coke, Classic Coke, and Cherry Coke? Or eight varieties of
potato chips in just one store? Or a dozen different brands of
running shoes? Or 27 different makes of automobiles, each with
endless optional extras?

What could be more American than a Friday night with the
kids, deciding whether it's pizza or hamburgers; and, if hamburgers, whether to eat at McDonald's or Burger King; and, if
McDonald's, whether it'll be a Big Mac or a Quarter Pounder;
and "for here or to go?" Then it's which of 14 movies to see at the
local cineplex, and afterward which of the tantalizing 31 flavors
to choose at Baskin-Robbins.

If we decide to stay home for the evening, *choice* is still the
magic word. In the "zap decade," we have *choice* in the palm of
our hands. The exclusive days of ABC, CBS, and NBC are past.

Now we've got 50 channels or more from which to choose. And at the commercial breaks we are also bombarded with choice. "You've Got the Option," touts the Optima Card. "Master the Possibilities," urges MasterCard, using language already familiar to a human-potential generation. And from among the highly competitive phone companies, we are told that AT&T is "The Right Choice."

Today's baby boomers are nothing if not consumers. Consumerism is America's new religion, and advertising provides its totems and icons. From *Choice*, the god of consumerism, comes the First Commandment of Choice written in stone: "Thou shalt have no other gods." And the Second is like unto it: "Thou shalt have the right to choose."

From Hamburgers to Morals

If only it were just hamburgers, ice cream, and TV channels. But Choice has also become the god of lifestyles. The Third Commandment of Choice, "Thou shalt have no closets," is observed with religious fervor on the streets of San Francisco and in West Hollywood. Ours is the era of openness and honesty. Whatever it is, "let it all hang out." I'm "free to be me!" Homosexuality? "It's just a sexual preference." Living together before marriage? "We may decide to get married later on." Cocaine and crack? "What's your drug of choice?"

The Fourth Commandment mirrors the throwaway consumerism of which Choice is god: "Thou shalt carry no excess baggage." It's not just the Styrofoam boxes in which the hamburgers are packaged that we throw away by the millions into already-maxed-out garbage dumps. Or the disposable Pampers, Kodak cameras, and even contact lenses.

Now, "throw away" has also become the hallmark of *morals* in a pro-choice generation. Want to trade in your wife for a younger model? There goes one marriage. Want to exchange your husband for someone who understands you better? There goes another.

Just to bolster the first four commandments, the Fifth Commandment of Choice echoes the Me-Generation rhetoric of the 60's: "Thou shalt choose to do whatever feels right for thyself." In a pro-choice generation, the sensual "If it feels good, *do* it" has evolved into a more cerebral "If it feels good, *believe* it." There are no helpless victims. We are responsible for ourselves through the decisions we make. We *choose* whatever happens to us. It's the message of *cosmic choice* taught by New Age gurus, from the late Baghwan Sri Rajneesh to "getting-in-touch-with-your-higher-Self's" Shirley MacLaine.

If there is any one problem with choice, it is the dulling of our senses. As CBS chief Howard Stringer has reminded us, now that most households have a choice of 50 TV channels, viewers have become bored by program choice, and rarely want to watch a program to the end.[1] There's been a similar problem with choice in sex: The more we see it on the screen and in magazine racks, the greater titillation we demand. Exposed breasts seem to beg the next step of full frontal nudity, which, when still not enough, insists on sadomasochism. Obscenity in the movies runs the same route. Can you remember when *darn* moved to *damn*, and when *damn* still wasn't enough?

The promiscuity of the 60's, 70's, and 80's left in its wake three decades of interchangeable sexual partners with numbed sexual senses. The smorgasbord of sex turned us into a nation of unfulfilled grazers. The tempting desserts at the beginning of the line became all that we wanted. No one was willing to wait for the main course. Then more dessert was put out, until there was nothing else from which to choose, and we quickly tired of it. We went through the motions of sexual grazing, but left the bedroom feeling empty and used. Perhaps encouraged by the threat of AIDS, or perhaps recognizing the emptiness of illicit sex, more and more people are making a different kind of choice—commitment.

Yet the relinquishing of sexual choice by an increasing number of people has hardly slowed the pace for others. Dulled as we are, whether in morals or in the marketplace, we apparently insist on the right to be dulled! In virtually every aspect of our lives, *Choice* has become God. And the crowds roar: "Long live *Choice!*"

The Road to Pro-Choice

The obvious questions are staggering: How in one generation did we ever manage to get to this point? How did personal choice in morals become as acceptable as personal choice in the marketplace? Where along the way did we lose our sense of a transcendent, unalterable, and universal point of moral reference? In short, how did *Choice* become god?

In one of his many books analyzing cultural decline in the West, author Francis Schaeffer tells of snow falling on a ridge near his alpine chalet in Switzerland. As he thinks about it, he realizes that the apparent unity of the mass of snow along the ridge is an illusion, because along the ridge is an imaginary line which is a watershed. As the snow melts on one side of that line, it goes into a small river which flows into the Rhine and makes its way to the cold waters of the North Sea. When the snow melts on the other side, it drains into the Rhone Valley into Lac Leman (or, as we call it, Lake Geneva), and from there into the warm waters of the Mediterranean—1000 miles from the North Sea.[2]

The origins of a pro-choice generation are found along many ridges, distant in both time and place. Seemingly insignificant events have combined like a thousand trickling streams into one mighty river of collective thought, bringing us to a pro-choice worldview as different from the paradigm of preceding generations as are the waters of the Mediterranean from those of the North Sea.

Without having the luxury in this book to fill in all the bright hues of American history over the past several decades, much less the more sophisticated shades of modern sociology, it is at least possible to sketch a brief collage of those watershed events and phenomena leading to the enthronement of *Choice* as God.

The World Wars—Since the two World Wars, America has been shaken out of its isolation to become aware of cultures that are radically different from our own. Before the wars, who really knew very much about other forms of government, or major world religions apart from Christianity and Judaism, or about how people of other races and nationalities thought? There were options out there which few Americans had previously known. For farm boys from Iowa, war was an eye-opening experience in every way. "How ya' gonna keep 'em down on the farm, once they've seen gay Paree?" asked the song perceptively. Wars on foreign soil brought a whole new world of choice to our own shores.

Between the two wars, even the Depression of the 30's made its contribution to choice by encouraging the freedom of travel, seen more immediately from the perspective of that generation as *necessity* of travel. For people in the Dust Bowl it was "California or Bust!" The nation was on the move, and it has been on the move ever since.

No longer do children automatically live in the same community as their parents. Where we live has become another exciting decision to be made. And we make it frequently, changing our place of residence many times over the years. A pro-choice generation is a generation of upwardly mobile nomads, moving about with the shifting sands of ever-changing career choices.

The wars brought changes in employment as well as in travel. While the men were away at the front, it remained for the women back home to take their places on the assembly lines, in the steel factories, and in many other male enclaves. Even when Johnny came marching home again, it seemed natural to many women to keep on marching to work.

With the wars had come industrialization and people pouring into the cities from off the farms. City-dwellers didn't need as many children as folks back on the farm, so family size dwindled. With smaller families and double paychecks, the "good life" ushered in an age of consumerism. Labor-saving devices and luxury items appeared in every store window, enticing Americans with more and more products from which to choose.

The experience of World War II, in particular, gave parents every reason to pamper their children by wanting them to benefit from the sacrifices which had been made. Little wonder that the postwar baby boom generation grew up with a certain expectation of freedom. And freedom came in waves.

Automobiles—What could have led to more freedom of choice than the increasing availability of the automobile? Initially the options were in the cars themselves. By the 50's and 60's your basic black Model-T had evolved into a two-tone gas guzzler, complete with tail fins and a landau roof. You want power windows? You've got 'em. Air conditioning? Of course.

More than just options on the showroom floor, automobiles soon began to reflect choices in the lifestyles of their owners. First it was the convenience of a station wagon—just right for those cross-country vacations with families of six, eagerly watching for the next set of Burma Shave signs. Then came the two-car garage, reflecting the mobility of a dual-career family shuttling back and forth between Little League, PTA, and the office. And finally the two-seater sports car, complete with cellular phone and portable fax machine, for a pro-choice generation of singles in the fast lane.

Communication—Who could have guessed the impact of technology in fostering choice among Americans? With the advent of the telephone, radio, and television, whole new avenues of communication were opened up, permitting what seemed to be unlimited options. Yet these were but a prelude to the real communication and information explosion which would come with the computer. With the computer-generated Information Age, choice became self-perpetuating: The more we knew, the more options we had; the more options we had, the more information we demanded.

Credit—Gone are the days when children bought savings stamps at school and took their nickels, dimes, and quarters to the bank in plastic Hopalong Cassidy "piggybanks." Now the quarters feed hungry computer games in the video arcade. Just as the good guys in Hollywood Westerns have been replaced by the Teenage Mutant Ninja Turtles, so too savings stamps and piggybanks now belong to a bygone era. Whether adults or children, ours is no longer a nation of savers, but spenders— even if we don't have the money. And that is where we took the quantum leap: The pro-choice generation is also the credit-card generation.

The inaugural BankAmericard promotion that sent its representative on a grand tour from Seattle to San Diego, armed only with a credit card, was an unqualified success. (When toll-keepers at the Golden Gate Bridge refused to accept the card, only a minor diversion was necessary in order to get a cash advance of 25 cents at a nearby Sausalito bank.) The successful tour told the story: It was the beginning of the credit generation. And *choice* took another giant stride toward godhood.

Choice is the god of instant gratification, and the credit card has become its guardian angel, promising on-demand money at the 24-hour automatic teller machine and on-demand purchases in the shopping malls where we regularly go to worship the god of choice. "On-demand" has been the creed of a pro-choice generation ever since.

The Pill—Women's lib didn't come when feminists burned their bras; it came when women got the Pill. And not a minute too soon, what with a free-swinging economy and even freer lifestyles, at once begging for and permitting smaller families. But it wasn't just a matter of limiting the size of the nuclear family; the Pill exploded into a full-scale revolution. Reproductive freedom begat sexual freedom on every front.

Greater freedom for sex *within* marriage became the impetus for sexual freedom *outside of* marriage. In a dizzying, whirlwind affair, sex soon became the mistress of *choice*. But sex was insatiable. Just as quickly, it took on other partners, for whom the Pill was not a factor. With but a whiff of sexual freedom, *hetero* became *homo*. And "sexual preference" was born.

Body Consciousness—We used to keep fit by working, walking, and eating wholesome home cooking. With the coming of fast food, fast cars, and sedentary jobs at the office, our waistlines have bulged in direct proportion to the atrophy of our muscles. And with endless leisure hours logged in front of televisions, we have deteriorated into a nation of listless "couch potatoes."

But to counteract the flab, we've also become a nation of joggers, slimmers, and cholesterol counters. Exercise, health food, and fitness are all the rage. Wimps are out, Adidas and Nike are in. Smoking has become almost a capital offense, and hard liquor is in a tailspin. Today's beautiful people are *Perrier* people.

What exercise and diet cannot accomplish, cosmetic surgery can. From facelifts, to tummy tucks, to morale-boosting breast enhancement, the body is now center-stage. A nation that once took bodies for granted—whatever their shape or size—is now a nation of body fanatics. We slim them, firm them, feed them, and dress them with a fervor once reserved for nourishing the inner person. Souls are the subject of religious burials; in the meantime, it's our *bodies* that count.

So it is that the pro-choice generation is a *body* generation. Deciding what's good for the body becomes an all-consuming passion. Either we control *it*, or it controls *us*. Little wonder, then, the logical progression: From lack of control, to taking control, to demanding a "right to control" our bodies.

Fat bodies get in the way of an active social life, so we are told by the dieting ads. And no one has to be told that pregnant bodies get in the way of careers and personal plans. The solutions become obvious: "Fat farms" take care of the fat; abortion clinics handle the rest. Choice is having control. Pro-choice is having a *right* to control.

Civil Rights—Rights come naturally for Americans. We are a people of natural, civil, and legal rights. If ever that were in doubt, it was resolved in the 60's with the civil rights movement for racial equality. It was the era of Martin Luther King and nonviolent demonstrations. It was the time when "Whites Only" signs came crashing down from restrooms, water fountains, and school classrooms. Segregation got a bad name, and integration achieved respectability. "Equal rights" and "Equal Opportunity Employer" became household terms.

However, "equal rights" quickly evolved from majority rule (with legal protection for the rights of those *not* in the majority) into *minority* rights (even if it meant inverse discrimination against those in the majority). And minority rights soon swept beyond racial injustice to sexual equality in the workplace (women's rights), to personal sexual freedom for homosexuals (gay rights), to personal reproductive freedom for women (abortion rights). There was a gradual slide from just causes to unjust causes: from morality to immorality, from legitimate women's rights (racial and employment equality) to illegitimate women's rights (homosexuality and abortion).

For many people, even *human* rights and *animal* rights have been put on the same level of importance. "Rights are rights!" seems to be the cry. *Choice* makes no fine distinctions among the plethora of rights that are demanded. Neither, it seems, does a pro-choice generation, which regards personal rights as untouchables. In a pro-choice generation, only two minorities have no rights: the unborn, and those who would defend them.

A Closer Look

Anyone interested in a closer look at the many forces at work behind the scenes will want to turn to such thought-provoking studies as Allan Bloom's insightful bestseller, *The Closing of the American Mind*, which focuses on intellectual and moral drift in higher education; and *Habits of the Heart*, by Robert N. Bellah and his team of sociologists, who explore individualism and commitment in American life.

Their studies, as well as others, focus in on a number of factors contributing in a special way to the birth of a pro-choice generation. It is worth a brief look at a half-dozen areas of American culture which these authors point out as having had a direct impact.

Choice in the Classroom

According to Professor Bloom, the roots of modern education

go back to philosopher John Stuart Mill and educator John Dewey, who taught us, in Bloom's words, that "no attention had to be paid to the fundamental principles or the moral virtues that inclined men to live according to them. To use language now popular, civic culture was neglected. And this turn in liberalism is what prepared us for cultural relativism and the fact-value distinction . . . ."[3] As Bloom points out, relativism has become the hallmark of American education. "What's happening now" is all that counts—however you, as an individual, perceive it to be.

❧ Through the avenue of cultural and moral relativism, *Choice* has become the only God permitted in the classroom.

"Dewey's pragmatism . . . saw the past as radically imperfect and regarded our history as irrelevant, or as a hindrance to rational analysis of our present."[4] Thus relativism in education has taught us that the moral choices of previous generations (generally informed by "higher" values which are no longer acknowledged as valid) are now ours to be made—in whatever way we wish to make them. The choice is ours.

It should not be surprising, then, that God has been taken out of the classroom. The issue is not primarily one of separating church from state. School prayers and controversies about after-school Bible studies on campus are merely popular distractions. The real issue is far more fundamental: *Reference to God in the classroom would be a thorn in the flesh to relativism.* By their very natures, a God of absolutes and a philosophy of relativism don't mix. It is not a battle between religion and secular education, but between *two different* religions: the biblical God of transcendent values, and the secular god of individual choice.

It is this difference which permits free discussion of homosexuality, condoms, and abortion (all seen as matters of individual choice) but not the discussion of biblical sexual morality, whose absolute standards preclude individual choice on certain issues. Through the avenue of cultural and moral relativism, *Choice* has become the only God permitted in the classroom.

Therapy, The Religion of Choice

If *Choice* is the God of relativism, therapy has become relativism's established religion. There has been an observable shift from minister to psychologist, from pulpit to couch, from eternal judgment to "nonjudgmental," from divine authority to "self-actualization." Robert Bellah and company note that therapy intentionally divorces one's values from the "faith of our fathers." As they see it, "The work of therapy is often aimed at so distancing us from our parents that we may choose, or seem to choose, freely, which aspects of them we will resemble and which not."[5]

A kind of unashamed self-worship is the result:

> The therapeutic ideal posits an individual who is able to be the source of his own standards, to love himself before he asks for love from others, and to rely on his own judgment without deferring to others. Needing others in order to feel "O.K." about oneself is a fundamental malady that therapy seeks to cure.[6]

With *self* having replaced *others*—and particularly the *great* "Other"—traditional "others-oriented" values are turned on their head:

> In its pure form, the therapeutic attitude denies all forms of obligation and commitment in relationships, replacing them only with the ideal of full, open, honest communication among self-actualized individuals.[7]

Ironically in an era of "right to privacy," the only sin is hiding our feelings! It doesn't really matter what we choose to do, as long as we are open and up-front about it. It's a matter of *form* over *substance*. You see it over and over again in a pro-choice generation. In therapy, *communication* is the exalted form, whereas how we *act* is the underplayed substance. Of course, it only follows that in a philosophy intentionally devoid of inherent values, substance *must* take a back seat to form. Form is all there is.

That is why in the abortion controversy, for instance, *choice*—the form—is promoted rather than *moral rightness*—the substance. Unable to claim a clear consensus on the moral rightness of abortion, abortion rights activists are left only with form—*choice*. It is predictable, therefore, that they should insist on being referred to as pro-choice rather than pro-abortion.

And self-fulfillment therapy further bolsters the pro-choice mentality by forbidding its worshipers from being intolerant of *others'* choices. Where the pulpit condemned, the couch accepts all. (All, that is, except intolerance of any kind. Like any religion, therapy condemns its own list of sins, of which intolerance is the cardinal sin.)

The modern therapist, as the high priest, becomes the example for all to follow. It doesn't matter what you think or do—the therapist gives a listening ear and a sympathetic nod. As Bellah's brief points out, "The therapist is not there to judge but to help clients become able to make their own judgments. . . . By taking each person's values as given or self-defined, the therapist seems to make no moral judgments."[8] The lesson is clear: "As you have seen me do," says the therapist, "go thou and do likewise."

In the midst of all this nonjudgmental relativism rises the central, unchallengeable truth of a pro-choice generation: "Morality" is to be distrusted. In its place is therapeutic contractualism, in which the question "Is this right or wrong?" becomes "Is this going to work for me now?" All that matters is individual choice, subjectively evaluated by a cost-benefit analysis.[9] Whether we are talking about divorce, homosexuality, drugs, or abortion, the only question is: "Do the pro's outweigh the con's?" "At the moment will I be better off *with* it or *without* it?"

When it comes to almost any other aspect of higher education, Professor Bloom writes as a coolly analytical, if concerned, observer. However, the professor becomes almost livid when he thinks of how therapy has crippled the young people in our pro-choice generation, especially through the avenue of guilt-free divorces for their parents. "Psychologists are the sworn enemies of guilt," says Bloom pointedly. "Psychologists provide much of the ideology justifying divorce—e.g., that it is worse for kids to stay in stressful homes . . . ." (In truth, the evil of stress is a distant second to the evil of abandonment.)

Professor Bloom concludes that "modern psychology at its best has a questionable understanding of the soul."[10] That should be no surprise. From Freud on down, much of modern psychology, with its roots deep in biological evolution, has denied the very existence of the soul. And afterlife. And a day of judgment. All of those "antiquated concepts" are related to the God of a different generation. In our generation, *Choice*, the god of therapy, sits enthroned on the analyst's couch and in the modern American mind.

Choice Learned Through Divorce

The tragedy of divorce in America is the penultimate symptom of choice becoming God. A high percentage of divorces reflect a commitment to the sanctity of *choice* rather than a commitment to the sanctity of *commitment*. Marriage has been reduced from a lifetime bond of love to a mutual contract in which both parties are free to choose—and thus free to break—their commitments, if only they are willing to pay the price for breach of the contract.[11] If choice always has its price—and it does—it is also true that, for a price, you can have your choice.

The report of Robert Bellah's team bears this out: "We would argue that the family is not so much 'fading,' as some have said, as changing. Marriage and the family, while still desirable, are now in several ways optional."[12] *Optional*—that's the key word for a pro-choice generation. Some even see divorce as an *enhancing* option: "That getting married, having children, and staying married are now matters of choice, rather than things taken for granted, creates a new atmosphere for marriage and a new meaning for family life,"[13] reports Bellah and company.

From this analysis, one could be excused for thinking that divorce is the best thing since sliced bread. In fact, Bellah's team cites one report that reckons "this new atmosphere creates more sensitive, more open, more intense, more loving relationships—an achievement of which America can justly be proud."[14] Surely someone is rattling our cage. Is even a pro-choice generation prepared to claim that divorce is something of which "America can justly be *proud*?"

In divorce we are tampering with the very essence of society, for the family is the glue which holds society together. Author and lecturer James Dobson has it dead right in emphasizing his "Focus on the Family." At the very heart of the crime problem is the disintegration of the family. At the core of drug abuse is a family structure in disarray. Warring gangs, the decline in public education, and burgeoning suicide among the young—all have their roots in the home.

Whether in the ghetto or in upper-class suburbia, the fractured family gives new meaning to our growing concern for the homeless. First and foremost, it is the children of divorce—by the tens of millions—that are truly America's "homeless." Many of them are homeless on the streets; many more are homeless in their own homes.

In the case of divorce, however, we are not dealing simply with a *symptom* of our pro-choice generation. Divorce is itself a *cause*. As Professor Bloom points out, "Children who have gone to the school of conditional relationships should be expected to view the world in the light of what they learned there."[15] And what they have learned through the cruelty of divorce is far different from what they are told when it happens:

> Children may be told over and over again that their parents have a right to their own lives, that they will enjoy quality time instead of quantity time, that they are really loved by their parents even after divorce, but children do not believe any of this.
>
> To children, the voluntary separation of parents seems worse than their death, precisely because it is voluntary.[16]

What children learn through divorce is that parents in a pro-choice generation have only a conditional attachment to each other, and, worse yet, even to them. Spouses are expendable. Children are expendable. Little wonder that children in a pro-choice generation have grown up thinking that their own children are expendable—whether born or unborn.

Choice in the Wake of Biblical Illiteracy

In previous generations, moral choices were informed by Holy Writ. However, the pro-choice generation is a biblically illiterate generation. On one level there is nothing explicitly sinister about that fact, since the pro-choice generation is an illiterate generation *generally*. For all those who would pick up this book and read it, there are millions who wouldn't. Not just this book, but *any* book. We are a generation of people who relate to visual images on screens, not to written words on pages.

Unlike books—television and rock videos are aimed at our *feelings*, and only rarely our *thoughts*. Hence we are less rational than intuitive when making moral choices, and we are certainly ill-informed regarding the history of how past generations have made moral decisions. The history of people in biblical times is even more remote to us. Divine revelation itself seems archaic in a time of moon walks and laser beams. How can ten commandments etched in stone many centuries ago on a barren Middle-Eastern mountaintop possibly compete with the slick packaging of trendy moral issues that comes our way daily on *Donahue* and *Oprah?*

> ❧ Having no grand vision of what life is all about, we are reduced to making ad hoc decisions based on opinion polls, media propaganda, or unabashed self-interest.

In many ways the church itself has contributed to the decline in biblical literacy. Liberal Christian clerics have stifled our reading with their own doubts, alleging that the Bible is filled with contradictions and is therefore untrustworthy. Big-name preachers have sometimes called more attention to their own glitzy persona than to the words of Scripture, and we've quickly forgotten even the memory verses we learned as children in Sunday school.

Headline-grabbing televangelists have held the Bible aloft in praise while denying the power of the gospel in their own lives. It's enough to make some people wonder, "Is *that* what the Book is all about?" At the opposite end of the church spectrum, authoritative religious bodies have imposed heavy-handed human tradition in the name of biblical truth—and when we didn't like what such human doctrine told us, we rejected the Bible itself, as if it were the source of our problems with the church.

For decades now, mainstream liberal churches have turned the gospel message of sin and salvation into a platform for political and social reform. The responsibility for helping us to make crucial moral choices fell by the wayside. Worse still, divorce, sexual freedom, and abortion were all condoned in the name of Christian love—even in the face of clear biblical teaching to the contrary. When the keepers of the Book could so easily ignore moral standards which even many nonbelievers would uphold, the credibility of the Book itself was undermined.

For reasons both within the church and without, biblical illiteracy abounds. And with biblical illiteracy comes choice in a vacuum. Religion is supposed to give us answers, but without a book of faith we are left with only the questions.

Allan Bloom is hardly your average defender of the faith. He is a philosopher and social observer, not a churchman. Nevertheless, Bloom laments the loss of one of the elements most fundamental to primary learning: knowledge of religion. "Real religion and knowledge of the Bible," says Bloom, "have diminished to the vanishing point."[17] Whether in the church or in the home—where religion once lived—"the dreariness of the family's spiritual landscape passes belief."[18]

Until relatively recent times, the Bible has always been the key resource for social discourse about moral issues confronting the nation. "With its gradual and inevitable disappearance," says Bloom, "the very idea of such a total book and the possibility and necessity of world-explanation is disappearing. . . . Without the book even the idea of the order of the whole is lost."[19]

The impact on personal choice is found in the valueless pragmatism of a pro-choice generation. Having no grand vision of what life is all about, we are reduced to making ad hoc decisions based on opinion polls, media propaganda, or unabashed self-interest. Without a given worldview consensus, which the Bible once provided, social dialogue is without anchor. Today, not only is biblical truth defended with embarrassed timidity by large segments of the church, but it is no longer even challenged by its opponents. They see no need to do so, since in their perception the Bible has been made obscure by cultural irrelevance.

With biblical illiteracy, both sides of the coin are covered for a pro-choice generation: Where there is no Book, there is no sin. And when personal choice becomes God, who needs a Book?

Self, the Object of Choice

It will shock no one to be told that the pro-choice generation is a generation of self. Shelves of books and stacks of articles have already been written on the ME generation. All that remains to be explored is in what way the ME generation has contributed to the enthronement of choice as God.

> &. As a *soul*, self sees itself in rela-
> tion to God. Self *without a soul* sees
> itself in relationship only to itself—to
> say the least, a redundant, imploding
> perspective.

Of course, ours is not the first generation to make its choices about careers, recreation, religious beliefs, sex, and marriage within an environment devoid of social pressure, necessity, and moral restraint. Bloom says the younger members of our pro-choice generation are simply "exaggerated versions" of Plato's description of young people in his day:

> [The democratic youth] lives along day by day, gratifying the desire that occurs to him, at one time drinking and listening to the flute, at another downing water and reducing, now practicing gymnastic, and again idling and neglecting everything; and sometimes spending his time as though he were occupied with philosophy. Often he engages in politics and, jumping up, says and does whatever chances to come to him; and if he admires any soldiers, he turns in that direction; and if it's money-makers, in that one, and there is neither order nor necessity in his life, but calling it sweet, free and blessed, he follows it throughout.[20]

Does this remind you of any young people you know today? Whether young or old, ours is a generation singing Walt Whitman's "Song of Myself," whose first line is, "I celebrate myself."

Depending on the critic, looking "selfward" may be viewed either as a healthy, positive act or as pure selfishness. On the positive side is the widespread idea that people must take responsibility for deciding what they want and for finding relationships that will meet their needs.[21] Of course, the word *responsibility* must be carefully scrutinized. What it can mean all too easily is taking *control* without accepting moral *accountability*—as seen, for example, when the IRA is quite happy to claim "responsibility" for terrorist bombings in Northern Ireland.

On the negative side is Alexis de Tocqueville's observation that "in democratic societies, each citizen is habitually busy with the contemplation of a very petty object, which is himself."[22] In one sense, *petty* is far from being the right word, given the more serious implications of hard-core navel-gazing. Professor Bloom is rightly concerned that "the self is the modern substitute for the soul."[23] As a *soul*, self sees itself in relation to God. Self *without a soul* sees itself in relationship only to itself—to say the least, a redundant, imploding perspective.

I say *imploding*, because the world of self collapses inward of its own weight. Pro-choice is not a good match for self in a vacuum. "If the self is defined by its ability to choose its own values," asks Robert Bellah, "on what grounds are those choices themselves based?" For most people who concentrate on self-direction, "there is simply no objectifiable criterion for choosing one value or course of action over another. One's own idiosyncratic preferences are their own justification, because they define the true self."[24]

But even if our choices could somehow be justified simply because we make them, how can we have any confidence that what we decide for ourselves is ultimately good for us? Should self be encouraged to decide against its own self-interest on a regular, ongoing basis?

Self-destruction through one's own choice—a kind of moral suicide, if you will—would be tragic enough. However, the implications present society at large with an even greater problem: How are we ever going to resolve moral issues of national importance—issues like the breakdown of the family; like values-education in the classroom; like the nagging issues of homosexual and abortion rights?

Bellah sees the problem clearly: "If selves are defined by their preferences, but those preferences are arbitrary, then each self constitutes its own moral universe, and there is finally no way to reconcile conflicting claims about what is good in itself."[25]

If this looks like the best argument yet in favor of pro-choice—that, since we cannot arrive at a consensus, everybody should be left to choose for themselves—not even *that* argument can expect ratification. By its own logic, pro-choice lacks moral force. If what is right is right solely in the eye of the beholder, even the idea of pro-choice cannot be *right*; it can only be *preferred*. Hence pro-choice cannot itself exist as a "right"—whether a "human right," a "legal right," or a "Constitutional right."

For something to be universally acknowledged as a "right," we must assume some identifiable point of reference on which all people can agree: some universal truth, some sense of rightness that transcends individual preferences. If pro-choice wishes the legitimacy of being a "right," then it must compete with all other "rights"—including the right to life. Are we prepared to defend the "right to decide" as being superior to even the "right to life"?

Retracing Our Steps

Self is fine in the marketplace. And who could argue that pro-choice is out of line at McDonald's? Choice is the American way. But pro-choice in matters of *morals* is a different story altogether. There was a time not that long ago when everyone recognized the difference. If it was a time when homosexuals were forced to stay in the closet, it was also a time when American families stayed together, and when children had a "home" to go home to.

No, it wasn't Camelot. Some couples *did* get divorced. Some children *were* on the street. And, yes, some women *did* die from back-alley abortions. But we didn't kid ourselves about right and wrong. We didn't try to rationalize immorality or demand that our personal preferences be given legal status. Nor did we treat human life as just another disposable commodity.

When *Choice* became God, all that changed. When *Choice* became God, we took a nap on the therapist's couch, dreamed of becoming self-actualized, and woke up with the morals of the marketplace.

T H R E E

Any Choice But God

The greatest question of our time is not communism versus individualism, not Europe versus America, not even the East versus the West; it is whether men can live without God.

—Will Durant

WITH TWO OUTS IN THE BOTTOM OF THE NINTH inning, and the Los Angeles Dodgers leading the Oakland A's 5-2 in the fifth game of the 1988 World Series, Oakland fans were on their feet yelling encouragement to Tony Phillips in a last desperate hope that he could keep the inning and the game alive. A win for the Dodgers would mean the end of the Series by four games to one.

On the mound, a slender 30-year-old right-hander from New Jersey threw down the resin bag and grabbed his belt to pull his pants up a notch. Then he adjusted his cap. Orel Hershiser had already shut out the A's in the second game of the Series. Supported by heroic hitting from a mix-and-match lineup that resembled an army of the walking wounded, Hershiser had walked four batters, allowed four hits, and struck out eight. Now, with two strikes on Phillips, the moment of truth had come.

Looking intently for a sign from catcher Rick Dempsey, Orel took a deep breath, tugged at his cap once again, then went into his stretch. The ball flew out of Hershiser's hand toward the plate. Phillips took a determined swing, only to hear the ball pop securely into Dempsey's glove. Phillips and the A's were out, the Dodgers had won the Series, and Orel Hershiser was on his way to unanimous MVP honors.

As Dodger manager Tommy Lasorda raced from the dugout and as teammates ran toward the mound, Orel Hershiser dropped to his knee, head bowed. Within moments he was swept up in the pandemonium of Dodger Blue. Of course there was also the prearranged Disneyland promotion: "What are you going to do next, Orel?" "I'm going to *Disneyland!*" (Two takes, just to make sure.) And then it was back to the clubhouse to face the onslaught of the media.

There was nothing unusual about the questions put to Hershiser by the cadre of sports reporters wanting to know the secret of his success. But there was something *quite* unusual about his response. "I know this isn't a religious show," said this curious man on national television, "but I just think the Lord has blessed me with composure. I thank God." Another question about his feelings upon winning the Series, and once again came an unexpected reply: "I thank the good Lord for giving me the opportunity to be involved in all of this." When asked what he was thinking about as he kneeled on the mound after the game-winning pitch, Orel said he was thanking God for his strength.

Not unexpectedly, the next day's *Los Angeles Times* was filled from front to back with stories of the Dodger victory. One article in particular caught my attention. "As Rick Dempsey raised his hand in celebration," wrote the reporter, "Hershiser paused at the mound *as if to reflect on the enormity of their achievement.*" Was this reporter the only person in Los Angeles—perhaps even the nation—who missed what Orel had said about thanking God for his strength? Did he somehow feel the need to cover up for Orel's embarrassing social gaff in involving God on such an inappropriate occasion? The article contained all the obligatory runs, hits, and errors, but there was no mention of Orel's personal faith. No mention of how Orel always praises God for his victories. No acknowledgment of any spiritual dimension in the midst of a secular event of great prominence.

What journalist in a pack of headline-hungry colleagues, all reporting the same event, wouldn't kill for a unique angle on the story—something that would transform the facts and figures into a piece of journalism with real human interest? And here it was, staring the media in the face—not just another "born-again" athlete who gratuitously throws in some trendy God-talk, but a man who actually incorporates his profession of faith into his profession of baseball.

But few, if any, of the reporters chased that angle. After all, what would they have done with it if they had ever caught up with it? Would they not risk their journalistic credentials by mixing the secular with the sacred? Doesn't everyone know there's a separation between church and state? Besides, surely the readers wouldn't venture past the first paragraph if too much mention was made of religion.

It's okay, of course, for Tommy Lasorda to talk about the "Big Dodger in the Sky," but no one wants to pursue seriously the reality of a God from whom Hershiser draws personal strength. No one dares question Orel about who his God is, why he has put his faith in God, or what kind of strength he gets from God.

In the days following the Dodger victory, Orel Hershiser was in great demand on the television talkshow circuit. Perhaps the highlight was an appearance on *The Tonight Show* with Johnny Carson. "Orel, they tell me you were singing hymns in the dugout between innings," observes Johnny. "Yeah, I was just singing some hymns to myself and trying to relax," says Orel modestly. "What hymns were you singing?" "Oh, uh..." "Sing one for us," Johnny insists. Hesitating momentarily, but desiring to please his host, Orel quietly sings the Doxology:

> Praise God from whom all blessings flow;
> Praise Him, all creatures here below.
> Praise Him above, ye heavenly hosts;
> Praise Father, Son, and Holy Ghost.

The audience applauds a pitcher who can also sing, and Johnny says politely, "Oh, that's really sweet."

Of course, there were no follow-up questions, like, "What is your personal relationship with God?" "Why is your faith in God so strong?" Or perhaps, "How do you relate something so profound as your faith to the relative insignificance of the game of baseball?" Yes, I know—Johnny doesn't do that kind of interview. Never mind that virtually all of his monologues contain some zinger directed at televangelists who have brought dishonor to religious faith in America. (Not that it isn't funny; who could help but laugh?)

Keeping Faith Separate

I know very little more about Orel Hershiser's faith than what I have just shared with you. One article did quote Orel as attributing his success to his wife and their Christian bond. And he says there was a time when success went to his head and he forgot his Christianity. What I *do* know is that Orel's faith is extremely important to him. Even more significant than that, Orel's faith is a *fully integrated* faith.

I don't know if God cares one way or the other about who wins a World Series. Actually, I rather doubt it. But surely God cares very much about whether we acknowledge him in all we do, and about whether we involve him in every part of our lives, including the choices we make every day.

Moral choice probably shouldn't expect a frontal assault, even from its enemies. If someone wanted to destroy personal religious faith, it is not likely that he would tell us straight out that religion is off-limits. No, he would be just as successful (and even come off looking respectably tolerant) by telling us: "Indulge yourself in religion all you want; just keep it in its place."

Orel Hershiser's crime was that he broke the rule and included God in a terribly secular activity. The offense was all the more flagrant because baseball is one of the most secular activities known to human experience. Let's face it—baseball is hardly one of man's more noble pursuits; it's a national *pastime*—just a very nice way to pass the time. So why insist on involving God?

If the opponents of morality can keep God within the four walls of churches and synagogues, then they have done their job well. They've isolated the infectious germ of religious influence. The secular world (everything *outside* those four walls of religion) can then go about its business unbothered—a kind of spiritual apartheid in which religion is both separate *and* unequal (and hopefully harmless). It's nice in its place, but should exist without meaningful representation in the halls of moral choice.

God on the Back Page

It's not only the sports page that excludes God; it's the front page as well. It wasn't so long ago that religious news was an integral part of regularly reported community affairs. Whole sermons would be reproduced, right there in the front section. But now most religious articles are put somewhere toward the back of the paper in a separate section, typically written by a designated religion writer, and perhaps only in the Saturday edition. The move is not necessarily part of some sinister secular-humanist conspiracy. As much as anything, newspapers reflect the interests of their reading audience. The point is that, other than in articles exposing fallen religious leaders, faith and religion no longer make front-page news.

The same is true if you're looking for God on major television networks. God simply doesn't show up in prime time. Of course, televangelists are available almost nonstop via the cable channels and independent networks, but where do you find God on ABC, NBC, or CBS? Perhaps a religious issue is explored on an occasional *60 Minutes* or *Nightline* segment. Otherwise, there's the late-night or early-morning religious-affairs program, but little else.

Even then, there is more than one way to exclude God in the media. It can be done through the tyranny of time. By way of example, I was recently invited to participate in one of those early-morning religious-affairs programs on a local NBC affiliate. The invitation came on the heels of the film controversy surrounding *The Last Temptation of Christ*. It was to be a discussion between a liberal theologian, myself, and the host of the program, regarding the nature of Jesus Christ: Was he human or divine? Quite an interesting topic, given enough time to articulate an issue that has engaged centuries of believers and skeptics in serious debate. The time alloted for *our* critical dialogue? Among the three of us, all of 12 minutes!

In the house of social discourse, religion is rarely an invited guest. Even then, its welcome is brief. But if you think about it, that should be no surprise these days. It's all about protecting our "right to privacy."

Sanitizing Public Perceptions

In *The Naked Public Square*, perhaps the most insightful book of our time regarding the privatization of public morality, Richard John Neuhaus tells of a small but significant event following Martin Luther King's assassination. An ecumenical memorial service was held in Harlem with numerous religious, political, and cultural dignitaries in attendance. The announcer covering the service said in solemn tones: "And so today there was a memorial service for the slain civil rights leader, Dr. Martin Luther King, Jr. It was a religious service, and it is fitting that it should be, for, after all, Dr. King was the son of a minister."

Why was a religious service fitting? Not because Dr. King *himself* had a deep religious faith, nor because King's call for racial integration was based on religious convictions, but only because he was a minister's son!

"How [do we] explain this astonishing blindness to the religious motive and meaning of Dr. King's ministry?" asks Neuhaus. "The announcer was speaking out of a habit of mind that was no doubt quite unconscious. The habit of mind is that religion must be kept at one remove from the public square, that matters of *public* significance must be sanitized of religious particularity."[1]

Neuhaus illustrates how the media sanitized King's civil rights movement of any religious connections:

> It regularly occurred that the klieg lights for the television cameras would be turned off during Dr. King's speeches when he dwelt on the religious and moral-philosophical basis of the movement for racial justice. They would be turned on again when the subject touched upon confrontational politics. In a luncheon conversation Dr. King once remarked, "They aren't interested in the *why* of what we're doing, only in the *what* of what we're doing, and because they don't understand the why they cannot really understand the what."[2]

The most surprising thing is how *religion itself* can be sanitized of religion. As a guest on the *Sally Jessy Raphael* program, I was matched against a woman claiming to have been Anne Boleyn in a previous lifetime. (I have recently come across another woman who makes the same claim with equal confidence.) We were on the program to talk about the relative merits of reincarnation and resurrection. When a member of the studio audience referred to what the Bible says in support of resurrection, I think even Ms. Raphael must have been shocked to hear herself say, "C'mon now. I don't want us to get off onto religion." What, pray tell, is a discussion regarding afterlife all about but religion?

Again, it's that habit of the mind that Ms. Raphael undoubtedly tripped on. These days all of us are indoctrinated in the need to separate public discourse from anything sounding too religious—certainly anything sounding like a biblical "book, chapter, and verse." Somehow it's not fair to the egalitarian exchange of private opinions. It introduces an external, objective source of authority which threatens to end the argument. Worse yet, it would herald the demise of America's ever-popular talkshows, which purport to resolve complex moral and social issues in convenient one-hour bites, on the basis of highly subjective personal opinions from the audience.

The bottom line today is that we have evolved in our thinking from an already-questionable *right* to privacy in matters of moral choice to a concerted effort on many fronts to make sure that all morality *remains* private. In fact, the former almost *requires* the latter. For if morality is allowed to "go public," it may well condemn the choices we want to make in private. If that should happen, then we obviously don't want to hear about it. It's like the old saw: "Don't confuse me with the facts; my mind's already made up." A pro-choice generation gives it only the slightest twist: "Don't bother us with your moral concerns; we've got the right to do what we want."

Privatizing the Private Square

If forces are at work to strip naked the *public* square by privatizing religious faith, one should not be surprised that it can also happen in the *private* square. History has shown that even religious institutions can allow their missions to be compromised by a "religion of neutrality."

Possibly the best illustration is the gradual secularization of church-related institutions of higher education. Anyone today who didn't know otherwise would find it difficult to believe that universities such as Harvard, Yale, and Princeton were founded as devoutly Christian schools. Today these institutions both reflect and foster America's new national religion: secularism.

Who knows exactly the order of events leading to the change? It's a chicken-and-egg situation. Did religious views change when church ties were severed, or were church ties severed because religious views had changed? It was undoubtedly a bit of both.

As between the churches and the universities, it was hard to tell whether the dog was wagging the tail or the tail was wagging the dog. But one thing is clear: When churches began to abandon their primary spiritual mission (often influenced by their own increasingly-liberal schools of theology), they lost any legitimacy for controlling the spiritual direction of those very schools.

Labels and Self-Perception

The process of secularizing religious institutions continues even today. However, the process has taken a somewhat different course in many cases. Although just as gradual and unnoticed at the earlier stages, radical change today often results from a subtle altering of the institution's projected image in order to achieve a more diverse constituency. Might a church-related university, for example, feel more comfortable describing itself as a "values-oriented" institution than one which is "Christ-centered?" Would the latter label offend too many people? It's not difficult to see that a carefully chosen label can help to privatize institutional ideals in order to achieve a broader range of acceptance.

Even more important is the way in which religious faith can be privatized in the heart of the individual. As individuals we often find ourselves using interesting "fudge labels": "I happen to be a Presbyterian." "I'm associated with the local Baptist church." "I was born Catholic." "My parents are Christians." "Of course I'm Jewish." "I guess I'm Protestant."

The question is, are we *really* Christians, *deep down*? Or if we're Jewish, does being Jewish *really* inform our decisions? Is what all of us believe simply inherited from our parents and in turn from their parents? Do we truly know *what* we believe and *why* we believe it, or do we simply wear various religious labels because they feel comfortable?

In our staunchly pluralistic society, how easy it has become for each of us to be simply a *cultural* Jew or a *hereditary* Christian! Unfortunately, when difficult moral issues have to be faced—

whether to divorce, whether to abort, whether to "pull the plug" on a dying loved one—meaningless religious labels hang in a terribly empty closet.

Bringing Private Morality Out of the Closet

It is dangerous enough to keep personal values private, but worse yet not to know for ourselves what those values even are. The price of privatizing morals can be staggering. Whether as an individual, a religious institution, or even a nation, the denial of a universally compelling, transcendent point of reference can tear us away from our moorings and set us adrift in a sea of moral uncertainty. Uncertainty which can lead to poor choices. Uncertainty which can lead to foolish mistakes.

Despite his faith in God, Orel Hershiser still occasionally makes poor choices and foolish mistakes. Sometimes the fastball he thought would strike out the batter sails over the left-field wall for a home run. Sometimes the curve ball he delivers gets straightened out for a line drive up the middle. And, like the rest of us, Orel Hershiser probably makes occasional poor choices and foolish mistakes off the field as well. After all, even true believers are still human.

But the lesson for all of us is that faith kept hidden—in other words, faith denied—will rob us of moral composure during those crucial times of decision when all the bases seem loaded and no relief is in sight. Privatized religious faith can neither inform nor sustain. Its ethical pretensions are but decorative stadium banners wafting in the breeze of popular opinion. Its determined liberal aims are but a swing and a miss. When secularist fans from the opposing team yell, "Any choice but faith!" it's time we shouted back, "Without faith, the ballgame's over!"

F O U R

Separating
Church And Choice

Things have come to a pretty pass when religion is allowed to invade public life.

—Lord Melbourne
(opposing abolition of the
slave trade)

NEWS ITEM: "A FEDERAL JUDGE RULED THURSDAY that an elementary school teacher could not keep or read religious books in his classroom, but ordered that a Bible removed from the school library be returned to the shelf.

"Fifth-grade teacher Ken Roberts kept the books—*The Bible in Pictures* and *The Story of Jesus*—for students to use during a 15-minute quiet reading period each day. Roberts said the religious books were among a 250-book collection and he never suggested that students read any specific book.

"The teacher also kept a Bible on his desk, which he said he sometimes read during the reading period.

"Kathleen Madigan, principal at Berkeley Gardens Elementary School in suburban Denver, ordered Roberts to remove the books because she felt they violated the separation of church and state. She also ordered Roberts to keep the Bible off his desk during school hours."[1]

News item: "Persistence upon the part of the Teaneck Menorah Committee has finally paid off with the Teaneck, New Jersey, Town Council. Last month, after several previous rejections, the Council approved the committee's request to erect an 8-foot-high menorah on the municipal green during the holiday season.

"For at least the last 50 Christmas seasons, town officials had been stringing lights on a large evergreen tree at the green. Mayor Francis Hall said there had never been any problems with that. Because the tree was part of nature and is adorned with lights rather than ornaments like a manger or angel, Mr. Hall said residents felt that the decorated tree reflected a general holiday spirit instead of a particular religious significance.

"But some Jewish residents felt otherwise. They said a decorated tree on public property was more appropriate to Christians than Jews. They wanted to see a symbol of their religious holiday, Hanukkah, placed alongside the tree."[2]

News item: "Omaha, Nebraska, high school students requesting permission to participate in an after-school Bible club have been denied access to classrooms. Bridget Mergens, organizer of the club, said she was denied permission to form the religious club by Principal James Findley. She said Assistant Superintendent James Tangdall told her the club would violate separation of church and state.

ào Somewhere along the line we have come to believe that separation between church and state means separation between *religious belief* and state.

"Omaha Westside High School had 30 other after-school clubs, including chess, scuba-diving, and community service groups. If the Bible club had been recognized, it could have been in the yearbook and had access to bulletin boards."[3]

Free Exercise at Risk

As these news items remind us, at almost every turn in recent years new questions have arisen regarding the propriety of long-standing traditions and institutions. We can think immediately of school prayers, nativity scenes, tax exemption for religious charities, and Sunday closing laws. Like never before, daily events in our lives are being accompanied by an old familiar tune, now being sung with uncharacteristic reverence as a national anthem: *the separation of church and state.*

If only that phrase presented nothing more than difficult Constitutional questions for legislatures, courts, and juries to decide! But today, in flagrant violation of its own guarantee, this Constitutional imperative has itself become the most sacred tenet of our new national faith, *secularism.* Somewhere along the line we have come to believe that separation between church and state means separation between *religious belief* and state: that it means separation between personal faith and secular activities; between going to the synagogue or church one day on the weekend and what happens the other six days of the week; between required chapel or religion courses in sectarian universities and "real" courses in math, science, and English literature; between the eternal principles of a higher law and pragmatic judicial decisions made in our courts.

The gradual separation between society and religious-based values found initial legitimacy in the courts. In fact, with the ever-increasing secularization of the courts themselves (the place where legal issues regarding expressions of religious faith are resolved), the process of secularizing society at large is self-perpetuating. And because the courts invoke the authority of Constitutional mandate to overturn legislation which violates their notion of religious neutrality, not even the representative voice of a religious majority can halt the slide toward officially sanctioned secularism. All the while, the free exercise of religion is suppressed still further.

In the struggle between religious faith and secularism, "neutrality" is by its very nature not neutral. Many Americans today would agree with this letter to the editor submitted in the aftermath of the Teaneck menorah dispute: "The philosophy of separation of state and church embodied within the establishment clause of the First Amendment requires that the separation be complete and unequivocal. It requires the state to be neutral with regard to religions, not to treat them all equally."[4] For the secularist, neutrality means *non-religion.* For the radical secularist, neutrality means *anti-religion.*

Consistent with this secularist interpretation of the Constitution, a growing sentiment among Americans today is that there is no place for religious faith or convictions in the public domain. Through various avenues, we have exalted the privacy of belief to the point of privatizing *all* belief, sometimes even our own. In the secular world of business, education, law, and politics, we regularly make crucial moral choices, believing all the while that we have no right to consult even our personally chosen religious faith.

Take, for example, the demand of some pro-choice advocates that Catholic justices not be permitted to rule on abortion issues (when, in fact, some Catholic justices—including Justice Brennan in *Roe v. Wade*—have already ruled *in favor of* abortion). After all, we are told, respectable religious beliefs ought to sit quietly in a church pew, thinking about heaven and redemption. They mustn't make their way from stained-glass sanctuaries into the classroom, courtroom, or family planning clinic.

Looking Back May Surprise Us

This has not always been the case, even for those whose religion was only a distant cousin to today's mainline evangelical Christianity. One thinks, for instance, of Benjamin Franklin, a card-carrying deist, hardly a Moral-Majority Fundamentalist. Yet when a committee revising the Articles of Confederation reached a bitter deadlock regarding the most appropriate Constitutional model, Franklin told the delegates that they needed to pray. If that weren't shocking enough (to *us*, that is; undoubtedly not to his colleagues), listen to a replay of his commentary on the place of God in their deliberations:

> We have been assured, Sir, in the sacred writings, that "except the Lord build the house, they labor in vain that build it." I firmly believe this; and I also believe that without His concurring aid we shall succeed in the political building no better than the builders of Babel. We shall be divided by our partial local interests; our projects will be confounded, and we ourselves shall become a reproach and byword down to future ages.[5]

Can you imagine the shock and disbelief if Senator Edward Kennedy were to make the same speech today in a deadlocked committee meeting? Would such an invocation of divine guidance, made spontaneously by someone other than the Senate Chaplain, become the subject of an ACLU lawsuit for violating the Establishment Clause? Even Senator Kennedy's more famous brother, a man sometimes associated with morally questionable personal conduct, was kindly disposed toward a mixture of government and religion (not to be confused with a mixture of government and the Catholic Church, of which he was a member, and about which many non-Catholics were alarmed during his campaign for election).

John F. Kennedy's assassination silenced not only one of America's most popular presidents, but also the message which he had prepared to deliver at the Dallas Trade Mart—a message extolling the virtues of biblical righteousness for a nation desiring to remain strong. Included in the speech, which he was never able to give, was this passage from the Psalms: "Unless the Lord watches over the city, the watchmen stand guard in vain."[6] Ironically, the passage Benjamin Franklin had quoted some 200 years before was taken from the same verse, Psalm 127:1.

At the time Kennedy was scheduled to read that verse, a nation was mourning in stunned silence. What a fitting tribute it would be if our nation could mourn in equally stunned silence at the death of its own sense of spiritual values!

The incongruity between Kennedy's public pronouncements about the social importance of biblical righteousness and his reputed behind-the-scenes lifestyle merely serves to underscore the personal danger of privatizing one's beliefs: Few of us live up to our own ideals, and most of us know the frustration of doing again and again that which we know we ought not to do. It's all the more reason why we must reject society's dulling of the moral conscience. If we do not always live up to the high standards of our public affirmations, without them we would lack even the motivation to try.

Separation of Faith and State?

If for many people morality remains a matter of dubious definition, few would deny its basic value, since hardly anyone wants to be thought of as immoral. The more difficult question for many people is the value of religion, particularly *organized* religion. Open up that subject and you soon hear cynical refer-

ences to the Crusades, the Inquisition, and other endless
cruelties done in the name of God. Yet these abhorrent chapters
in the history of religion too easily obscure the quiet, steady
contribution of religion to the moral and political structures of
innumerable civilized societies.

Kennedy was one in a long line of presidents to attribute
America's strength to religion. Even the very first holder of the
high office of the President of the United States not only paid
tribute to religion's general beneficence, but saw a vital connection between the morality to which even a secular society would
pay homage and the biblically-based religion which now happens to stand in such disfavor among America's intellectual
elite.

In his Farewell Address, George Washington pulled no punches
regarding the dangers of privatizing religion:

> Let us with caution indulge the supposition that
> morality can be maintained without religion. What-
> ever may be conceded to the influence of refined
> education on minds of peculiar structure, reason
> and experience both forbid us to expect that na-
> tional morality can prevail in exclusion of religious
> principles.[7]

Washington's warning is not only instructive regarding the
futility of removing religion from the public square, but is also a
compelling lesson that, in the minds of the nation's founders,
"separation of church and state" meant something radically
different from today's pervasive religiphobia. For the founders,
the word "church" meant just that—*church*, not *religion*. It meant
a *particular, officially-recognized* church and not *religion in general*.

As much as a church-controlled *state*, the founders feared a
state-controlled *church*. Therefore, Constitutional protections
against the establishment of religion were intended primarily
for the protection and preservation of the *church*, not the state.
No, not a particular church established by law, as was the case in
various of the original colonies, but *churches and religion in general*.

Far from privatizing religion, the goal of the founders was to
incorporate religion into the social, political, and moral fabric of
a new nation under God. In order to insure the free exercise of

religion toward that goal, it was necessary to prohibit any one church from being established to the exclusion of all others.

Establishment, as had already been proved to be the case in England, was more of a barrier than a bridge to political freedom. Establishment, with its typically authoritarian structure and politicized agenda, had a nasty tendency to stifle individual faith and political belief. Both moral and political choice became less a matter of religion-informed conscience than a matter of church-imposed rules dictated under the guise of divine doctrine.

What could be clearer historically than the primary motivation of many of America's colonists: To achieve religious freedom! Not freedom *from* religion, but freedom *for* religion!

What must not be forgotten, therefore, is that separation between church and state was not an end in itself. For the founders, the importance of separation was its indispensable role in fostering the free exercise of religion, so that unfettered religious faith could have free play in the formation of a new social order. Unlike today's purveyors of conventional secular wisdom, the founders were not hostile to religion, even if it might have an impact on law, government, and politics.

Quite to the contrary, the founders *wanted* religion to have such an impact. They saw in religious faith the bedrock foundation for the rights and responsibilities assumed in a democratic society. Not surprisingly, therefore, the political choices they made were unashamedly informed by their common appeal to a public square in which God held center position and in which religious faith sat in a place of honor.

When Church and State Collide

The current abortion debate has sparked anew the conflict regarding the appropriate distance to be maintained between church and state. One case in particular has sharpened the focus. In the run-up to last fall's special California senate campaign, Democrat Lucy Killea, a Catholic, challenged the Republican candidate, Carol Bentley, in a heavily Republican district. The campaign became a substantially single-issue struggle when Killea bombarded voters with pro-choice TV ads and mailers. Typical of Killea's pro-choice campaign was this position message:

> I have very strong feelings about privacy—feel-
> ings not shared by my opponent. She argues
> government should outlaw abortions—and dictate
> a woman's family planning options. I don't think
> that's any of government's business.[8]

Despite being a clear underdog, Killea defeated the pro-life
candidate in her own Republican stronghold. Was it because
Killea was considered the better candidate for the office? Not
necessarily. Was it because the voters agreed with Killea's pro-
choice stance? Not really. Although the campaign had turned
into a single-issue affair, no one doubts that the campaign
turned on an event hardly anyone could have expected.

Three weeks prior to the election, Roman Catholic bishop
Leo T. Maher made Killea a national *cause célèbre* when he barred
her from receiving Communion because of her pro-choice campaign. In a letter to Killea, the bishop set forth his reasons for the
unusual action:

> No popular vote or public opinion can change in
> any way the divine law that directs and guides
> mankind. In this case, we continue our pastoral
> endeavor of proclaiming . . . that life is an absolute
> value. The pro-choice movement is a pro-death
> movement. . . . [Because your position on abortion
> puts you] in complete contradiction to the moral
> teaching of the Catholic Church . . . I have no other
> choice but to deny you the right to receive the
> Eucharist in the Catholic Church.[9]

Maher undoubtedly was influenced in his decision by the
statement of the National Conference of Catholic Bishops just
days before, that "no Catholic can responsibly take a 'pro-
choice' stand when the 'choice' in question involves the taking
of innocent life."[10] In a statement to reporters, Maher explained
further: "We're doing this because the politicians have failed to
recognize their obligation to bring their Catholic faith and
morality into the public arena. We are trying to teach them,
direct them, that this is their obligation."[11] He said his action
was "more pastoral than political."

Nevertheless, in the wake of Maher's action and the resulting backlash it evoked from Catholics and non-Catholics alike,

many bishops carefully distanced themselves from similar action. Among pro-choice Catholic politicians whose bishops could yet take similar action are Senator Edward Kennedy, New York Governor Mario Cuomo, and California Attorney General John K. Van de Kamp. The bishops obviously face the dilemma of how to influence Catholic politicians without appearing to tear down the wall between church and state.

Maher's action drew the ire of columnist Martin Schram, who contrasted it with the words of John F. Kennedy to a gathering of Protestant ministers in 1960:

> I believe in an America where the separation of church and state is absolute—where no Catholic prelate would tell the President how to act. . . . I do not speak for my church on public matters and the church does not speak for me. Whatever issue may come before me as President—on birth control, divorce, censorship, gambling or any other subject—I will make my decision in accordance . . . with what my conscience tells me to be in the national interest, and without regard to outside religious pressure or dictate. And no power or threat of punishment could cause me to decide otherwise.[12]

Is this the same John F. Kennedy who believed passionately in the need for a national righteousness informed by biblical principles? Were the cynics right to dismiss such pious talk as patronizing "civil religion"? Or, indeed, is there a difference between religious influence generally and specific sectarian doctrine? Are we now in the arena where separation of church and state has the right emphasis on the term *church*?

A Matter of Discipline

A closer look reveals that a different dynamic was at play in the Killea incident. Instead of telling voters who to vote for, Maher was exercising his authority as a bishop to discipline one of his flock whose single-issue abortion politics flew in the face of church teaching. Even Killea acknowledged, "I knew I was in disagreement with the church hierarchy. . . . Perhaps they're trying to make an example out of me."

Here we get to the heart of the matter. Abortion itself was only a peripheral concern. Nor was it a church-state issue. The real question was *what right a church has to discipline its own members.* As one *Los Angeles Times* editorial put it, "The Killea race was treated by some as less a California Senate contest and even less a debate about abortion rights than as a kind of a plebiscite on how the Roman Catholic Church chooses to discipline its members." As such, the issue is not whether the church can invade the state, but whether the state can invade the church. That is, should the church have a legitimate right of privacy regarding in-house discipline of its own members?

At its best, public attitudes toward church discipline depends upon whose bell is being rung at the time. In the sensational Oklahoma case in which Marian Guinn was disfellowshiped by church elders for her illicit affair with the former town mayor, *Donahue* and other talkshow audiences sided with the self-confessed adulteress. By contrast, when the General Assemblies of God ousted Jimmy Swaggart following his admission of sexual improprieties with prostitutes, national sentiment was in favor of church discipline.

A church's involvement in political matters often swings on the same whimsical pendulum of public approval. Few eyebrows were raised in 1962 when Archbishop Joseph Rummel of New Orleans excommunicated members of his flock for attempting to hinder racial desegregation of schools. Even fewer objections have been raised at the role of clergy in South Africa who have called for civil disobedience to end apartheid; or Pope John Paul II's role in the chain of events leading to democratic government in Poland; or his condemnation of right-wing death squads in El Salvador and censure of an unjust Jean Claude Duvalier in Haiti.

NBC News producer Arthur A. Lord notes that "it is somewhat hypocritical, then, for Americans to feel that it is commendable for the Catholic hierarchy to try to effect social change in all those other places, but it is taboo for them to do it here." Lord even treads one brave step beyond by reminding us that "the Vatican's activism is understandable. The Pope, as a young man growing up in Poland, was acutely aware that during World War II, Pope Pius XII did virtually nothing to prevent the Nazi slaughter of Jews, Slavs, Poles and other 'undesirables'."[13]

I suspect that William F. Buckley, Jr., has got it just about right: "The question that people really ask themselves is: Do I agree with the moral position taken by this clergyman? If the answer is yes, then they manage to reconcile church and state. If the answer is no, then we hear from the *New York Times* that 'to force religious discipline on public officials risks destroying the fragile accommodations that Americans of all faiths and no faith have built with the bricks of the Constitution and the mortar of tolerance.' "[14]

At the time of the Killea controversy, an obscure newspaper blurb caught my eye: "Walt Disney Attractions, which leases and manages the Queen Mary in Long Beach, has fired three mustachioed employees for refusing to abide by company policy that bans facial hair."[15] Naturally, the men were consulting their lawyers.

As one of the bearded persuasion, with even more facial hair than a mustache, I suppose I should join them in a class-action suit. But Disney's personal-appearance policy, like Roman Catholic doctrine, has no force in my life. I am neither an employee of Disney nor a Catholic. And although I admire both the high standards of the Disney organization and the moral commitment of the Catholic Church, if it meant having to shave off my beard, or to submit to the spiritual authority of the Pope, I would join neither constituency.

The story, however, is a simple reminder of how most people today find virtually any sort of imposed standards somehow un-American. If even personal grooming policies barely meet the test, church doctrine can't be far behind. In the case of Killea, separation of church and state gets twisted out of all proportion with a demand that there be separation between church and *church*. Now we insist that the church not even intrude into the lives of its own members!

Are we to understand that a woman may freely choose to expel "part of her body" (as feminists put it regarding abortion) even if her own life is not at stake, but that a church (the body of the faithful) cannot expel a part of itself which threatens its very spiritual life? Choice for secularists, but not for the church?

John K. Roth, professor of philosophy at Claremont McKenna College and a pro-choice Protestant, cautions against stripping the church of its own spiritual jurisdiction:

> As a bishop, Maher is responsible for his church's integrity no less than elected political leaders are

responsible for the integrity of their government. In good conscience, he can no more allow members of his church to reject its teaching with impunity—especially when the actions of a particularly-visible member have the effect of contradicting that teaching publicly—than elected political leaders can blithely allow lawbreakers in their jurisdiction to proceed unhindered.[16]

Sanity on the Brink

When church discipline affects a politician it might be understandable that a rights-conscious society would mistake it for a church-state violation. But church-state mania is stretched beyond all reason when it is gratuitously employed to justify opposition to the Catholic Church's position against the use of condoms to achieve safe sex. As AIDS activists picketed Catholic masses from New York City to Los Angeles last fall, national ACT UP organizers said they were sending the "Catholic Church hierarchy a clear message: Stop peddling your religion's morality. . . . This chronic meddling is a violation of the legal separation of church and state."[17]

> ❧ Abortion is a transcendent moral issue precisely because it transcends all religious beliefs and even outspoken nonbelief.

Is this to say that Catholic bishops have lost the right of free speech simply because they happen to appeal to a transcendent moral law which condemns the free sex tenets of America's newest religion, *secularism*? Does a right to *free sex* now supersede even the Constitutional right of *free speech*?

Sometime, somehow, the mad misuse of church-state separation must come to an end. When it reaches the point that religious faith has no proper place even within churches themselves, much less in society at large, then we have lost all sanity.

Also sometime, somehow, we must give up the notion that

abortion is solely a *Catholic* issue, or even a *Christian* or *Judeo-Christian* issue, and least of all a *fundamentalist* Christian issue. Maintain an irrational separation between church and state in America if you wish, and even forbid the Catholic Church to speak its mind on the subject if you must, but you still have Hindu's greatest-ever advocate, Mahatma Gandhi, saying forcefully: "It seems to me as clear as daylight that abortion would be a crime."

No one has been more outspoken in behalf of the pro-life conscience than Dr. Bernard Nathanson, formerly a card-carrying pro-choice advocate who was co-founder of the National Association for the Repeal of Abortion Laws (NARAL) and director of the world's largest abortion clinic. (He described himself as "an agnostic Jew.") In 1979 he published *Aborting America*, which exposed the roots of the abortion industry, and more recently he has produced both "The Silent Scream" and "Eclipse of Reason," two controversial pro-life films which are anathema to pro-choice supporters. Says Dr. Nathanson: "Even if God does not exist, the fetus does."[18]

Abortion is a transcendent moral issue precisely because it transcends all religious beliefs and even outspoken nonbelief. Only religious bigotry allows pro-choice supporters to summarily dismiss opposition to their cause as nothing more than the narrow-minded religiosity of the Catholic Church and Bible-belt fundamentalists.

Hard Lessons from the Eastern Bloc

At stake ultimately is the free exercise of religion—as much a Constitutional right as the so-called separation of church and state. Think of the irony in these times of great human rights movements for freedom. For over 50 years, Communist regimes in Eastern Bloc countries have lived with a total (that is to say *totalitarian*) privatization of religious faith, enforced by officially-atheistic secular governments.

At the very time secularism in America is doing all it can to drive religious faith underground, those who have been the victims of that same elitist "enlightenment" for decades—together with its attendant loss of personal freedoms—are finally managing to throw off the shackles of spiritual ignorance and "go public" with a personal faith too long suppressed!

What does the collapse of atheistic Communism tell us if not that a society without God cannot succeed? That denial of the

Creator is a denial of the sanctity of life and by extension a denial of human rights? In that regard, you can rest assured that there is a direct tie between how a society treats its people and how it views the sanctity of life, even from the moment of conception.

It is no coincidence that, with but rare exceptions, Communist countries have encouraged abortion as a form of birth control. In fact Lenin in 1920 pioneered in liberal abortion. And you can be sure that official government support of abortion has had nothing whatsoever to do with any Western notions of some fundamental "right to privacy."

The statistics in the Soviet Union alone are mind-boggling: Each year one in five women terminates a pregnancy, and 90 percent of all first pregnancies end in abortions. For every 100 births there are at least 106 abortions—in all, between 7 and 8 million "official" abortions. Add to those figures abortions performed outside hospitals and medical clinics, and there may be as many as 12 million or more abortions annually.[19] Quite literally, abortion is the Soviets' idea of contraception.

Romania's now-notorious *prohibition* of abortion was no exception to Communism's low view of human life. The Ceausescu regime was hardly pro-life as we know it; it was simply nationalistic. Romania lies in a part of the Balkans where nationalism still leads to racial conflagration. Therefore it felt its survival was dependent on an increase in its population in order to hold its own and preserve its frontiers. In 1964 Romania's annual population growth stood at about 2.5 percent. Worried by this, the Ceausescu government set a target of 30 million Romanians by the year 2000.

To accomplish that goal, both contraception and abortion were prohibited. If feminists greatly exaggerate when they speak of *American* women's bodies callously being used to manufacture babies, they aptly describe official government policy in *Romania* for the past 20 years! Sanctity of life was not at issue, nor protection of family values, nor concern about the physical and psychological side-effects of abortion. Abortion was illegal because it did not suit state interests. Had *over*population been the problem, abortion would just as easily have been *mandated*, as it is for all practical purposes under the strict population control policy in Communist China.

Under the atheistic secularism of Eastern Europe (outside of Romania) recurrent abortions have been the traditional form of contraception. Dr. Tim Rutter, a consultant to Marie Stopes International, a pro-abortion health organization, reports that it is not unusual for a woman in her 20's to have had seven or eight terminations.[20] A nation's government does not have to be totalitarian in order to encourage the killing of millions of the unborn (note Japan, for example), but a political system having a low view of human *rights* could hardly be expected to have a high view of human *life*.

Replacing Religious Faith

Because today's secular journalists and politicians have all but shoved God and religion out of the picture, they have left what Richard John Neuhaus calls the "naked public square." As a result, social, political, and moral decisions are now made in a vacuum, or so it would at first appear. But the truth is, as Neuhaus points out, that every vacuum begs to be filled, first by anarchy and then by totalitarianism. What's filling the vacuum at the moment is the pro-choice moral anarchy of materialistic secularism. Who knows what totalitarian future is waiting in the wings, whether a backlash religious fanaticism or a godless socialistic state?

1989 was the year that Communism died in Eastern Bloc nations. Hopefully the 1990's will be remembered as the decade that the naked Red Square in Moscow became clothed again with transcendent moral conscience. What more of a lesson do those of us in the West need? If we continue to separate church and state in the way liberals and secularists urge today, we will get more than we ever bargained for. All we have to do is ask the millions of people who have suffered under Communist rule, whose bundle of freedoms—including both free speech and the free exercise of religion—has been denied under the banner of progressive, socialist secular humanism.

As Roanoke College professor Robert Benne points out, "Mikhail Gorbachev himself seems to be a recent convert to the social utility of religion. In promising to relax oppressive restriction on religion, he almost paraphrased our own George Washington's opinion that religion and morality are the twin pillars of healthy national life."[21]

Gorbachev has been joined by other Eastern Bloc Communist leaders moving in the same direction. Benne reminds us of what a radical shift in attitudes toward religion this move represents: "The leaders who once condemned religion for being an opiate that diverted the attention of workers from unjust social conditions are now intent on using religion to rescue their societies from calamity."[22]

However, the Communist leaders' pragmatic use of religion for economic resurrection undoubtedly will have spiritual spin-offs not yet fully comprehended by a nonbelieving hierarchy:

> There is a great likelihood of major religious renewals in the Eastern Bloc countries. The human spirit's aspiration for transcendent truth has been bottled up for decades by ideological and social practices that have attempted to reduce the human horizon to a drab one-dimensionality.
>
> The religious bodies that have resisted this pressure and kept the faith have gained enormous respect from the people and now offer them a liberating alternative to a failed Marxist vision. Catholics in Poland and Hungary, the Eastern Orthodox in Russia, and Lutherans in East Germany have remained credible islands of moral and spiritual transcendence in a flat sea of state-enforced materialism.[23]

Religious renewal will indeed strengthen the moral fiber that holds together marriages, families, and the workplace—in short, the nation. But what Eastern Europeans and Soviets will learn, and what we Americans must relearn, is that true religion does more than craft a useful morality; true religion is about obedience to God and faith in his leading.

Professor Benne brings us back to the need for yet another national movement to achieve integration—but integration this time between private and public morality, between religious faith and social justice. "Obedience to God," says Benne, "does not end with private, personal morality. It extends, as indeed the prophet extended it, to the public life of the society." Yet that is not always easy or comfortable, for "the prophetic call for justice is discomforting to every nation."

In the public life of American society, the prophetic call for renewed spiritual values may be hard indeed, requiring fresh looks at divorce, homosexuality, pornography, and abortion. Indeed, fresh hard looks at housing the homeless, feeding the hungry, and ridding the nation of its many substance addictions.

Secular humanist programs devoid of any spiritual dimension will no longer do. Separating the state from religious faith is as passé as empty Marxist promises. In America, as in Eastern Europe, the time has come for a spiritual revolution. In this unprecedented time of global optimism, all of us, like all of them, need "a measure of what the Russians call *dukhovnost*— the spiritual life of the people."[24]

FIVE

Through The Eyes of Radical Feminists

The party seeks power for its own sake . . . we are interested only in power . . . the object of power is power.
—George Orwell in *1984*

LAST NOVEMBER, ALONG WITH MILLIONS of other viewers, I watched extended live television coverage of one of the largest pro-choice rallies ever held across America. Yet I was genuinely puzzled as I watched, since of the many women I personally knew who had had abortions (some of them married, some single), not one of them had emerged emotionally unscathed. For none of them had the decision to abort been a happy decision. In each case it had been an agonizing, soul-wrenching, guilt-producing decision.

Even now after many years, when anniversaries of the abortion itself (or the baby's projected "due date") come around, these women still relive the nightmare and struggle with residual feelings of guilt and loss. Sometimes, when they hold another mother's newborn infant, they fight back tears at the thought of what might have been. Even newspaper and magazine articles on abortion can be daily reminders of the pain of their decision.

By contrast, what I saw as I viewed the pro-choice rally in Washington D.C. were 150,000 banner-bearing women shouting wildly and waving placards demanding a right to have an abortion. I couldn't help but ask myself, "Who are these women? What prompts a woman to get up in the morning, get dressed, have breakfast, drive many miles—perhaps even fly in—to be part of a crowd of people yelling loudly about the right to kill an unborn child in their womb?

Even if a woman believes she has a right to make such a decision, how, I kept asking myself, could she be so insensitive to the tragic reality of abortion, both for the unborn and the mother? Even if one believed that abortion ought to be permitted without restriction, how in the face of such a traumatic personal choice could anyone participate so blithely in an occasion having all the markings of a clamorous pep rally for the local football team?

The next question to cross my mind was how many of the women protesting that day had themselves had abortions. Always appreciative of the fact that, as a man, I cannot possibly understand the complex dynamics confronting pregnant women, I nevertheless wondered about the women at the rally. Did *they* know what it was like to have an abortion? While I supposed that many of them in fact did not know, I also guessed that many did. How then were these women different from all the women I knew who had suffered so greatly from their abortions—not one of whom would have joined the sometimes-circuslike atmosphere of the pro-choice rally?

One woman who *does* know what it is like to have an abortion—in fact *two* abortions—is Kim C. Flodin, a freelance writer. Her recent pro-choice *Newsweek* article, unusually frank both about her abortions and her mixed reactions to them, confirms my suspicions about how difficult it must be, even for those who have experienced it, to articulate politically the personal agony of abortion:

> I can say, despite the blood and the grief, I'd do it all over again—even though it makes me immeasurably sad and I still choke a little when I remember the dream boy on the beach [her second "son," as she imagined him].
>
> But I still cannot find the guts to march for choice. My friends, even those privy to my past, think it's

circumstantial—the marches always seem to be poorly scheduled for my busy life. But I know that in the end I can barely stomach the politics of this debate. Though I understand its necessity, I hate the sloganeering. I hate it because I cannot reduce my complicated set of emotions to the bold-faced type of a placard.[1]

As I watched the Washington demonstration, I still couldn't figure it out. How could women who have gone through abortion experiences be so unaffected, so insensitive to destroying what they claim to be a part of themselves? Was it because the women I knew were mostly women whose consciences were informed by religious teaching? (Some of them did *not* have religious backgrounds.) Was it perhaps because, as appears to be the case with many homosexuals, they had a deep need to secure public acceptability for conduct which, behind a facade of liberation, haunts them with guilt?

≥ More and more Americans are being led to accept that it is a good thing to have the *right* to do what is widely acknowledged to be *not a good thing*.

Or was it possible that television viewers across the nation were witnessing a quite-unashamed demand for unfettered personal freedom, even at the cost of human life, if necessary?

Even now I can't seem to shake the impact of what became the battle cry of the rally. As the momentum of the events reached a crescendo, Molly Yard, President of the National Organization for Women, called out from the platform: "My sisters—and men of conscience—join your hands together and TAKE THE POWER!" In eager response to her leading and to the singing of Kay Weaver, the crowd roared out with approval, over and over again: "Take the power! Take the power! Take the power!"

As I watched the screen in total amazement, it finally sank in. So *that* is what the pro-choice rally was all about—*power!*

Feminine power. And homosexual power (as reflected in T-shirts saying, "Abortion is not the only issue," worn by members of the Progressive Student Network). Pro-choice was nothing less than power politics for special-interest groups. What a far cry from the personal agony of lives which have been scarred by the decision to abort! If *power* is what it's all about, I thought, then we have lost the soul of America. If *power* is the motive behind pro-choice, then we have completely abandoned a sense of our own humanity.

Perhaps the crowd's orchestrated chant to "take the power" should not have been so surprising. What else *could* they have chanted? Not even the most callous person among them could have shouted, "Kill the fetuses! Kill the fetuses!" And that alone speaks volumes. Almost no one believes that abortion itself is a *good* thing. Most pro-choice advocates readily admit that abortion is a regrettable, last-resort act of violence. Yet more and more Americans are being led to accept that it is a good thing to have the *right* to do what is widely acknowledged to be *not a good thing*.

Gazing in stunned disbelief at this brazen display of abortion politics, I kept wondering how it all could have happened. As a law professor, of course, I knew how it had happened from a legal standpoint. It happened in 1973 when the Supreme Court restricted states in outlawing abortions in *Roe v. Wade*. But I also knew that the Court had based its decision on a supposed right of privacy rather than on any notion of feminist power. So, except for understandable feminist concern that the 1989 *Webster* decision heralded an erosion of that right, what was the underlying impetus for this revitalized pro-choice activism?

More than a Right of Privacy

One might suppose that feminists were thrilled with the decision in *Roe v. Wade*. However, that is not the case, at least not with all feminists. Gloria Steinem (whose own abortion "had taken place in a time of such isolation, illegality, and fear that afterward, I did my best to just forget"),[2] says of *Roe v. Wade* that "its solution was the compromise of *reform*, not *repeal*. . . . The goal was to get the government out of reproductive decision-making" altogether.[3] Even *Roe v. Wade's* viability cutoff standard is generally seen as an unacceptable compromise of women's rights.

As with any supposed cohesive group—whether fundamentalist Christians, Marxists, or Jews—it should not be surprising that feminists have differences among themselves. Where many feminists were pleased with the formulation of a right of privacy to protect reproductive control, thereby assuring sexual freedom and economic independence, more radical feminists weren't so sure. They saw the right of privacy as but another means by which men could control women and have more sexual access for themselves.

Radical feminists challenge the assumption of both proponents and opponents of abortion that women have a significant say in sex. Not only do women not wish to conceive, say some feminists, but they do not wish to have the intercourse which results in conception. If the idea of privacy is to recognize a tension between governmental intrusion and personal autonomy, radical feminists claim that personal autonomy doesn't exist in the first place. When it comes to sex, women don't act autonomously. Sex invariably is done in male ways on male terms with male power over the consequences.

Choice Through Male Eyes?

Hence the basis for the feminist charge that men were all too willing to "grant" women the right to abortion in order to preserve their own access to sex—to take away any last excuse that women might have for not having sex with them. In the words of Andrea Dworkin, "Getting laid was at stake."[4] Given the substantial financial support supplied to the abortion rights crusade by the Playboy Foundation, radical feminists may well be warranted in drawing this conclusion. Add to this the fact that a significant percentage of abortions are the result of young men putting pressure on their pregnant girlfriends and you begin to wonder if the feminists aren't right.

For feminists, proof of this sinister-plot-in-sheep's-clothing is found in the male-dominated government's refusal to provide public funding for abortion, upheld by male-dominated courts. They argue that, at least for economically disadvantaged women, the recognized right to a private decision regarding abortion does not translate into public support for that decision, thereby rendering any private right of choice illusory.

Yet if the feminists' thesis is correct—if there is in fact an ulterior reason for men to support women's right to abortion—

then what explains the number of men who bitterly oppose abortion? Are they men who have overlooked the reality that freer abortion means freer sex for themselves? And why would the same male judges who supported abortion as a matter of privacy turn right around and deny a right to public funding?[5] Have they forgotten the purpose of their conspiracy?

On the other hand, if other feminists are correct in arguing alternatively that men want control over abortion in order to keep women from destroying the babies through which men's potency is affirmed and their immortality assured, then why has the male-dominated Supreme Court held that *Roe v. Wade* denies the biological father a right to veto the woman's decision to have an abortion?

Whatever the merits of the alternative pleading by feminists, the bottom line is their claim that men remain in control of abortion. To that extent, they say, women still do not have a meaningful right of choice, either regarding abortion or sex itself. Puzzling throughout feminist literature, however, is an absence of suggested alternatives. Surely radical feminists are not calling for a reversal of *Roe v. Wade*. Nor, we can safely assume, do they want abortion recriminalized. So what more do they want?

What they seem to want is an *absolute* right to abortion in which the state not only refuses to *interfere* but also actively *intervenes*, if necessary, to assure public funding in support of such a right. One can imagine the outcry, of course, if the government were to reverse its policy of passivity regarding the human fetus and intervene affirmatively on behalf of the unborn! Whether private choice ought to be subject to the intervention of public choice depends upon what choice is being made and whether we agree with it—another reminder of how complicated the issue of choice becomes when relegated solely to the balancing of competing interests without the benefit of a more universal point of reference.

Yet the greater goal of radical feminists, like Catherine MacKinnon (*Toward a Feminist Theory of the State*), would appear to be societal affirmation of their claim that sexuality is both *male* and *forced*. That sexuality is definitively *male* is the acerbic intent of MacKinnon's opening sentence in her chapter on abortion: "Most women who seek abortions became pregnant while having sexual intercourse with men."[6] That sexuality is virtually always *force* is seen in her complaint that "abortion policy has never been explicitly approached in the context of how women get pregnant; that is, as a consequence of intercourse under conditions of gender inequality; that is, as an issue of forced sex."[7]

Radical feminists suggest that the abortion issue would simply fade away if only we would come to appreciate that sex, as sex, is violence, and that if abortion is an act of violence, it was born in turn out of another act of violence: male-imposed heterosexual intercourse. In her book *Of Woman Born*, Adrienne Rich explains the connection:

> In a society where women entered sexual intercourse willingly, where adequate contraception was a genuine social priority, there would be no "abortion issue." . . . Abortion is violence. . . . It is the offspring, and will continue to be the accuser of a more pervasive and prevalent violence, the violence of rapism.[8]

But of course the "rapism" of which Rich speaks is not the same as the crime of rape for which a man might be found guilty in a court of law. What Rich and other radical feminists are saying is that even sex between intimates (perhaps *especially* sex between intimates) is best defined as forced intercourse. As Catherine MacKinnon puts it: "Rape and intercourse are not authoritatively separated by any difference between the physical acts or amount of force involved but only legally, by a standard that centers on the man's interpretation of the encounter."[9] As she sees sex, "the major distinction between intercourse (normal) and rape (abnormal) is that the normal happens so often that one cannot get anyone to see anything wrong with it."[10]

In light of this perspective, it is indeed surprising to find the following discussion of "rape fantasies" in one of feminism's classic publications, *Our Bodies, Ourselves*:

> What about rape fantasies? Some people say that if we fantasize about having sex forced on us, that means we want to be raped. This is untrue: totally

unlike actual rape, fantasizing about rape is voluntary, and does not bring us physical pain or violation. For those of us who grew up learning that "good girls" don't want sex, a fantasy of being forced to have sex frees us of responsibility and can be highly erotic. It can allow us the feeling of being desired uncontrollably.[11]

One can only imagine the protest that would ensue if such positive encouragement were given for "rape fantasies" in a male version of *Our Bodies, Ourselves*!

Choice Without Consent?

Assuming for a moment that all sexuality, including sex within marriage, is unequally weighted in favor of men, and that therefore sexual expression in some sense may always be considered "forced," how would radical feminists propose to change things? By eliminating all heterosexual intercourse? Surely not. Then *what*? Only sexuality to which the woman "consents"?

But at this point we face the criticism that sexual "consent" is meaningless in a male-dominated society. If women don't consent under the fear of being physically harmed for refusing to have sex, then they consent because of the fear that refusal might make them unacceptable to their partner, or perhaps because of an ever-present fear that a nonviolent partner could always *turn* violent.

If radical feminists are right in claiming that sex and pregnancy generally happen without women's consent, how are we to account for the millions of women each year who claim, apparently voluntarily, that they joyfully choose to have children despite the attendant physical pain and limitations on mobility and career goals? Are we really to believe that they have been "forced into motherhood," as radical feminists urge? Is the "maternal instinct" simply a male myth? Is the ticking of a woman's "biological clock" just so much sexism? What explains the thousands of unmarried women each year (many of whom are feminist Lesbians) who decide to have children through artificial insemination, if necessary, in order not to miss out on motherhood? Forced sex and forced pregnancy do not seem to align with common experience.

Nevertheless, for the radical feminist, choice about sexuality is never fully free, fully chosen choice. It is never completely voluntary choice. Therefore all sex is forced sex. And therefore all abortions are the result of forced sex.

Legislation by Definition

Surely this allegation must raise a serious question for those who would urge that abortion be permitted in at least the two exceptional cases of incest and rape. If the law were to give approval to abortion in those instances, would not radical feminists next press the case that supposed inequality in the privacy of the bedroom (so much the more so in marriage where sex is *expected* of a woman) is tantamount to rape? Would they not urge that *all* sex resulting in conception is conception by force, and therefore subject to abortion? If that scenario seems incredibly farfetched, so did the decriminalization of abortion the day before the decision in *Roe v. Wade* was handed down.

The language of *forced pregnancy* is already in place, as we can see from an article in *Ms.* magazine by Rhonda Copelon and Kathryn Kolbert. Analyzing the oral arguments in *Webster v. Reproductive Health Services* (April 1989), they lament that "no one asked Fried [who argued on behalf of the government] why a state directive to a woman to suffer an unwanted pregnancy was not a 'very violent intrusion' into her life—albeit an invasion only women can experience."[12] Pregnancy—"a very violent intrusion"?

It's easy to forget that we've actually been down this road before. Statutes once permitting abortion only when the mother's health was at risk were amended to include both physical and *mental* health. The result of this seemingly benign amendment was to push the door wide open for abortion on demand. It was simply a matter of interpretation. The term "mental health" was sufficiently elastic to permit virtually any kind of emotional distress over an unwanted pregnancy to warrant an abortion.

Taking the position that all sex is to some degree "forced" is undoubtedly not only out of step with the common experience of most women, but it can have undesirable implications for sex which truly is forced. When all sex is considered rape because consent is never complete, the form of rape where there is not even a *pretense* of consent is tragically minimalized. That is one

of the dangers of well-intended attempts to legislate against so-
called "marital rape" (at least where a couple is not legally
separated). Such legislation may only serve to trivialize the
threat to women by those who would brutally force intercourse
outside the context where a woman has any choice whatsoever
over who her sexual partner might be.

Power and the Powerless

In urging the need for greater choice for women, feminists
assume (with questionable empirical support) a condition in
which half the human race lacks virtually all choice. In that
light, the abortion issue for radical feminists is an issue of
political power—getting it, sharing in it, exercising it. (Eventually turning the tables and dominating with it themselves?) If
that proposition were ever in doubt, the picture becomes clear
when pro-choice rallies appear on the television screen as real-
life drama. It's that cry again: "Take the power! Take the power!
Take the power!"

> ᪣ Are pro-choice feminists vic-
> timizing human fetuses by using the
> same logic with which they see them-
> selves being victimized?

For radical feminists, abortion is seen as a means of balancing the interests. But therein lies the weakness of their cause.
For if abortion is simply a matter of power politics, then even the
"oughtness" which they seek on behalf of women is dependent
upon the "isness" of political power from which they feel disen-
franchised. Because power in a democracy is a matter of
majority rule, then either the men who already are thought by
feminists to be in control politically, or those previously identified with the Moral Majority (whom feminists seem to hate
more than men generally), or even the majority of America's
women (who are personally opposed to abortion) will have the
final say.

Nor does an emotive call for protection of the powerless
present the best argument in favor of abortion when there is

none more powerless—and therefore more in need of protection—than the all-too-vulnerable human fetus. Seen in that light, feminist rhetoric is all too easily turned on its end by comparison. For example, it is said that women have had little choice but to be limited by terms which men set. In abortion, the human fetus has no choice but to be totally eliminated by terms which *women* set! Again, it is urged by feminists that women's status is second-class, and too often that is the case. Even so, as between the mother and the fetus in an abortion, the unborn is painfully and fatally second-class.

ટ Could it be that, deep down, feminists know they would lose the battle if it were fought on the turf of basic morality?

Of course these comparisons are based upon an assumption about the nature of the human fetus that many feminists (and nonfeminists) would find unacceptable. Setting aside at this point a fuller discussion of the specific question of whether the fetus is a person, it is fitting at this point to observe that what feminists say about their own plight as women could be said with equal force about the aborted fetus. With reference to how men view women, for example, Catherine MacKinnon talks about their "excitement at reduction of a person to a thing, to less than a human being, as socially defined."[13]

Are pro-choice feminists victimizing human fetuses by using the same logic with which they see themselves being victimized? As suggested elsewhere, the making of moral choices on the basis of self-serving redefinitions is in itself morally questionable. The reason, of course, is that redefinition—whether of slaves, women, or human fetuses—is not simply a word game. Addressing the way in which she believes men objectify women, MacKinnon unwittingly tells us how women likewise objectify the human fetus in abortion: "The mechanism is force, imbued with meaning because it is the means to death, and death is the ultimate making of a person into a thing."[14]

Flight from the Moral Arena

One fact stands out among all others: Feminists lose the force of their argument on abortion when they abandon the high moral ground they rightfully claim on issues of pornography and sexual abuse. As with both pornography and sexual abuse, feminists must come to see that abortion is not a matter of power, but of morality.

Thomas Paine, in his debate with Edmund Burke over the validity of the French Revolution, could have been addressing today's radical feminists when he said: "It is power and not principles that Mr. Burke venerates; and under this abominable depravity he is disqualified to judge between them."[15]

Feminists who rightly decry the abuse of power in forcible rape of women's bodies seem unable to understand the similarity of their quest for power to be used in the forcible rape of the fruit of their own wombs.

It is here that less radical feminists present a far stronger case by at least talking in terms of what they see to be competing moral interests (the love which might be withheld from an unwanted child, the questionable quality of life for those born with debilitating diseases, etc.). By contrast, radical feminists make no appeal to morals. Is that simply a matter of strategy or because they know they risk losing the battle if it is fought in the moral arena?

MacKinnon says that, for feminists, it's a matter of priorities: "Women's embattled need to survive in a world hostile to their survival has largely precluded exploration of these issues." With some chagrin, she notes that "if the fetus has *any* standing in the debate, it has more weight than women do."[16] Therefore, radical feminists simply cannot afford the luxury of engaging the moral issue regarding the status of the fetus. Any conclusion favoring the fetus would threaten what they see to be the more important cause, feminism itself.

In a recent editorial, journalist John Leo—for the most part a feminist sympathizer—shared his concern about how feminists, in Jason DeParle's words, "'wish away a very real collision' between female autonomy and our moral obligations toward developing life":

> For me, the problem is not feminists' pro-choice stance, but that the stance has no moral context. All

the emphasis is on rights. None is on the morality of using those rights. It is as if we were back in the 1850's: No one is talking about whether slavery is wrong; instead, the whole discussion revolves around the question of whether each slaveholder has a basic right to decide the issue for himself.[17]

Could it be that, deep down, feminists know they would lose the battle if it were fought on the turf of basic morality, and that the childlike response "But I *want* to do it!" is all they can legitimately cling to?

John Leo suggests that there are other reasons as well:

There is an obvious tactical reason why no moral discussion has taken place under feminist auspices: Any such debate could split the pro-choice constituency, a large portion of which thinks abortion is wrong.

But it goes beyond that. For years, feminist leaders have treated moral discussion of abortion within the movement as a betrayal or, at best, a distraction. "To even raise the question of when it's immoral," argues Kate Michelman, head of the National Abortion Rights Action League, "is to say that women can't make moral decisions."[18]

Is that also to say that women cannot be *persuaded* about the moral decisions they make? That there is no place for moral dialogue, even for women who may not have made up their minds on a given moral issue? The real reason seems more apparent: Feminists know that, if they have managed up to this point to keep a toehold on the issue of *pro-choice*, they are dangling precariously from the precipice of public opinion on the issue of *pro-abortion*.

Toward a Greater Vision

In the place of law, politics, and power struggles, what we need is a greater vision of who we are as male and female—that is, to understand why we have gender in the first place, whether biologically, reproductively, emotionally, or even spiritually. We need to be honest enough to ask the hard questions about gender and bold enough to buck the shallow self-righteousness of conventional wisdom when it accuses of sexist blasphemy anyone who dares to believe that equality in value doesn't necessarily mean sameness in role or function.

In the place of law, politics, and power struggles, what we need is a new appreciation of transcendent values, both moral and religious. We need to see that the higher law can be more effective than mere secular law because it lays greater claim to a person's actions than any human law can claim; that it calls each person to his highest aspirations rather than to minimalist conduct; that its rewards and punishments are greater than any human system can ever devise.

What radical feminists risk in pro-choice extremism—particularly with regard to abortion—is the dismantling of the very moral imperative to which they lay claim in pursuit of their own cause. The challenge of human existence is not to "take the power!" The challenge of human existence, both for feminists and nonfeminists, is to choose the good of others over ourselves.

Especially the good of those who are powerless to defend themselves.

SIX

Whales, Furs
And Human Life

*What irony that a society confronted with plastic bags filled
with the remains of aborted babies should be more concerned
about the problem of recycling the plastic.*

—Winifred Egan

THE PRO-CHOICE GENERATION is a *Green* Generation.
Ours is the generation of protecting the planet—of international concern about the Brazilian rain forests, nuclear waste,
vanishing elephants, and the greenhouse effect. We're all about
recycling and bicycling. Smog, acid rain, and industrial pollution have our undivided attention. Finally. Thankfully.

Who would ever have thought that airline flights would be
smoke-free, or that *Perrier*—a name synonymous with nature's
purity—would have to remove from the shelves millions of
bottles and cans of its popular sparkling water at the mere hint
of cancer-causing benzine? Who would have dreamed that,
even in the 70's, construction on a Tennessee River dam could be
temporarily halted because of a tiny, virtually-unknown snail
darter, or that in the 80's and 90's logging of old-growth Douglas
fir in Oregon would be brought to a standstill to protect spotted
owls threatened with extinction?

It's been a long, slow process of expanding global awareness of our fragile environment. Perhaps no organization has done more to contribute to our awareness than Greenpeace—often militant, often controversial, almost always successful.

The brochure that recently dropped through the front-door mail slot at my English country hideaway records the victories.

"Against all odds, Greenpeace has brought the plight of the natural world to the attention of caring people. Terrible abuses to the environment, often carried out in remote places, have been headlined on television and in the press.

"Greenpeace began with a protest voyage into a nuclear test zone. The test was disrupted. Today, the site at Amchitka in the Aleutian Islands is a bird sanctuary.

"Then Greenpeace sent its tiny inflatable boats to protect the whales. They took up position between the harpoons and the fleeing whales. Today, commercial whaling is banned.

"On the ice floes of Newfoundland, Greenpeace volunteers placed their bodies between the gaffs of the seal hunters and the helpless seal pups. The hunt was subsequently called off.

"Peaceful direct action by Greenpeace has invoked the power of public opinion which in turn has forced changes in the law to protect wildlife and to stop the pollution of the natural world."[1]

Under the banner "Join us and help save the natural world," Greenpeace has successfully launched political candidates in Britain and other European countries, thereby extending their already significant lobbying capabilities. While their tactics are confrontational in character, the results which they achieve have been applauded by some of the most conservative of political action groups.

Endangered Wildlife; Endangered Human Life

I keep wondering what our reaction might have been if the Greenpeace brochure presented above had included the following paragraph: "In Atlanta, Georgia, Greenpeace activists picketed on sidewalks outside of Planned Parenthood clinics, protesting the annual killing of 1.5 million unborn children in the wake of the 1973 *Roe v. Wade* decision legalizing abortion. In a recent Supreme Court ruling, this legalized slaughter of innocents has now been abolished." The conspicuous absence of such a paragraph ought to raise important questions for a pro-choice generation about the relative rights of endangered *wildlife* and endangered *human* life.

Associating the fictitious abortion protests with Atlanta will cause most of us to think of the well-publicized Operation Rescue protests in Atlanta and elsewhere which have caused so much consternation among pro-choice advocates, and, for different reasons, even among many pro-life supporters. Although they may be getting a bum rap regarding abortion-clinic bombings for which they were not responsible, unfortunately Rescue's protesters have allowed themselves to become associated in the minds of the public with unloving attitudes and conduct unbecoming Christians.

Without more fully discussing at this point the merits of Operation Rescue's tactics in opposition to abortion, suffice it to say here that such tactics typically are no more confrontational than the tactics employed by Greenpeace, which generally have been well-received by environmentalists. Nor, for that matter, have pro-life's methods of protest differed in kind from the now-hallowed civil rights protests of the 1960's.

❧ How do we justify being activist in the rescue of wildlife, but adamantly opposed to the rescue of human life?

In whatever way we might regard the "activist" protests of environmental or moral advocates generally, the point is that widespread approval of Greenpeace tactics undoubtedly stems from widespread approval of Greenpeace goals. Likewise, widespread disapproval of Operation Rescue's tactics undoubtedly stems from widespread disapproval of Operation Rescue's goals. Rather surprisingly, the *green* generation is also generally a *pro-choice* generation.

And that raises the more important question: How in the world have we managed to reach the point where preventing baby seals from being killed in Newfoundland and the Orkney Isles captures our social conscience, but preventing unborn humans from being killed in abortion clinics across America is somehow repressed within the recesses of that same social conscience? How do we justify being activist in the rescue of wildlife, but adamantly opposed to the rescue of human life? Wouldn't even "potential human life," if one prefers that characterization, represent a greater value than nonhuman life already in being? If necessary, what whale, dolphin, porpoise, or sea turtle would we not sacrifice to save just one human life?

Of all people, Greenpeace activists certainly ought to appreciate the value of just one human life. When the Greenpeace ship *Rainbow Warrior* was sabotaged and sunk in the harbor at Auckland, New Zealand, by French secret agents, a Greenpeace photographer was killed, setting off an international incident. Despite the twisted logic of those who planned the sabotage, there was an all-too-familiar ring to it. Human life became dispensable when it became *inconvenient,* in this case to the plans of the French government to proceed with their nuclear tests. What's so wrong, twisted logic seemed to be asking, about taking one human life if it gets in your way of preparing to take hundreds of thousands of lives, if necessary?

Of course, that latter figure was what concerned Greenpeace in the first place: nuclear holocaust—the loss of hundreds of thousands (and perhaps millions) of human lives. We've seen that word *holocaust* before. And the numbers involved were in the millions. I understand why many people get upset at the comparison, but how can we escape the obvious parallel with the estimated 25 to 30 million human fetuses killed since abortion was legalized in 1973? If you like, cut that number in half. But whatever million mark we choose, can it be anything less than a holocaust?

If I were to quote Jerry Falwell's reference to legalized abortion as *"biological holocaust,"*[2] reaction undoubtedly would be predictable along political and religious lines. Pro-choice advocates would surely cry foul. I suspect they would say that comparing "terminations of pregnancy" with the genocide of living, breathing, out-of-the-womb human beings is unfair, emotive argumentation. However, I am still struck by our seeming double standard, right down to the very language we use. This news quote from Greenpeace spokesman Mike Hagler demonstrates what I mean:

Asia's drift net fishing fleets may be slaughtering more than 100,000 dolphins a year in the Pacific, the environmental group Greenpeace said on Thursday.

"It's what I would call an *ecological holocaust* going on," said Mike Hagler from the Greenpeace ship Rainbow Warrior II, which is monitoring 20 drift net boats from Japan and Taiwan in the Tasman Sea between Australia and New Zealand.[3]

It's perfectly acceptable to speak of an *ecological holocaust* when we're concerned about the killing of 100,000 dolphins a year, but distasteful and off-limits to speak of a *biological holocaust* when we're talking about the 1.5 million unborn who get caught in the drift nets of abortion clinics each year! If there is any improper use of the word *holocaust*, surely it must be its use when referring to the killing of animals. Associated as it is with the greatest inhumanity to man in modern history, the word *holocaust* deserves more respectful use.

> ❧ **One would think that Greenpeace and Operation Rescue ought to join together in common cause. "For Life and Planet" might be the slogan;** *Greenpeace Rescue* **could be the name.**

Dolphins are intelligent, contributive, and lovable creatures—well worth extraordinary efforts to save—but they are not touched with the same human spirit that was quenched in the ovens of Dauchau and Auschwitz. Unlike the victims of the Holocaust, dolphins are not possessed of a soul which lives beyond death. They are valuable, but not invaluable; precious, but not sacred. That's where Operation Rescue has a leg up on Greenpeace. Theirs is the rescue of humanity itself—body, soul, and spirit.

Until far too late, the world was not aware of the hidden human destruction taking place inside the privacy of concentration camp ovens. That part of the Holocaust was not unlike the private deaths of dolphins in drift nets, hidden beneath the surface, where (apart from the watchful eye of Greenpeace) the world takes no notice. How much more abhorrent, then, the silent screams of the unborn, killed in the now-Constitutional privacy of unwilling wombs.

Divergence in Worldviews

One would think that Greenpeace and Operation Rescue ought to join together in common cause. "For Life and Planet" might be the slogan; *Greenpeace Rescue* could be the name. But, surprisingly enough, never would there be stranger bedfellows. Without taking a poll of their respective members, it is probably safe to say that each organization is motivated by entirely different life perspectives.

Labels too often overgeneralize, distort, and mislead, but the constituency of Greenpeace is likely to be politically liberal, ideologically left of center, and unabashedly secular. By contrast, members of Operation Rescue most likely are politically conservative, ideologically right of center, and intensely religious.

> &. **Modern man and modern woman have made a rubbish tip of the womb. It too was once a thriving oasis of life.**

I'm tempted to point out, perhaps not entirely fairly in this context, that the political liberals are concerned with saving animals and the political conservatives with saving human life. For the purpose of discussion I simply suggest that behind each of these very different organizations is a quite different understanding of the meaning of life, beginning with its origins. Although pro-choice and pro-life advocates do not always fall into similarly-predictable categories, I suspect that even in this arena of life and origins we are faced with the same fundamental conflict between the two groups.

The Greenpeace story, for example, begins with the headline "Planet Earth is 4600 million years old." What follows tells the tale:

If we condense this inconceivable time-span into an understandable concept, we can liken Earth to a person of 46 years of age.

Nothing is known about the first 7 years of this person's life, and while only scattered information exists about the middle span, we know that only at the age of 42 did the Earth begin to flower.

Dinosaurs and the great reptiles did not appear until one year ago, when the planet was 45. Mammals arrived only 8 months ago; in the middle of last week man-like apes evolved into ape-like men, and at the weekend the last ice age enveloped the Earth.

Modern man has been around for 4 hours. During the last hour, Man discovered agriculture. The industrial revolution began a minute ago.

During those sixty seconds of biological time, Modern Man has made a rubbish tip [garbage dump] of Paradise.[4]

Starting with the assumption that life has evolved biologically, and that man was once animal, it is perhaps not surprising that Greenpeace would so closely identify its mission with animals. Naturally, its passion for peace, as in the name Green*peace*, reflects the high value placed on human life as well. Hence the campaign to prevent nuclear disaster. Even so, one must ask why more energy is directed toward the welfare of animal life in the sea than toward the welfare of human life in the womb. Death comes to each form of life when forcibly removed from its proper environment.

Environmentalists, more than anyone, surely must recognize that in the last millisecond of time, as they count it, modern man and modern woman have made a rubbish tip of the womb. It too was once a thriving oasis of life.

Ascendancy of Animal Rights

Perhaps nothing has served to alert us more to the incongruity of concern as between animals and unborn humans than recent animal rights activism over the wearing of furs. Thousands of women will no longer wear their coats in public for fear of humiliation, and models are paid extra for the social stigma of wearing mink coats. Actress Kate O'Mara now writes her refusal to wear fur into her contracts, after she was forced to wear it in episodes of *Dynasty*. Some women have become so frightened at the prospect of being accosted in the street by violent anti-fur protesters that fashion designers have started producing ranges that include *bullet-proof* mink coats!

If there is anything that particularly piques pro-choice advocates about anti-abortion campaigns it's the heart-tugging picture they show of an 18-week-old baby in the womb sucking his thumb. (Hardly a match, one might note, for the emotionally-provocative bloodied corpse of a back-alley abortion victim pictured in the feminists' handbook, *Our Bodies, Ourselves*.)[5] But such vivid reminders of actual life in the womb are child's play compared with the emotional ammunition being used by anti-fur protesters.

Take, for example, their poster depicting a woman in a fur coat and the bloodstained body of a fox. Or the vitriolic ad campaign against the use of leg-iron traps which has included such messages as "Get a feel for fur—slam your fingers in a car door."

Hollywood celebrities, including Liza Minnelli, Norma Shearer, Elton John, and a host of others, can get on the trendy animal-rights bandwagon behind that kind of free-swinging protest propaganda, but most of Hollywood is outraged when pro-life literature tells it like it is and vividly describes what happens to the unborn in the process of an abortion. Cybill Shepherd, for example, has lent her name in a Foreword to *Over Our Live Bodies*, in which author Shirley Radl objects to pro-life's emotional film "The Silent Scream." ("It does not show the woman, for that would draw attention away from the fetus," laments Radl.)[6]

Judge for yourself whether this description of vacuum aspiration, the most common method of abortion (used between six and twelve weeks), goes beyond fair play:

> The cervix is gradually enlarged and stretched using a series of metal dilators. A suction tube similar to that used in menstrual extraction, but larger, is attached to an electric vacuum pump and inserted into the uterus. At a pressure many times greater than that of a household vacuum cleaner,

the tube tears apart the tiny fetus and sucks the pieces into a jar. After 12 weeks, the head of the baby is too large and too hard to be sucked out whole, and may first have to be crushed with special forceps.[7]

It is true that anti-abortion literature may sometimes have overly embellished the stark reality of abortion (although never more blatantly than Shirley Radl's emotionally charged description of a back-alley abortion).[8] But the fact remains that there is a stark, grim reality to abortion killings, a reality no less inhumane than the pain experienced by animals caught through violent means. How then can a pro-choice, "caring" generation recoil at the thought of leg-iron traps for animals, yet remain untouched by the horror of human death at the end of a suction tube?

The Great Gap

One doesn't have to believe in biblical creation to appreciate that there is a yawning gap between man and animals. The divine quality possessed by men and women in the human race does not extend to lesser creatures not imbued with the human spirit. That gap is what permits us to swat flies and trap mice without experiencing postdeath trauma.

In that regard, animal-rights activists display a grand naivete, if not also a high level of hypocrisy, when they attend anti-fur fund-raisers wearing wool suits and leather shoes, and dining on chicken and fish. As one wag has suggested: "Today fur. Tomorrow leather. Then wool. Then meat."

When God created the universe, he made man a trustee and guardian of the earth, to exercise control over fish, birds, live-stock, and insects—whether for food, clothing, and shelter, or for industry or any other supportive role that animals might legitimately play.[9] This doesn't mean we are to regard animal life as fair game for cruelty. The ancient laws of Israel were careful to instill a respect for animals, as seen, for example, in this injunction: "Do not muzzle an ox while it is treading out the grain."[10] And one of my favorite laws, which can have no other meaning than to promote caring and sensitivity: "Do not cook a young goat in its mother's milk."[11]

Despite such precedent for treating animals with respect, we don't put people in jail for killing a rabbit or a fish for the sheer sport of it, even if we happen to disagree with it. We *do* put people in jail for taking *human life* just for the sport of it, and especially when they take human life in hatred and anger. What, then, is the difference? Is it dictated merely by cultural tradition? Is it simply a matter of religious teaching—particularly Judeo-Christian teaching? Surely no one need press a case that this distinction has been made universally throughout all cultures, regardless of century, politics, or religion.

Toward the Sanctity of Human Life

More important than arrogantly distancing ourselves from lower animals is the vital importance of bringing ourselves closer to our own humanity—to understand why, in contrast to the killing of bugs and beasts, an act of abortion is so often attended with post-abortion trauma. We cook vegetables without any moral compunction, and we may also kill animals, but we take human life only under the most compelling of circumstances.

As we've already seen Woody Allen's character, Judah, say in response to his brother's suggestion that he kill his mistress: "I can't believe I'm talking about a human being. Jack, she's not an insect. You don't just step on her."[12]

There's something special about human life that cannot be matched in lesser creatures. Human life is qualitatively different from all other forms of life because, in some unique way, it is like God. Deny the truth of that fact and no human right or liberty is secure, for, as someone has suggested, "If man is not made in the image of God, nothing then stands in the way of inhumanity."

Whether or not we can adequately articulate it, we intuitively know that human life is special. It commands our highest attention and deserves our particular protection. You may wish to call it the human spirit. Some say it's that "magic spark." The biblical word is *soul*. It's the *soul* that makes us special. It's the *soul* that defines us as different from other creatures. It's the *soul* that makes human life sacred.

I confess I don't fully understand how a one-day-old zygote that is conceived when egg meets sperm possesses a soul. It's as mysterious to me as the miracle of conception itself. What I think I do know is that the soul's existence does not depend upon the fully developed baby being born alive, having the breath of life. There is simply no quantum leap in the nature of a human being from the moment just before birth to the moment immediately after birth which would suggest that some kind of "ensoulment" takes place as the baby emerges from the birth canal.

&. In the highest sense of the word God is pro-choice. It is God who *gave* us moral choice. But it is that very Creator-endowed gift of choice which compels us to be pro-life.

If the existence of the soul itself is a matter of religious faith, so be it. Only the most faith-defiant person would deny hope and expectation of an afterlife. Nor is it just the Christian's belief in resurrection. From the afterlife preparations within ancient Egyptian pyramids, to Hindu and Buddhist belief in reincarnation, to the American Indian's happy hunting ground, humankind on the whole has universally believed in man's transcendent spiritual component.

In *Crimes and Misdemeanors*, after Judah visits the scene of the crime and sees Dolores' dead body with the eyes still open, he is shown in a flashback talking to Dolores about her eyes:

> Dolores: Do you agree the eyes are the windows of the soul?
> Judah: Well, I believe they're windows, but I'm . . . I'm not so sure it's a soul I see.
> Dolores: My mother taught me I have a soul . . . and it'll live on after me when I'm gone. And if you look deeply enough in my eyes . . . you can see it.[13]

Later, in remorse, Judah describes to his brother Jack the emptiness of Dolores' eyes as her body lay on the floor:

> I went to her place after. I saw her there . . . just staring up. An inert object. There was nothing in . . .

behind her eyes if you looked into them. All you
saw was a . . . black void.[14]

Whether intended or not, in this brief dialogue Woody Allen
has captured the essence of the human soul. Even when the eyes
are still intact, without the soul the body is "an inert object." It is
nothing but a shell—"a black void." It's the human soul that fills
the void. It's the soul that survives the grave.

But exactly what is that transcendent part of the developing
fetus which eventually survives the grave? Another mystery.
Whatever the nature of the soul, it is not exclusively confined
within the living cells of the human body, or else it would decay,
like the body itself, in the ground where it is laid. Our brain is
not our soul. Our gray-celled creativity is not our soul. Our
intelligence alone is not our soul.

Scientist Carl Sagan is on shaky ground to suggest that
"thought is our blessing and our curse, and it makes us who we
are."[15] Even the lower animals can think. Sagan knows that, and
futilely attempts to separate us by saying that "our one great
advantage, the secret of our success, is thought—character-
istically human thought. We are able to think things through,
imagine events yet to occur, figure things out."[16] But even
Lassie knows when the house is burning. Dogs and cats can
"figure things out." We are not just different *by degree*; we are
different *in kind*. We have moral sensitivity and a soul fit for
eternity which no other species has.

Our soul is the mirror image of God within us. We are *not*
God, but we are *like* God. We are like God in being spiritual in
nature. And—most importantly for a pro-choice generation—
we are like God in possessing moral consciousness and the free
will to choose.

Yes, in the highest sense of the word God is pro-choice. It is
God who *gave* us moral choice. But it is that very Creator-
endowed gift of choice which compels us to be pro-life, recognizing that human life, uniquely imbued as it is with a Godlike
soul, is therefore sacred: off-limits to human control; off-limits
to human experimentation; off-limits to human choice; and off-
limits to human "termination" in the womb.

Greenpeace has done a good thing to remind us of how
badly we treat dolphins and whales. And environmentalists are
right to call our attention to an ailing planet. But it is a terrible

mockery of values to save Mother Earth while ignoring the callous killing of her children. Because of pro-choice, the most threatened life on the planet is the life in a mother's womb. The time has come to decide. Is human life a cause we can choose to ignore?

SEVEN

Creation, Evolution And The Right To Choose

The care of human life and happiness, and not their destruction, is the first and only legitimate object of good government.
—Thomas Jefferson

IN A PRO-CHOICE GENERATION, to be pro-*choice* is to be pro-*rights*. In a pro-choice generation, a woman has a right to control her own body. A right to control her own reproductive capabilities. A right to choose when and whether to have children. A right to choose an abortion. In short, as the Court held in *Roe v. Wade*, a right to privacy. Or, as one pro-choice banner put it: "A woman's right to abortion is akin to her right to be." (An interesting proposition, considering that at least half of all aborted fetuses are female.)

But how do we know that a woman has a right to all of these things? Does *saying* it loudly enough and often enough make it true? Is it true simply because the *Supreme Court* says it's true? If so, would women's rights no longer exist were the Court to change its mind? That chilling prospect undoubtedly is the very possibility that has spurred pro-choice advocates to renewed vigor in the wake of the recent *Webster* decision.

Most of us assume that fundamental rights—like the rights to life, liberty, and the pursuit of happiness—are linked to our Constitution and its almost-sacred Bill of Rights. But where do *those* rights come from? If the Court in *Roe v. Wade* didn't think there was another source of rights, apart from the Constitution itself, their judicial fabrication of a "right to privacy" would never have seen the light of day. Search as you will, you will never find a right to privacy mentioned in the Constitution, not even in the 9th or 14th Amendments. And certainly not a right to abortion.

It is not the Constitution which ultimately guarantees human rights, but the principles stated in that other hallowed American document, the Declaration of Independence. I once ran across this illuminated version: *"We hold these truths to be self-evident"*—that is, so plain that their truth is recognized upon their mere statement—*"that all men are created equal; that they are endowed"*—not by edicts of emperors, or decrees of Parliament or acts of Congress, but *"by their Creator with certain inalienable rights"*—that is, rights which cannot be bartered away, or given away, or taken away except in punishment of crime—*"and that among these are life, liberty, and the pursuit of happiness, and to secure these"*—not grant them but secure them—*"governments are instituted among men, deriving their just powers from the consent of the governed."*

Nice words, but do they really mean anything? It's that word *Creator* I'm most interested in. Did Thomas Jefferson, who wrote these words, really believe in a Creator? Do the familiar phrases "*created* equal" and "endowed by their *Creator*" actually mean *so made by their Creator* or are they meaningless euphemisms?

Of course, we hear many references to "a Higher Power," or "Our Maker, or "The Almighty." Printed on our money, it's "In God we trust;" in our pledge of allegiance, "One nation under God;" and in courtroom oaths, "So help me God." Even the oral arguments in *Roe v. Wade* were prefaced by the words "God save the United States and this Honorable Court," with which the Supreme Court opens all its sessions. But do we really believe in a Creator who is the ultimate source of the basic human rights which we both expect and demand?

The Origin of Human Rights

For over 125 years, the divine origin of man's humanity has

been convincingly stripped away through scientific and educational propaganda which has reached brainwashing proportions. At a very deep level, the distracting (for some) issue of Creation versus Evolution is one of the fundamental reasons why there is such an impasse in the ongoing abortion debate.

No, not so much whether creation of the entire universe could have happened within the biblical time frame, or whether Darwin's theory of gradual evolutionary ascent can maintain credibility in the face of still-unexplained gaps in the fossil record, but whether it can be said with certainty that human life is not in some way qualitatively different from animal life. Whether there is a quantum leap between man and animal. Whether human life is truly unique.

❧ If our existence is the result of mere chance, then all fundamental human rights are at serious risk.

I am certain that secularists must see the fundamentalists' apparent fixation on creationism as continuing proof of the myopic, narrow-minded, anti-intellectual persons they regard fundamentalists to be. After all, every right-thinking person in the world *knows* that we have evolved from lower species, and that notions of special creation proceed from ancient myths, to be believed only at the peril of being out of touch with reality.

Even today's liberal Christians seem to be embarrassed by the debates (such as those recently occurring before the State Board of Education in California) which keep cropping up about what explanations of life's origins should be included in biology textbooks. Can't the Bible and Darwinism be reconciled by *theistic* evolution, they ask? Couldn't God have created man through a gradual, evolutionary process? Why should Christians have to look like fools in the eyes of their secularist friends?

For most people, frankly, the entire discussion is absolutely irrelevant—something fundamentalists have to resolve in order to prevent their Bible (and thus their religious beliefs) from collapsing, but of no interest to anyone else. *"Get real,"* a secular world seems to say, if it takes any notice at all. Hardly anyone—

and I'm afraid this includes some creationists as well—is being thoughtful enough to distinguish between *micro*evolution (adaptation *within* species, which obviously is provable) and *macro*-evolution (evolution from *one* species to *another*, a speculative theory yet to be proven).

And never mind that in the heartland of secular thought—Harvard University—no less eminent a paleontologist than Stephen Jay Gould is saying that Darwin's notion of predictable progressive evolution is so much claptrap. In his new book, *Wonderful Life*, based upon the Burgess Shale findings, professor Gould says that the human race did not result from the survival of the *fittest* but of the *luckiest*. "Replay the tape a million times from a Burgess beginning, and I doubt that anything like Homo sapiens would ever evolve again."[1]

Not only are there enormous gaps in the fossil record (which one would not expect to encounter if there had been a steady progression from amoeba to man), but in the supposedly 530-million-year-old Burgess Shale there is a disparity in anatomical design far exceeding the modern range throughout the world (calling into question what, until recently, has been the sacred dogma of upwardly ascending multiplication of life forms.)

I don't propose to resolve in this book all the issues of man's origin, but it is imperative that we attempt to tie together some loose ends. For there are indeed some loose ends to our thinking—*significant* loose ends; *troubling* loose ends.

We face them right away when we consider the pro-choice position on abortion. If our existence is the result of mere chance, then all fundamental human rights are at serious risk. There can be no ultimate guarantor of those rights, whether the "right to life" or the "right to decide." If, however, we owe our existence to divine design, then the "right to decide" is forced to compete with a sacred "right to life," and what real contest can that be? In asking hard questions about life's origins, nothing could be clearer than that attempting to hold hands with both *fundamental human rights* and *evolutionary beginnings* is asking the impossible.

So we return to the crucial question: Is our reference to the *Creator* just a catchall expression for a generic national God? Or is it possible that the nation's founders actually did intend to say that our fundamental human rights exist by virtue of a divine act of creation?

A Nonbiblical View of Creation

Thomas Jefferson was a deist. Deists were "rationalists," believers in the ultimate rule of Reason and the scientific advances of Enlightenment Europe. For deists, God was a benevolent deity whose essential characteristic was *order*. It was the vast orderliness of the universe which compelled deists, through their reasoning processes, to believe in a God sufficiently powerful and intelligent to bring that order into existence. But the God of the deists closed up shop after Creation and went home. He no longer intervened in the affairs of humankind whom he had created.

Therefore Jefferson was not a Christian as we might think of an evangelical Christian today. Nor would he ever have described himself as a Southern Baptist or a member of the Moral Majority. With some massaging, particularly regarding his belief in Creation, Jefferson today might be a Unitarian, or even a convert to the New Age movement. Certainly, deists like Jefferson and Thomas Paine (whose writings played a significant role in the founding of our nation) were often bitterly outspoken against the authority of the Bible.

In fact, I don't know of a more caustic rejection of Christianity than this one contained in Paine's *The Age of Reason*:

> It is certain that what is called the Christian system of faith, including in it the whimsical account of the creation; the strange story of Eve, the snake, and the apple; the amphibious idea of a man-god; the corporeal idea of the death of a god; the mythological idea of a family of gods, and the Christian system of arithmetic that three are one and one is three, are all irreconcilable, not only to the divine gift of reason that God has given to man, but to the knowledge that man gains of the power and wisdom of God by the aid of the sciences, and by studying the structure of the universe that God has made.[2]

A Jerry Falwell, James Kennedy, or Pat Robertson he was not! Yet Paine's categorical rejection of Christianity and biblical revelation must not cloud the force of his underlying belief in

Creation. It was not the *fact* of Creation that Paine questioned, but what he took to be a "whimsical account" of that Creation. By use of "the divine gift of reason that God has given to man," Paine had no doubt that we are all part of a "universe that God has made."

> ❧ **Are we to look proudly upon an "American way" that teaches 12-year-olds about abortion as an option, but censors any teaching about Creation as an option?**

It is possible, of course, that Charles Darwin might have changed Paine's mind 65 years later, when he published *Origin of Species*. Darwin's scientific bent certainly would have coincided with Paine's own deist perspective. It is even possible that Darwinism might be the reason we no longer see many deists around. (Darwin's personal ambivalence about God ultimately yielded to a confirmed atheism.) But Paine's hypothetical Darwinian conversion is not altogether a foregone conclusion. Paine was fiercely convinced of an intelligent, purposeful First Cause, who had brought order and meaning into existence by his eternal power:

> Everything we behold carries in itself the internal evidence that it did not make itself. Every man is an evidence to himself that he did not make himself; neither could his father make himself, nor his grandfather, nor any of his race; neither could any tree, plant, or animal make itself; and it is the conviction arising from this evidence that carries us on, as it were, by necessity, to the belief of a first cause eternally existing, of a nature totally different to any material existence we know of, and by the power of which all things exist; and this first cause, man calls God.[3]

Of one thing I am certain: Paine would not have looked kindly upon efforts by Norman Lear's People for the American

Way to exclude any mention in public schools of the Creator to whom Paine and Jefferson attribute the very basis for "the American Way." (Should we expect the Declaration of Independence to be the next target for exclusion from the classroom?)

Nor, I suspect, would Jefferson and Paine be the least bit pleased that People for the American Way fraudulently passes itself off as "a constitutional liberties organization." Does it make sense that an organization dedicated to Constitutional liberties would insist that only one view of life's origins be permitted in institutions dedicated to the search for knowledge? Freedom of thought, but only for those who agree with the current conventional wisdom? Is *that* the American way—not having a right to *informed* choice?

Are we to look proudly upon an "American way" that teaches 12-year-olds about abortion as an option, but censors any teaching about Creation as an option? In the Soviet Union and Eastern Bloc countries, we have witnessed the exclusivity of the party line falling under the weight of its own fear of self-exposure. That is, after all, the reason for censoring another person's viewpoint: It threatens to disclose the weakness in your own. Censorship wins the argument through imposed silence from the other side.

But just as in single-party Communist societies, the day will also come when the right to choose in our own country will permit an honest choice between elitist-imposed secularist ideology and what is now officially censored opposition. When that day comes, Evolution dogma will be seen as every bit as much an enemy of the people as the social-evolution Marxist dogma which it inspired.

I can almost see Paine's look of incredulity if he were to read a recent *Los Angeles Times* article by People for the American Way's spokesman, Michael Hudson. "Science is science and faith is faith," says Hudson superciliously,"[4] as if to suggest that creationism can only be accepted by blind religious faith, and as if to suggest that only mindless Bible-thumpers could possibly believe in Creation.

Obviously no Bible-thumper himself, Paine adamantly insisted that Creation was the only reasonable conclusion a person could draw regarding the origin of the universe. Deists such as Paine and Jefferson did not have to accept the first chapter of Genesis in order to reasonably conclude that man is not the product of chance origins. From reading Paine's works, you get the feeling that he would find Stephen Jay Gould's "lottery theory" to be just so much scientific sophistry. Paine more likely would agree with Einstein's elegant statement that "the most incomprehensible thing about the universe is that it is comprehensible." The God of deism was a God of order, not chaos.

Therefore, once again I suggest that the jury is still out on whether Darwin might have convinced Paine and Jefferson to throw away their reasoned conviction that our universe, together with immutable principles of morality and justice which give rise to human rights, is the result of a purposeful, intelligent Creator. What we hear from Thomas Paine is nothing but derision at the suggestion by today's secularists that the *Creator* referred to in the Declaration of Independence is merely a euphemism:

> Do we not see a fair creation prepared to receive us the instant we were born—a world furnished to our hands that cost us nothing? Is it we that light up the sun, that pour down the rain, and fill the earth with abundance? Whether we sleep or wake, the vast machinery of the universe still goes on. Are these things, and the blessings which they indicate in future, nothing to us? . . . Or is the gloomy pride of man become so intolerable that nothing can flatter it but a sacrifice of the Creator?[5]

What a telling indictment: Intellectual pride that demands the death of a Creator in order to keep itself alive!

Paine gives us an important clue here as to what he might have said to Darwin, had the two of them been able to sit down together to talk about life's origins. "Great, Charles, maybe you do have something there in your theory of how biological life developed. But what's your explanation for gravity, light, air, energy, water—the sun, the moon, and the stars? How does your amoeba-to-man evolution even begin to explain all of these other things?

"In fact, how do you explain the incredible coincidence that all of those nonbiological factors came together in such perfect harmony that your theory of biological progression could even get rolling?"

I feel confident that Paine would put those same questions to today's intellectual elite who believe with such condescending self-assurance that creationism is unworthy of a reasoned mind. In the middle of his famed treatise, the *Age of Reason*—a classic defense of Enlightenment's scientific rationalism—Paine pauses to insert Addison's paraphrase of the 19th Psalm:

> The spacious firmament on high,
> With all the blue ethereal sky,
> And spangled heavens, a shining frame,
> Their great original proclaim.
> The unwearied sun, from day to day,
> Does his Creator's power display,
> And publishes to every land
> The work of an Almighty hand.
>
> Soon as the evening shades prevail
> The moon takes up the wondrous tale,
> And nightly to the listening earth
> Repeats the story of her birth;
> Whilst all the stars that round her burn,
> And all the planets in their turn,
> Confirm the tidings as they roll
> And spread the truth from pole to pole.
>
> What though in solemn silence all
> Move round the dark terrestrial ball?
> What though nor real voice, nor sound,
> Amidst their radiant orbs be found?
> In reason's ear they all rejoice,
> And utter forth a glorious voice;
> Forever singing as they shine,
> THE HAND THAT MADE US IS DIVINE.

"What more does man want to know" asks Paine, "than that the hand or power that made these things is divine, is omnipotent? Let him believe this with the force it is impossible to repel, if he permits his reason to act, and his rule of moral life will follow course."[6]

The Implications of Origins

What's so important about Paine and Jefferson believing in a God of creation? As Paine correctly saw it, our rule of moral life flows as a matter of course from how we view our origins. Merely compare the social implications that suggest themselves respectively from Jefferson's *"created equally"* and Darwin's *"survival of the fittest."* Which suggests a greater commitment to human rights? Which do we know had greater appeal to Adolf Hitler? And if "survival of the fittest" raises a horrific specter of inhumanity to man, imagine where we are headed with Gould's *"survival of the luckiest"*! One shudders to think how that might translate regarding questions of abortion and euthanasia.

If you remain unconvinced about the tie between the Creator and our basic human rights, no better case has been made than in a recent article by Anselm Atkins ("Human Rights Are Cultural Artifacts") in *The Humanist*:

> Those of us who deny that we were created by any creator are drawn ineluctably to the conclusion that no naturally endowed rights exist.
>
> It is curious that Ayn Rand, a committed atheist, did in fact believe in natural rights—such as the "right to life." In this, she was inconsistent. Perhaps her trouble was that, like so many other philosophers, she failed to take seriously the implications of our evolved biological condition: that, at first, there was mute mud and nothing else; then our species, among others; and, last of all, the things we invented (the totality of culture).
>
> Like any educated person... Rand "believed in evolution," but it hardly influenced her thinking.... If, on the other hand, Rand had made evolutionary biology the cornerstone of her philosophical anthropology, she might have avoided this contradictory position.[7]

Atkins rightly points us to the philosophical schizophrenia in which we have indulged for over a century. We want all the natural human rights which we have come to enjoy, without acknowledging the Creator by whom they are bestowed. In the struggle for abortion rights, feminists can appeal only to what they *want* or to what they think they *need*. Ultimately their appeal cannot be affirmed in any court higher than themselves. Pro-life advocates, on the other hand, will eventually win the day, because they appeal legitimately to a Higher Court of human rights. "Pro-life" and "right to life" are inseparable Siamese twins.

Again, Atkins brings us to the reality of what happens when we divorce ourselves from the notion of a Creator:

> Rights make no sense in nature. There are simply biological entities doing what they must do, wanting what they must want, and getting what they can get—living by hook or by crook and then dying. Humanity is part of this.[8]

Where there is a fundamental belief in chance origins, we may *choose* to act more nobly than Atkins pictures us acting (especially in a society which maintains a Judeo-Christian, Creator-affirming framework), but we are not inherently *encouraged* to live nobly. Nor, more importantly, can we demand our "rights"—whether it be the "right to life" or the "right to reproductive choice." In nature without a Creator, there are no "rights."

It is no mere coincidence of linguistic phrasing that our basic human rights are listed in this order: life, liberty, and the pursuit of happiness. The freedom to order our lives as we wish—the liberty which expresses itself in personal rights—must never take precedence over the right to life. As applied to the pro-choice/pro-life controversy, the idea is not to diminish the rights of women, but only to secure the superior right to life. For if the right to life itself cannot be assured, then no other liberty is secure, not even for women.

If Anselm Atkins is right, that "we add 'rights' to our social expectations as new desires are felt and better goals envisioned," then he is also right in recognizing that "the guarantor of our social rights is the society in which we happen to live."[9] No better proof of this can be found than in *Roe v. Wade*, in which an entirely new "right" was invented, and in the recent *Webster* decision, in which that "right" was then limited. The Court gives, and the Court takes away. If the Court is all there is, then pro-abortionists have a "right to be worried." And so do we all. For if the Court can deny the right to life to any part of humankind, then all of us are at risk.

The Founders' Views on Abortion

Have you ever wondered how the founders—those who wrote the Constitution—would have viewed the issue of abortion? For a rights-conscious Thomas Paine, it was very clear that human life itself is a natural right, given by God—in fact, the *foremost* natural right.

For a pro-choice, pro-*rights* generation, the following explanation from Paine's *The Rights of Man* deserves careful reading and reflection:

> Every history of the creation, and every traditionary account, whether from the lettered or unlettered world, however they may vary in their opinion or belief of certain particulars, all agree in establishing one point, *the unity of man*; by which I mean that man is all of *one degree*, and consequently that all men are born equal and with equal natural rights, in the same manner as if posterity had been continued by *creation* instead of *generation*, the latter being only the mode by which the former is carried forward; and consequently every child born into the world must be considered as deriving its existence from God. The world is as new to him as it was to the first man that existed and his natural right in it is of the same kind.[10]

Human *procreation*, says Paine insightfully, is but the ongoing divine handiwork of God's *original* creation. Human conception is a ceaseless miracle of life, worthy of protection. Hence, a natural right to life.

Contrast that view with current evolutionary justifications for abortions and you quickly find life cheapened rather than elevated. In a current biology text, beneath the picture of a newborn infant, the question is raised: "When did this particular human life begin? When the sperm encountered the egg? When the embryo became a fetus, visibly human? At the first heartbeat? The first brain wave? When the infant became viable as an independent entity?" Note how the answer then moves subtly away from a *particular* human being to a biological continuum, thereby justifying the abortion of a "particular human life":

In the evolutionary sense, none of these events marks the beginning of life. Life began more than 3 billion years ago and has been passed on since that time from organism to organism, generation after generation, to the present, and stretches on into the future, farther than the mind's eye can see. Each new organism is thus a temporary participant in the continuum of life. So is each sperm, each egg, indeed, in a sense, each living cell.[11]

Once a human being is reduced to "the blink of an eye from the perspective of the biological continuum," the stage is set for terminating a pregnancy in the blink of an eye. What is one life snuffed out in 3 billion years of evolutionary process?

Almost lost, at the bottom of the same page, is the *real* answer to the question of when life begins—the answer Paine and Jefferson would have given us, and the answer that any biology text would give if the issue of abortion were not at stake: "Development in most species of animals begins with fertilization—the fusion of egg and sperm."[12]

Never in their wildest imagination would the nation's founders have included among fundamental human rights a right to abort the unborn. It would have been both unnatural (in violation of the natural order and the laws of nature) and immoral (in the killing of humankind resulting from God's perpetuated process of creation). In a somewhat different context, but under the appropriate title of *Common Sense*, Paine confirms the obvious: "But Britain is the parent country, say some. Then the more shame upon her conduct. Even brutes do not devour their young, nor savages make war upon their families."[13]

"Even brutes..." Not even animals. Not even animals which, although they share the breath of life, do not share the image of divinity. Paine chooses animals to shame humans, driving home his point by the very chasm that exists between human and nonhuman life. If, typically, not even *animals* destroy their offspring, how much more outrageous it is that *humans* should do so!

And what is it, Thomas Paine, that compels the equality of humankind and the unique rights which flow therefrom? "The expressions admit of no controversy," says this deist who doesn't believe in the Bible: " 'And God said, let us make man in our own image. In the image of God created he him: male and female created he them.' "[14] As even Paine was willing to acknowledge from a biblical source he did not otherwise acknowledge, the uniqueness of man—male and female—is man's participation in the spiritual nature of God.

In the battle over abortion, the issue is not simply a woman s right to decide. The greater issue by far is whether there is a Creator who has declared human life sacred and thereby pre-empted our right to say otherwise.

PART 2

The Battle
Over Abortion

EIGHT

If Wombs Had Windows

I am a Jew. Hath not a Jew hands, organs, dimensions,
senses, affections, passions? . . . If you prick us, do we not bleed?
If you tickle us, do we not laugh? If you poison us, do we not die?

—Shylock
in *The Merchant of Venice*
(by William Shakespeare)

THE MOST FAMOUS PASSAGE in the 1973 abortion case of *Roe v. Wade* is typical of the blinkered insight which we have come to accept as normal in a society intent on elevating personal choice above all other moral considerations. Denying the obvious to a degree unworthy of schoolchildren, prestigious Supreme Court Justices rationalized the legalization of abortion on the basis of admitted ignorance.

"We need not resolve the difficult question of when life begins," said Justice Blackmun for the Court. "When those trained in the respective disciplines of medicine, philosophy and theology are unable to arrive at any consensus, the judiciary, at this point in the development of man's knowledge, is not in a position to speculate as to the answer."[1]

Having renounced the right to proceed on the basis of speculation, the Court then legalized abortion upon what could only be speculation that human life did *not* begin before birth, or, at the least, before some even more speculative point which the

111

Court termed "viability." With that intellectually dishonest leg-erdemain, the Court proceeded to do exactly what it said it could not do: It resolved, at least for the issue before them, "the difficult question of when life begins."

If the Court can easily sidestep the issue of when life begins, society cannot. Sometimes a Court decision is ahead of its time and is eventually ratified by a public reluctant to accept the consequences of what it knows to be right. Such was the case with the Court's decision in *Brown v. Board of Education*, which heralded America's move toward racial integration. In its heart, America knew that racial segregation was wrong. But in the almost two decades since *Roe v. Wade*, the Court's "nondecision decision" about the beginning of life has never been ratified by society. In its heart, America knows that human life begins before birth.

In Search of the Real Issue

It is frequently said that no question relative to abortion is more crucial than when human life begins. Virtually all choices, so it is said, will be made upon some assumption about the answer to this question. And to some extent that may be right, for on the surface, pro-choice and pro-life advocates will never make progress toward mutual understanding as long as they differ on this issue. Yet this question may not, in fact, be the dividing line.

> ❧ In its heart, America knew that racial segregation was wrong. In its heart, America knows that human life begins before birth.

For pro-life advocates, human life begins at the moment of conception. Period. For that reason, they oppose not only abor-tion but also the deliberate destruction of human embryos done under the guise of "research." They object to embryo biopsy designed to seek out the "defective" embryo, which involves the death of most of the embryos—whether normal or abnormal—as well as any *in vitro* fertilization (IVF) where unused human embryos are discarded. From their perspective, a human life is destroyed with each discarded embryo.

In some ways embryo destruction is morally more reprehensible than abortion. Whereas no woman deliberately gets pregnant in order to have an abortion, in embryo research some embryos are deliberately conceived with the intention to destroy them.

In a similar vein, increasing numbers of women are beginning to realize that certain forms of "contraceptives"—including the IUD, or coil (now largely in disuse because of adverse side-effects), and the so-called "morning-after" pill—are in fact abortifacients. That is, rather than *preventing* conception, they cause the miscarriage of embryos at a very early stage in their development *subsequent* to conception. And whereas they work prior to implantation of the embryo on the wall of the uterus, the new French-developed RU486 abortion drug—benignly termed a "contragestive" pill—causes the implanted embryo to die as the uterine lining falls away when the woman starts bleeding.

Mimicking the Court in *Roe v. Wade*, many pro-choice advocates tend to talk about viability as the key dividing line, abortion being a basically unlimited option before that point. However, apart from scientists engaged in embryo research (who argue that the line ought to be drawn at a number of arbitrary points, from 14 days to 56 days) I have yet to find in pro-choice literature a categorical denial of the pro-life position that human life begins at *conception*. To the contrary, what I read from the pro-choice camp is that, "of course, there is no quantum leap between conception, embryo, fetus, and baby."

Indeed, how could anyone claim otherwise? Dr. Jerome Lejeune, professor of genetics at Medical College in Paris, France (who was awarded this country's Kennedy Prize for his discovery of Down's syndrome), cogently points out that "if a fertilized egg is not by itself a full human being, it could never become a man, because something would have to be added to it, and we know that does not happen."[2]

Perhaps the best proof of this proposition, at least tacitly accepted by both sides, is in vitro fertilization, where a laboratory-developed embryo in inserted into a woman's uterus. If in vitro fertilization tells us anything, it is that the *embryo*, even before such time as it is arbitrarily classified as a *fetus*, is unquestionably human life. Otherwise, what woman wanting to give birth to a child would permit something which is neither human nor alive to be placed into her uterus?

The only articulated pro-choice dissent I have heard to the proposition that human life begins at conception has come in the form of debased ridicule of a type which I am certain even most pro-choice advocates would find distasteful. Responding to the straw-man argument that biological life does not *begin at,* but rather is *continuous from,* the living cells in the female ovum and male sperm, an ethics professor in a recent Oxford debate gleefully taunted his pro-life opponents with the proposition that women ought to say "Hail Marys" monthly over the toilet bowl (during menstruation), and that masturbation would be mass genocide.

Apparently the masturbation illustration is now making the rounds. Even Carl Sagan has stooped to the same low level of academic argument, asking, "So is masturbation mass murder?" and "Why isn't it murder to destroy a sperm or an egg."[3]

Apart from causing one to marvel at the shallow intellectual prowess displayed by those who are supposed to be at the pinnacle of academic learning, one is forced to conclude that ridicule in this form is, after all, the only answer a person can make to the obvious proposition that human life begins at conception. Although human sperm and eggs are *alive* in the male and female, they do not form a new, unique human *life* until they merge in conception.

It should also be noted, of course, that there is a vast difference between the spontaneous abortion of fertilized eggs in a woman's menstrual discharge and the voluntary removal of an embryo or fetus in an abortion. In the woman's menstruation, no choice whatever is made; by contrast, no intended abortion occurs *without* a conscious choice.

The point is that, *biologically* speaking, there can be no question but that human life begins at the moment of conception. And because no one has stepped forward to seriously suggest an alternative, any other conclusion is unthinking nonsense.

Surely Carl Sagan cannot be serious in suggesting that "despite many claims to the contrary, life does not begin at conception: It is an unbroken chain that stretches back nearly to the origin of the Earth, 4.6 billion years ago. Nor does *human* life begin at conception: It is an unbroken chain dating back to the origin of species, tens or hundreds of thousands of years ago."[4]

How can one present so facile an argument with a straight face? The question is not whether the *human race* can be aborted but whether individual *human beings* can be aborted. No human being has existed for millions of years. Each of us had a distinct beginning. Such Saganesque sidestepping of the question merely exposes the depth of intellectual dishonesty to which one must go in order to avoid the obvious.

Unfortunately, the *biological* conclusion is not the end of the matter. And that is precisely where the *real* disagreement lies. The true primal question is: By what standard shall we define "human life"? Will it be the biological standard, or, as the Court suggested, perhaps a *philosophical* or *theological* standard?

Herein lies the crux of the abortion debate. And it is here that pro-life and pro-choice advocates find no room for common ground. For if the *biological* standard is to be applied, as pro-life advocates insist, then the ballgame is over. They win by default. The case is closed. Pro-choice advocates are helpless to prove otherwise. Beyond any shadow of a doubt, biological human life begins at the moment of conception.

It should be noted, incidentally, that "life from conception" is a moot consideration in virtually all cases of abortion apart from fetal experimentation in which embryos are intentionally destroyed. Typical methods of abortion today do not occur "at conception." No woman even recognizes the moment that occurs. Abortions take place weeks and months after conception, at a time when there is a recognizable, distinctly human fetus in being. If there were ever any doubt about whether human life begins "at conception," those doubts can no longer exist at the point where most abortions actually occur.

From Conception to "Personhood"

If, on the other hand, a *philosophical* standard is to be applied, as pro-choice advocates urge, then "human life" does not begin until there is "personhood." Up until that point virtually any disposition may be made of human fetuses, embryos, or so-called "pre-embryos" (a recently coined term of convenience not even used in animal embryology) which are the subject of human vivisection.

It is important to note, parenthetically, that once having drawn the line at "personhood," pro-choice advocates must be willing to live by that choice. Repeatedly, I see pro-choice advocates casting aspersions on "designer abortions" in which the decision to abort is based merely on a gender preference. (Take, for example, the Women's Center survey of six clinics in Bombay, India, which deplores the fact that out of 8000 amniocenteses done, 7999 resulted in abortions of *female* fetuses!)[5] Yet drawing the line at "personhood" forecloses any legitimate moralizing about the kind of choices one makes before that line is crossed.

As Jo McGowan reports from India, "When the issue is sex determination and 'the selective abortion of girls,' [feminists in India] call it female feticide. But when the issue is reproductive freedom and the abortion of male and female fetuses, they call it a 'woman's right to choose.' It won't work. They can't have it both ways. Either they accept abortion or they don't."[6]

In fact, drawing the line at "personhood" gives carte blanche to virtually any disposition imaginable before that point is reached. In the near future, for example, doctors are considering the possibility of transplanting ovarian tissue from aborted female babies to menopausal women, enabling them to produce ova for conception. Without being unreasonably alarmist, one can foresee the time when pressure could be put on the mother of the "contributing fetus" to have an abortion at the *appropriate* moment, and also a not-so-future time when aborted fetuses could be cannibalized for other "spare parts," as is already the case with fetal brain tissue in the treatment of Parkinson's disease.

What shall we say, for instance, to the woman whose father is dying of Parkinson's disease, who intentionally gets pregnant and then aborts the fetus so that the father can make use of the tissue? In the notorious case of 43-year-old Mary Ayala, we are already halfway to that point. Mrs. Ayala and her husband decided to risk pregnancy in order to produce a donor to save their 17-year-old daughter who needed a lifesaving bone marrow transplant. The baby was tested in the womb and found to be a compatible donor.[7]

"But what if the fetus had *not* been compatible?" many doctors are now asking. "Would they have then aborted the fetus and decided to try again?" If that possibility seems shocking, we must remember that, once we establish the line of personhood, we are bound by it, even in the most outlandish circumstances. Unfortunately, there will be many people for whom this argument is not the least bit disturbing. They are quite prepared to draw an artificial line and let the chips fall where they may. But are *we* prepared to do that?

Bound by the potentially bizarre implications of what we determine "personhood" to be, how then shall we define it? If, as is often proposed, it is the point when the developing fetus or baby is a "self-conscious or rational being," then a human being, philosophically speaking, may not become a person for months, perhaps years, after birth. Wide latitude indeed! In the hands of secularist philosophers and pop psychologists, "personhood" exists only at the mercy of trendy psychobabble.

William Sloane Coffin, a United Church of Christ clergyman and president of Sane/Freeze Campaign for Global Security, insists, along with many others, that there is a difference between "potential life" and "actual life." Don't we all *act* as if there are differences, he asks in an article entitled, "Life, Yes; But Is It Yet Human Life?"

> When a fetus aborts spontaneously, we grieve for the parents, hardly at all for the life no one has seen. We don't have funerals for unborn children. No one urges the same punishment for a mother who aborts a fetus as for one who murders her child. And no one, to my knowledge, has applied for Social Security nine months before his or her 62nd birthday![8]

By that reasoning, of course, eight-month-old babies could be aborted just a month before they otherwise would have been delivered. At that point the baby is still "unseen," and there is no way, even under *Roe v. Wade*, that the mother would be prosecuted for murder.

The futility of this approach to determining "personhood" is seen in the case of the baby to which Mary Ayala has given birth in order to save her older daughter. Having been created purely for a single objective, the baby in the womb could well have been considered an *object*. On the other hand, even before her birth she was treated as a *person*, right down to being given the name Marissa-Eve.

From the moment of her planned conception, this little fetus was to be the "person" who would save her older sister's life. She was the one "person" whose unique genetic makeup—as an extension of her parents—made her the compatible donor who could not be found in a nationwide search of millions of other "persons." Far from being unseen in the womb, Marissa-Eve was clearly seen through the eyes of medical science as the perfect *person* for the role for which she had been created. Fortunately for Marissa-Eve.

Laws Pregnant with "Personhood"

As for not charging an aborting mother with murder, the truth is that we don't classify all homicides in the same category even where there are *adult* victims. The drunk driver who accidently kills another motorist will not be charged with murder in the first degree, but typically with some form of manslaughter. Yet that difference is not a statement by society that a drunk-drive victim was any less human than the victim of a cold-blooded premeditated killing.

ご **The Supreme Court has pandered to the interests of feminists who demand the right to do an immoral act which, if done by anyone else, would result in time served in prison.**

Many people might be surprised to learn that unborn fetuses can in fact be the subject of both manslaughter and murder charges in many states. As recently as 1970, an amendment to the California Penal Code provided a charge of murder for the unlawful killing of "a fetus," which a later court decision defined as being a *viable* fetus. Unquestionably a viable fetus—even without any other vested legal rights—has sufficient personhood to be given the law's protection.

Rev. Coffin is right, of course, to point out the obvious anomaly that a woman can choose, even beyond the point of viability in many cases, to kill her own unborn child, whereas if anyone else did it—including her husband—he could be prosecuted for murder. This anomaly only serves to underscore the extent to which the Supreme Court has pandered to the interests of feminists who demand the right to do an immoral act which, if done by anyone else, would result in time served in prison.

This point is emphasized all the more in a recent California case in which it was alleged that a former boyfriend intentionally caused the death of a woman's 18-week-old fetus. Valerie Morales testified that Jose Velasco beat her after he discovered she was pregnant by her current boyfriend, and when she refused Velasco's demand that she have an abortion. Velasco was prosecuted under a 1985 statute which allows for an extra five years to be added to a felony sentence if a crime committed against a pregnant woman results in the loss of a *nonviable* fetus.

The paradox here is obvious. The law under which Velasco was charged protects even a *nonviable* fetus against a violently caused killing, whereas if Morales had yielded in fear to Velasco's demand that she have an abortion, her child would have had no protection whatsoever under the law. Apart from revealing the confusion created by *Roe v. Wade's* disastrous ruling, this case is a reminder of how the California law regards even nonviable fetuses with sufficient personhood as to be worthy of limited protection.

Little wonder, therefore, that feminists and civil liberties organizations are thrown into a quandary as to which side of the fence to be on. In order to maintain the right of abortion-on-demand, they adamantly deny the "personhood" of nonviable fetuses. But in order to protect women and their unborn babies from violent assaults by other people, they must tacitly admit the "personhood" of those same fetuses.

Should we be surprised, then, at the statement of Carol Sobel, an attorney with the American Civil Liberties Union, and one who has done a great deal of work in reproductive rights cases? As reported in the *Los Angeles Times* in connection with the Velasco case, Sobel noted that it is extremely difficult—even in cases in which a woman is beaten—to prove the cause of a fetus' death, given the number of spontaneous fetal abortions resulting from inadequate prenatal care or other health factors, such as venereal disease.[9]

As a former criminal prosecutor, I can give you my own stories about the nightmarish difficulty of proving cause of death. But given the death of an apparently healthy 18-week-old fetus within a few days of the beating alleged in this case, Sobel's facile explanation of spontaneous abortions from inadequate prenatal care has a decidedly hollow ring, as if caught in the contradictory quagmire of liberal doublespeak about fetal "personhood."

No less a feminist than Gloria Steinem gets caught in the same quagmire when protesting the fact that *Roe v. Wade* "enshrined a limited idea of state interest in a fetus." "How can [the law] differentially apply to two people who may be legally separate, but who actually inhabit the same body?"[10] asks Steinem, in what has to be the concession of the century. And, of course, that's the whole point. The state *must* enshrine a protective interest in the fetus because it *is* a separate person within its mother's body!

"Personhood" Is Not Dependent upon Recognition

Rev. Coffin's scenario about the way we usually treat the unborn, as if they were not persons, might seem reasonable at first glance, since we *do* treat the unborn differently. But how we *act* does not always tell the whole story. For example, I continue to be struck by the way in which we react to human death on a grand scale. If a jumbo jet with 350 passengers aboard crashes on takeoff from Chicago's O'Hare Field, it makes national media headlines, and everyone is talking about it. But if, on the same day, 10,000 people in Bangladesh are killed in a monsoon, that story will find its way to the bottom of page 1, if it makes the front page at all. That was 10,000, as in *ten thousand*, as in TEN THOUSAND individual, living human beings. As in 28.5 times the number of individual, living human beings killed in the airline crash!

When 350 people die at one time in America, there are identifiable relatives and friends whose dramatic television interviews about their loved ones tug at our heartstrings. And because the ill-fated passengers were people who looked like us and spoke our language and *might have been us*, given other circumstances, we identify with them and join as one to mourn their loss. However, the deaths of 10,000 people in a distant country hardly seem to touch a sympathetic nerve. Is that because they are any less human than we are?

To bring the analogy even closer: Because of malnutrition and unsanitary conditions, each *day* (365 days each year, year in and year out) the equivalent of 20 faulty jumbo jets filled with little children crash in India alone! UNICEF goodwill ambassador Liv Ullman reports that in 1988, 4 million children under the age of five died in squalid conditions in the world's largest democracy.[11] Are the deaths which occur on any one of those days ever found on the front (or even back) pages of our newspapers? Does the fact that we can so easily ignore them mean that the children never existed or that they did not possess human value?

In the case of the people of Bangladesh, we undoubtedly fail to react any more strongly than we do because these people do not happen to look like us and do not speak our language. We simply don't relate to them as we do to people in our own English-speaking Western culture. If 10,000 people were killed in a London disaster, for example, you can be sure that we would sit up and take notice! But the way we act, or react, doesn't mean that the people of Bangladesh did not also have identifiable family and friends who could tell us heartrending stories about their lost loved ones. Nor does it tell us that they were any less human than 350 Americans—nor any less entitled to life.

The fact that we generally do not have funerals for unborn children says nothing about their being any less human than we are. As with 10,000 unknown strangers who die in Bangladesh, and 4 million children of India who die shortly after birth, we are caught in the trap of not appreciating sufficiently the loss of those people who may not fully look like us and cannot yet speak to us.

And on what grand a scale we ignore them! One-and-one-half million a year die, not from airline accidents or natural disasters, but intentionally, at our own hands. That's 1.5 million, as in *one million five hundred thousand*, as in ONE MILLION FIVE HUNDRED THOUSAND individual, living human beings. As in 4285 times the number of individual, living human beings killed in our hypothetical airline crash!

To bring reality even closer to home, that is one human death by abortion every 22 seconds of every day, day in and day out. Put another way, by the time you finish reading this paragraph, another unborn child will have been killed. As John Ankerberg demonstrates so graphically, by the year 2000 (based on current figures), we will be approaching 50,000,000 (that's *50 million*) abortions in the United States alone in the 25 years which will have passed since *Roe v. Wade* was decided in 1973. This means that, by the end of this decade, we will have killed *30 times the number of Americans lost in all of our wars from the Revolutionary War down to the heartbreak of Vietnam!*[12]

Richard John Neuhaus questions our attitude toward the fact that "so many people are killing their sons and daughters. Lest that seem to be stating it too sharply," says Neuhaus, "one might say that each year since 1973 in America about 1.5 million lives have been terminated that, if not terminated, would have resulted in sons and daughters."[13] (And from the time you finished reading the last paragraph until this point, yet another one of those "sons" and "daughters" was just killed. Another 25 will die while you are reading the remainder of this chapter.)

Does "Personhood" Depend upon Legal Standing?

In article after article, pro-choice advocates acknowledge, in the words of Rev. Coffin, that "it goes without saying that a fertilized egg in a woman's uterus is human in origin and human in destiny." Nevertheless, Coffin and other pro-choice writers doubt whether that is enough to warrant calling a fertilized egg—as do proposed state laws—a human being with "all the rights, privileges and immunities available to persons, citizens and residents of this state."[14] (That statutory language may indeed overstate the case, if interpreted to mean that the fetus is to be vested with all *adult* legal rights and privileges.)

Of course, their concern echoes that of the Supreme Court itself in *Roe v. Wade.* Had it not rejected the notion that fetuses are "persons," the Court would have been forced to give the unborn all the protections of the 14th Amendment, including the right to life.

However, the Supreme Court's argument was simplistic when first propounded, and it remains just as superficial today despite its frequent repetition. Simply because an unborn child cannot legally own property, inherit his father's estate, or sue for tortious conduct against himself does not mean that he is not a human being worthy of legal protection. If that were the case, then we could justifiably dispose of a 12-year-old who, because he is not an adult, cannot vote, sign a legally binding contract, or—even with his parents' consent—get married.

The reason that an unborn child cannot inherit his father's estate is the same reason that Athina Roussel, the 5-year-old daughter of the now-deceased shipping heiress, Christina Onassis, cannot inherit an $840-million fortune until her eighteenth birthday. Neither little Athina nor the unborn child is yet capable of assuming that responsibility. Athina and the unborn child are different only by age and venue—not by personhood. Based upon relative maturity, the adult human being is given full legal rights and responsibilities; the child, partial legal rights and responsibilities; the unborn, neither legal rights nor responsibilities.

However, just as an adolescent child—whose legal rights are limited—is nevertheless fully a human being worthy of the law's protection, so too is the unborn child who has no vested legal rights. And in this there is a grand irony. When the Court in *Roe v. Wade* permitted substantially unrestricted abortions principally in the first two trimesters of gestation, it tacitly recognized the "personhood" of unborn children in the third trimester, and thus their "right" to the law's protection. But of course third-trimester fetuses are just as lacking of "rights, privileges, and immunities" as their first- and second-trimester brothers and sisters, who for that very lack were deemed not to be "persons"!

The masks covering moral compromises have a tendency to fall off at the most embarrassing times. Maybe it's impossible for us to act with perfect logic all the time, but how can we feel comfortable about life-and-death choices based on human reasoning which is obviously and embarrassingly contradictory?

The Historical Tragedy of "Personhood"

We who are part of the American experience have already witnessed the ease with which human reasoning can be distorted in order to justify the dehumanization of fellow human beings. I'm not speaking figuratively of, say, "dehumanizing" working or living conditions, but of a literal declaration that certain human beings were not "persons" worthy of the law's protection. A century before *Roe v. Wade*, in the *Dred Scott* case of 1857, the United States Supreme Court held that blacks were "non-persons," and therefore could legitimately be owned, bought, and sold as slaves.

Although black slaves obviously had hearts, brains, and healthy human anatomies from a biological perspective, the Supreme Court, using logic reminiscent of *Roe v. Wade*, held that blacks were non-persons in the eyes of the law. Blacks became "persons" only when *set free* by their owners—just as we are urged to believe that a fetus becomes a "person" only when *born*, or perhaps at some point shortly before birth. And the arguments in 1857 look suspiciously familiar. According to slave owners, declaring black slaves to be "persons" would have catastrophic economic and social costs. And would it not be inhumane to set the blacks free, only to send them out into a hostile environment for which they would be ill-equipped?

Here again there is a grand irony at work. When America finally came to its senses and rejected the *Dred Scott* decision, at the cost of half a million lives in the Civil War, the 14th Amendment to the Constitution was passed, guaranteeing equal protection and due process of law. How sad it is, then, that a century later the Court in *Roe v. Wade* would turn the 14th Amendment from a protective shield into a sword of destruction by once again denying personhood and the law's protection to human life. If the 14th Amendment stands for anything at all, it stands as a monument to the moral debasement which occurs when, by the convenient manipulation of language, we refuse to protect human life.

Can We Really Know When Life Begins?

Deep down, most pro-choice advocates seemingly realize that attempting to define a human being in terms of "personhood" not only has embarrassing historical precedent, but also defies the very consensus that the Court in *Roe v. Wade* wished to achieve. Therefore, what one most often hears—echoing the Court's own words—is that, since no one knows for certain when human life begins, each woman must be allowed to decide that issue for herself. But in what other circumstance would we ever take so cavalier an approach to human life?

For several days following the disastrous San Francisco earthquake of 1989, an entire nation sat glued to its television sets, hoping against hope that survivors would be found in the pancaked remains of the Nimitz Freeway. Among the dedicated rescue workers, no one was prepared to say, "We don't really know that anyone is still alive in the rubble, so we're going to go ahead and demolish the whole thing. After all, the people who were trapped in their cars are *probably* dead by now." What could have been more unthinkable? Until they knew for certain that no one else was alive, they risked their own lives in order to make sure.

> ❧ **If, in fact, we cannot decide when human life begins, then we cannot safely assume that it *hasn't* begun.**

And who can forget the heart-tugging news that, against all odds, that diabetic, 58-year-old teddy bear of a man, Buck Helm, had been found alive after 89 hours of being trapped? Even when he died unexpectedly 28 days later, no one had any second thoughts about the efforts which had been made to rescue him. Would even the most coldhearted person suggest that Buck Helm should have been left in the rubble because he would prove not to be *viable* outside the womb of concrete in which he was encased?

When it comes to human life, we dare not play games with either doubts or definitions. If, in fact, we cannot decide when human life begins, then we cannot safely assume that it *hasn't* begun. At a minimum, the almost universal agreement that an unborn fetus is both *human* and *living* must raise a presumption in favor of *human life*. Are we prepared to find out that we've been wrong all along in denying the obvious?

Beyond the Question of When Life Begins

I fully appreciate what I know is the frustration of many people at pro-life's dogged insistence that what is killed in an abortion is a human being. But the issue simply won't give up; it continues to haunt us. It is pivotal and inescapable, no matter which way we turn. Aware of the seeming impasse, however, let me suggest that we may have shortchanged our analysis on both sides of the controversy by concentrating on the question of *when* life begins. The most important question is not *when*, but *what*?

Just as an *egg* is not a *chicken*, so a zygote or embryo or fetus is not a *fully developed* human being. For that matter, neither is a newborn *infant* a fully developed human being. However, the point is that there is more involved than simply a question of timing. Timing addresses only the question of *when*.

Rather than asking questions like "Which came first, the chicken or the egg?" we would do well to take a closer look at both the chicken *and* the egg. As for eggs, we eat them without moral compunction. But it's obviously not because an egg is not yet a chicken, because we also eat *chickens*—again, without moral guilt. Whether it's an egg or a chicken—regardless of its stage of development—we feel free to kill it and eat it *because it is not human life.* The same goes for caviar and fish, veal and prime rib.

Simply because a human fetus is not an adult human does not mean it is any less a human being. It shares the same essence in both forms. If we would not kill an innocent *adult* human being, how can we kill a *fetal* human being? At their different stages of life they nevertheless are one-in-the-same. Like a chicken and an egg, they share the same unique nature. *Unlike* a chicken and an egg, they are both sacred human life.

Looking at the *what* rather than the *when* of human existence makes it possible to have an altogether different appreciation for the pro-choice characterization of a fetus as "a potential human being." In the words of Dr. Denis Cavanagh, "While it might be more convenient to regard the fetus as "a potential human being," I submit that he is in fact "a human being with potential."[15] Surely this must give new meaning to those people who are caught up in the various human potential movements. If human potential is all about the quality of life, then quality of life begins in the womb.

Neonatal physician Dr. Thomas Elkins reminds us that quality of life in the unborn is easily recognized, and heroically fought for, on the other end of the hospital from the abortion unit:

> We don't treat the fetus as a potential person. We have been approaching the fetus as a patient for a long time, especially in the third trimester when it is still a fetus. We can do a lot of things for that fetus that basically elevate it in every way and every sense to personhood. We operate for the benefit of the fetus—we do it every day. We monitor the fetus—we do it every day.
>
> We intervene when it appears ill and rush in to save its life. And I mean we rush. It's a two-minute dash to the C-section room to get out a fetus who has collapsed its cord. It's a dash for a life we feel is very, very personal.

So, to say that the fetus is only a potential human life is to miss some of the quality that we have already placed in it.[16]

Quality of life *outside* the womb cannot be divorced from quality of life *inside* the womb, where there are fetuses who possess the same human "qualities" as do we on the outside. It is as true in the first trimester as in the third, or else third-trimester fetuses would never have developed from first trimester embryos. Eight-month-old babies in the womb do not suddenly appear from nonhuman embryos. Only our inability to appreciate the uniqueness of human life itself permits us the foolishness of asking when life begins.

Looking Inside the Womb

All of us know that for most purposes "seeing is believing." We know, too, that "a picture is worth a thousand words." Misleading as graphic illustrations, photographs, and other visual evidence can sometimes be, we tend to put well-placed reliance upon what we can see with our own two eyes. By contrast, it is also easy for us to ignore what we *can't* see. "Out of sight, out of mind" is all too true for most of us.

Therefore, when it comes to deciding the point at which human life begins, we tend to rely on what we can physically see for ourselves. That is one reason why, in the Western world, a person's life is reckoned from the day he or she comes out of the womb. However, not every society is limited to visual confirmation. Paradoxical as it is in light of their widespread practice of abortion, the Chinese (overestimating by three months) have traditionally counted a child one year old *at birth* in recognition of the unceasingly active life that has already taken place.[17]

I'm convinced that if wombs had windows, the abortion debate would be over, once and for all. For years, like millions of other Americans, I had only the vaguest notion of what actually took place in an abortion. I assumed that the procedure to "terminate a pregnancy" was simply the removal of a glob of cells having no similarity whatever to a human being. But most of us would be shocked to see how highly developed the typical aborted fetus really is, even at very early stages.

I wish there were some way I could adequately picture for you the amazing development that has been captured so beautifully, for example, by Swedish photographer Lennart Nilsson.

His photo essay, "Drama of Life Before Birth," in the April 30, 1965, edition of *Life* magazine remains a classic record of the human odyssey from conception to birth. Long before the abortion controversy reached full stride, Nilsson wrote dispassionately: "The birth of a human life really occurs at the moment the mother's egg cell is fertilized by one of the father's sperm cells."[18]

Nilsson's photo of a 3 1/2-week-old embryo is accompanied by this surprising caption:

> This embryo is so tiny—about a tenth of an inch long—that the mother may not even know she is pregnant. Yet there is already impressive internal development, though not visible here. This embryo has the beginnings of eyes, spinal cord, nervous system, thyroid gland, lungs, stomach, kidney and intestines. Its primitive heart, which began beating haltingly on the 18th day, is now pumping more confidently. On the bulge of the chest, the tiny buds of arms—not yet visible—are forming.[19]

At 6 1/2 weeks, shortly before the embryo (meaning "to swell") is called a fetus (meaning "young one"), Nilsson shows us a "baby in miniature," though at this point it is lacking the sharp features of what we would recognize as a newborn infant. Says Nilsson:

> Though the embryo now weighs only $1/30$ of an ounce, it has all the internal organs of the adult in various stages of development. It already has a little mouth with lips, an early tongue and buds for 20 milk teeth. Its sex and reproductive organs have begun to sprout.[20]

The 11-week-old fetus is nothing less than a "tiny teenager," exercising newfound independence and letting his presence be known:

> Bones, including the ribs, are now rapidly forming. The body wall has grown from the spine

forward and is joined at the front—like a coat being buttoned. All the body systems are now working. Nerves and muscles are synchronizing with the young bones so that the arms and legs can make their first movements. Soon the fetus' living quarters get more cramped, and as it gains steadily in strength, the mother will begin to feel the sharp kick and thrust of foot, knee and elbow.[21]

It is important to note that, by this point in time, the largest number of abortions will already have taken place. The incredible developing life described by Nilsson—far from being the "glob of cells" that many of us once thought—has been killed either by menstrual extraction (up to five or six weeks) or by vacuum aspiration (between six and twelve weeks).

If the fetus is allowed to live to the sixteenth week, "the body has filled out fantastically, quite recognizable now as a baby. The eyes are still closed, but the nose, lips and ears finally look like nose, lips and ears." At 18 weeks, "this fetus is clearly sucking its thumb. This pre-natal practice prepares the baby to feed spontaneously as soon as it is born. It can go through the motions of crying, too."[22]

Here again, we must face the fact that many fetuses are aborted each year, even at this advanced stage. Although *relatively* few (when compared with the vast majority of typically six-to-ten-week abortions), the overall numbers are still such that many hundreds of the more advanced fetuses become victims of abortion. Picturing a thumb-sucking, crying fetus is not just phony phenotype argument or soppy sentimentalism. It is a vivid reminder that what we naturally associate with newborn babies *outside* the womb—whom we regard as persons—is already associated with unborn babies *inside* the womb.

Finally, Nilsson brings us to the 28th week:

> Here the development of the fetus is virtually completed, and some premature babies are born no older than this one. [Twenty years on from this assessment, some premature babies are now surviving from 21-22 weeks.] The extra time in the womb gives it added strength and health and time

to acquire from its mother precious, though short-term, immunity to a number of diseases.[23]

Nilsson's words accurately describe the biological developments, but his pictures tell the real story of what it means to "terminate a pregnancy." It is no more possible for a fetus to be just a little bit human than it is for a woman to be just a little bit pregnant. It seems that our "old-fashioned" parents and grandparents knew what they were talking about all along: A woman is not just *"pregnant"*; indeed she is *"with child."*

When it comes to abortion, unfortunately, seeing suffices for believing. If it *looks* like a baby, it *is* a baby. If it *doesn't*, it *isn't*. Perhaps that explains why so many people of faith are concerned about the unborn. They accept the teaching that we are to walk by faith and not by sight. They have learned the lesson that a morality based on physical sight alone lacks true insight into the invisible, spiritual world of which we are also a part.

One such man, Israel's King David, was able to perceive the unseen world of the womb through the eye of faith in the One who had made him. His words give masterful articulation to Nilsson's photos of the developing child:

> For you created my inmost being; you knit me together in my mother's womb. I praise you because I am fearfully and wonderfully made; your works are wonderful, I know that full well. My frame was not hidden from you when I was made in the secret place. When I was woven together in the depths of the earth, your eyes saw my unformed body. All the days ordained for me were written in your book before one of them came to be.[24]

If you can't obtain a copy of Nilsson's *Life* article, don't miss "The Making of Me" film shown in the Wonders of Life Pavilion at Disney's Epcot Center. The film, written and directed by Glenn Gordon Caron, creator of the "Moonlighting" television series, includes many of these and other startling photographs of fetal development by Lennart Nilsson.

In order to appreciate more graphically what is involved in a typical abortion, the drawings on the next page depict a life-sized eight-week-old fetus (in darker gray) and an enlarged close-up. At eight weeks, you may recall, the fetus is making the transition from an embryo to a fetus. The key distinction lies in the formation of the first real bone cells that begin to replace the cartilage. At this point, too, all his major organs are in place.

If wombs had windows, we could no longer refuse to acknowledge the existence of this little person. Nor could we continue to rationalize the right to kill. If wombs had windows, the charlatan charade of whether there is "personhood" would come to a screeching halt. Pro-choice is nothing less than *blind* choice that slams the windows shut.

Let's not continue to fool ourselves: "Pro-choice" on the issue of abortion means a dead baby. Otherwise there is no reason to have that choice. Those who say they are *anti-abortion* but *pro-choice* are saying nothing more than that they wouldn't personally kill the baby, but that it's all right if others do. Either way, our little one is dead.

NINE

Phantom Choices

Once impregnation has taken place, it is no longer a question of whether the persons concerned have responsibility for a possible parenthood; they have become parents.

—Helmut Thielicke

IN 1981 *THE PHILADELPHIA INQUIRER*, along with a number of other newspapers, reported the following story: A woman's scream broke the late-night quiet and brought two young obstetrical nurses rushing to room 4456 of the University of Nebraska Medical Center. The patient, admitted for an abortion after a 19- or 20-week pregnancy, had been injected 30 hours earlier with a salt solution which normally kills the fetus and causes the patient to deliver the dead fetus in a process similar to a miscarriage.

This time, though, something had gone wrong. When nurse Marilyn Wilson flicked on the lights and pulled back the covers, she found—instead of the stillborn fetus she had expected—a live 2-pound, 3-ounce baby boy, crying and moving his arms and legs there on the bed. Instinctively, Wilson clamped and cut the umbilical cord.

A second nurse, Joanie Fuchs, gathered the squirming infant in loose bedcovers, dashed down the corridor, and called to other nurses for help. From that point, accounts vary. Either the baby was bathed, baptized, and wrapped in a blanket before being placed in a warmer, or he was deposited on the stainless steel drainboard of a sink in the maternity unit's Dirty Utility Room.

Whatever the location, other nurses gathered and gaped, unsure of what to do. Finally a head nurse telephoned the patient's physician, Dr. C. J. LaBenz. "He told me to leave it where it was," the head nurse testified later, "just watch it for a few minutes, that it would probably die in a few minutes." LaBenz himself said later that another doctor at the scene advised him that the infant's chances of survival "were so bad that heroic measures were not warranted." The boy died two hours after birth.[1]

A tough decision. A tragic ending. Great latitude for Monday-morning quarterbacks. Second thoughts undoubtedly abound, and there's obviously grist for the moralists' mill. (For instance, had it been a "baby" they expected, heroic efforts would have been made to keep the "baby" alive.) But two things are clear: First, given the premature birth, the baby might have died in any event. Second, without the abortion, the fetus in all likelihood would have developed into a perfectly healthy baby.

The purpose of the illustration, however, is to draw us to the endless arguments swirling around the word *viability*. Says the Court in *Roe v. Wade*, a pregnancy may be terminated prior to the time when the fetus is *viable*—that is, capable of living on its own outside the mother's womb. *Prior* to viability we have a *fetus* which legally may be aborted; *after* viability we have an *unborn baby* which (typically under state laws) may not be aborted except where there is threat to the mother's life.

The Viability Fraud

The problem with viability—or "quickening," or even first, second, and third "trimesters"—is that we can never be sure where along the line of gestation we happen to be at any given time. The ancient idea of "quickening" attempts to draw a significant line when the mother first feels movement in her womb. But what if there is movement which she does *not* feel? (In fact, there is more movement *before* "quickening" than *after*. The mother feels movement when the baby has outgrown his "playroom" and has his movement restricted.) Even modern pregnancy tests—varying as they do, depending on the point of time by which they are calculated—are not always helpful in determining the now-familiar, but Court-invented, "trimesters."

Not even pro-choice advocates are completely satisfied with notions of viability. Consider, for example, Carl Sagan and Ann Druyan's objections:

> Why, exactly, should breathing (or kidney function, or the ability to resist disease) justify legal protection? If a fetus can be shown to think and feel but not be able to breathe, would it be all right to kill it? Do we value breathing more than thinking and feeling? Viability arguments cannot, it seems to us, coherently determine when abortions are permissible. Some other criterion is needed.[2]

Any way you look at it, arbitrary line-drawing after the moment of conception (including Sagan's own "onset of human thinking" criterion) is doomed to failure. Thus the needless tragedy in Room 4456 of the Nebraska Medical Center. What they expected was a *fetus*. What they got was a *baby*!

One can argue the issue of viability all day long, but it doesn't alter the fact that, in this case, the baby boy which was born in room 4456 actually lived apart from his mother's womb, even if only for two hours. For two crucial hours, the baby was living *independently* of his mother. If, as some would argue, the fetus in the womb is only "potential life," for at least two hours this baby was a breathing, crying, kicking, *alive* human being. Chances are, however, that his tragically brief life was recorded by neither a birth certificate nor a certificate of death, as would have been the case had he been a *wanted* baby.

There are two critically important lessons to be learned from this abandoned baby's brief life. (If we can learn them, perhaps his short life will not have been lived in vain.) The first is that arbitrary lines of viability are a hopelessly inadequate basis upon which to make life-and-death decisions. Too many different standards are possible: Are we in the United States or India? Which decade do we live in? What medical equipment is available? The line of "viability" changes with each day's advance in medical technology.

As Carl Sagan has pointed out, "A morality that depends on, and changes with, technology is a fragile morality; for some, it is also an unacceptable morality."[3]

Whatever the circumstances, there is a far more important point to be made. Because we know that the baby in this case could survive for two hours on his own *outside* the womb, we also know that he undoubtedly would have continued to live a normal, healthy life *inside* the womb, where he was meant to be until fully developed.

The fraud of viability is exposed when we stop to think that a fetus outside the womb is like a fish out of water, or an egg taken from the nest, or an astronaut in outer space without his space-suit. In each case, viability ceases outside a proper environment.

If it were possible for some force to suck us off the earth and deposit us on some unfriendly distant planet, we too would be out of our element and most likely would die. Would our lack of viability outside the security of Mother Earth thereby make us expendable while still in her womb?

With but rare exceptions, *every* baby is viable if left in the womb until birth. With but equally rare exceptions (including our tough little two-hours-old Nebraskan), *no* fetus is viable when forcibly removed from the womb by abortive means.

In that light, any talk of viability is meaningless. It's a distractive irrelevance. It's a phantom issue designed to permit choices where, without such contrived distinctions, no choice legitimately could be made. In this case, in order for choice to become God, choice had to be invented. And here Shakespeare is proved to be frightfully right: When the Court first practiced to deceive, with its manufactured "right to privacy," it became necessary to weave an entire web of deception, including the legal fictions of "trimesters" and "viability."

Even many feminists agree. Rhonda Copelon and Kathryn Kolbert confirm for us that "viability is widely seen by commentators less as an unassailably logical line than as a compromise between the feminist view that the law cannot treat the fetus as separate until born and the anti-choice view that the fetus is human life from fertilization."[4]

Justifying abortion on the basis of viability is disingenuous. If *any* fetus survives apart from its mother, it is indeed an exception to the rule. Fetuses aren't *meant* to be viable outside the womb. For that matter, a child's dependence does not end even with his or her birth. Without continuing physical and social nourishment from its parents over the ensuing days and months, even the newborn infant would be "nonviable."

One last chilling thought. If ever there were any doubt about the issue of viability, of one thing there can be absolutely no doubt: Neither a fetus, nor an infant, nor an adult is viable once killed.

Where Viability Finds Legitimacy

Pro-choice advocates and Supreme Court Justices are grasping at straws when they speak about viability. The way they apply viability to kill perfectly healthy fetuses makes viability a sham and a farce. As so used, the notion of viability, with its built-in license to kill, is immoral and unworthy of civilized minds. However, despite "viability's" general inappropriateness, there is that rare, tragic instance in which the issue of viability is legitimate. Some fetuses truly are *not* viable. Because they lack a life-sustaining anatomy, they are not capable of living once they are born, even if carried to full term.

Such is the case, for example, with a fetus which is anencephalic. Here the brain simply does not exist in a form capable of directing the body's critical functions. No matter how long the fetus is able to survive inside the protection of the mother's womb, there is no possibility of survival on the outside. If an argument were to be made for abortion based upon lack of viability, this exceptionally rare instance would have to be the limit of such an argument. For here "viability" takes on its proper meaning. Here the fetus in the womb—from conception to delivery—is "as good as dead."

Before modern medical scans could detect such fatal fetal conditions, parents first learned of their child's nonviability when the child was delivered stillborn. Today the possibility of advance warning induces most parents of anencephalic fetuses to abort. Even those who oppose the typical eugenic abortion for abnormal fetuses may not be as quick to condemn a decision to abort in such a case. However, I have been touched recently by the decision of a friend's daughter to carry her anencephalic baby to term, and also by a truly heartwarming story of yet another expectant couple who rejected their doctor's advice, deciding instead to continue the pregnancy until natural birth.

Dr. Daphne Watkins, a general practitioner at the Mary Potter Health Centre in Nottingham, England, tells of one of her patients, a happily married woman of 30, already with a daughter of nine and a son of seven, who had not planned to have another child. At 15 weeks a scan revealed that the fetus was anencephalic. As a matter of course, the consultant obstetrician advised termination of the pregnancy.

To everyone's surprise, the woman and her husband decided against an abortion. Dr. Watkins says the parents clearly were not taking refuge in unreasonable hopes, having carefully read all the information that had been supplied them concerning their child's condition. What Dr. Watkins relates about the subsequent delivery of the child speaks volumes about how even a truly "nonviable" fetus can become the object of love and concern:

> As soon as the parents had decided to have the baby, they had told their son and daughter. The wider family had been skeptical about the decision, but the children had quickly joined in the plans for the birth and helped choose the baby's clothes.
>
> The birth, which was induced, took place in hospital, and I was present. The delivery was by hospital midwives, who knew the circumstances and were skilled and supportive. The mother received an epidural, the labor was smooth and the delivery was normal. The baby boy was stillborn.
>
> The father and I took the baby to the end of the delivery room, where a midwife dressed him. His father gave him the name the parents had chosen, and afterwards he was always referred to by his Christian name. The midwife arranged his bonnet to hide his abnormal skull and returned him to his mother. She welcomed him with cuddles. A nurse and I took photographs of mother, father, and baby.[5]

A poignant ending, indeed—one that we might wish all parents would choose. Yet it would not be at all surprising if other couples in a similar situation would choose another course. The thought of carrying a baby who is "as good as dead" could be a horrible prospect to an expectant mother. However, no life-and-death choice is made without attendant costs.

Sometimes the choice is between grief and guilt, or between *grief without guilt* and *guilt accompanied by grief.*

❧ Guilt about abortions was not invented by the Pope.

Dr. Watkins highlights this "choice of the horribles," referring to a letter written about the mother by a doctor from the Clinical Genetic Service:

> I was most interested to find that your patient is much more emotionally intact three months later than the majority of women I have seen who have undergone a later termination on genetic grounds, and clearly neither partner feels the guilt that is unfortunately associated with a decision to interrupt a pregnancy, whatever the reason. In fact, I found it most instructive to listen to them and particularly to learn that the mother still found the pregnancy and birth fulfilling.
>
> Six months after the birth the mother was still grieving, but she told me she had no feelings of guilt. A termination might have allowed some patients to forget the episode more quickly, but experience of the birth had remained a part of their lives. However, it was being dealt with in a balanced and guilt-free way.[6]

"Few women choose to continue a pregnancy in which the fetus is not viable," concludes Dr. Watkins. "However, the decision to terminate such a pregnancy may be more traumatic for some women and their partners than allowing nature to take its course."[7]

Why the Guilt? Why the Trauma?

Guilt about abortions was not invented by the Pope. Post-abortion trauma is not the dastardly creation of the Moral Majority to punish believers and nonbelievers alike for having killed their unborn children. Guilt and post-abortion trauma are subjects of virtually all feminist literature dealing with termination of pregnancies. You find guilt and post-abortion trauma in non-Christian societies as well as in Judeo-Christian cultures.

> ?◦ **Newly created life is so much a part of who the mother is as a giver of life that aborting the fetus is tantamount to ripping out a part of her own self.**

The universality of post-abortion guilt extends, for example, to Shintoist and Buddhist Japan—hardly a Judeo-Christian nation, less yet a Catholic nation. An article in London's *Sunday Times* shows a picture of thousands of tiny statues in a Japanese temple, which the writer of the piece describes as being "mute testimony to the sad story of Japan's abortion industry":

> The effigies, in stone, plaster, or plastic, represent children conceived but never born. The temple, at Kamakura, is one of scores across Japan. . . .
>
> Mineko, a 19-year-old student, came here after her overnight abortion in a clinic. She bought a statue and committed it to the care of Jizo, the Buddhist guardian deity of children. After prayers, she said: "This soothes my heart. I felt so bad about it."
>
> On the altar strewn with dolls and baby clothes lie memorials from guilt-stricken parents. "We promise to give birth to you next time. Please forgive your bad mum and dad," reads one message to an unborn child. "We'll never forget you," says another.[8]

In America, Japan, and even officially atheistic societies such as the Soviet Union, some degree of guilt or post-abortion trauma almost invariably accompanies abortions, whether of "wanted" babies aborted for medical reasons or of "unwanted" babies aborted for so-called social reasons.

"There is no question about the emotional grief and mourning following an abortion," says Dr. Julius Fogel, an obstetrician-gynecologist who has performed 20,000 abortions. "There is no question in my mind that we are disturbing a life process."[9] According to journalist John Leo, "One researcher says that '*only*' 1 percent of women who abort, or about 16,000 women a year in America, are 'so severely scarred by post-abortion trauma that they become unable to function normally.'"[10] Although *severe* post-abortion psychiatric complications may be thought to be relatively uncommon, it is not at all unusual for abortion to result in feelings of regret and remorse.

If, as pro-choice advocates urge, nothing more is being aborted than a collection of cells, or merely a vaguely defined embryonic organism, then why all the guilt, why all the trauma? With surgery to remove an appendix, or liposuction to remove excess fat, there may be some residual pain, but not guilt or emotional trauma. Abortion, by contrast, is rarely free from psychological aftershocks—even if, for some, the tremors on the moral Richter scale are but a slight blip. Almost never is there no moral tremor at all.

What is it, then, that causes that "loss of innocence," as it was put by one young woman who otherwise denies any greater moral repercussions from her abortion? I suggest that the answer lies in what feminists have affirmed all along: that the fetus within the womb *is* a part of a woman's body—not to be confused, of course, with being *the same as* her body, or *indistinct* therefrom. ("Test-tube" babies ought to put an end forever to that foolish notion. Are we to assume that the week-old embryo in the lab is part of the petri dish in which it is cultured?) But newly created life is so much a part of who the mother is as a giver of life that aborting the fetus is tantamount to ripping out a part of her own self.

And not just part of herself which is a useless organ, like an appendix, or unwanted fat cells, as in a liposuction, but a part of her that is distinctly *not* a part of her: a part of her that is *more* than her, a part of her that is *different* from her, a part of her that is *another person*. (It is perhaps something like what we mean when we refer to being "part of" someone we love.)

Referring to the statistics he previously cited regarding the incidence of post-abortion trauma, John Leo affirms the obvious: "Findings such as these do not constitute an argument against abortion. But they certainly tell us we are not in the realm of tonsillectomies."[11]

What, after all, is reproduction all about? It's about duplication and continuity. Just as humankind is made in the image of the *Creator*, the fetus is made in the image of the *procreators*. The mother has part of herself invested in the life form conceived within her. The fetus is not a *generic* human life but a *special* human life. It is special to the *father* and special to the *mother*. It is unique to them.

If, therefore, abortion is morally wrong, it is one of the most *personal* wrongs one can ever do. For if abortion is the wrongful killing of another, there is also a sense in which it is *moral suicide*. It is killing a part of one's own self. It is self-denial, self-abasement. Abortion carves a hole in the human soul. *That's* why there is guilt. *That's* why there is post-abortion trauma. And, as we have already seen, a woman doesn't have to be particularly religious to experience it.

In fact, that is why there is so much *pre-abortion* trauma. Lost in all the talk about post-abortion trauma is the agony which accompanies a decision to abort in the first place. Hardly any abortion—even if it is an "abortion of convenience"—is a *morally* convenient abortion, even for hard-core pro-choice advocates. Rare is the woman who doesn't have second thoughts about going through with it. Not even the relative ease with which an abortion is performed (compared with major surgery) provides much solace. Intuitively, women know that what they are about to do is qualitatively different from any other medical surgery, or even elective cosmetic surgery.

Guilt Worthy of Warnings

In light of the post-abortion trauma experienced by most women having abortions, the Supreme Court ought to rethink its decision in *Roe v. Wade*. In criminal cases, the Court insists on the giving of "Miranda warnings" before an accused is interrogated by the police. (You have the right to remain silent. You have the right to an attorney, etc.) The purpose is to make certain that a confession is "voluntary." Whether or not it is "voluntary" depends upon whether there has been *informed* consent—that is, does the accused know of all the potentially harmful implications of the choice he is about to make in giving a confession to the police?

In the same spirit, the Court should have mandated *"Roe warnings"* for any woman contemplating an abortion. The consequences are not always immediately evident. In fact, guilt postponed is often guilt compounded. Removing a baby from the *womb* is the easy part; removing the aborted baby from the *mind* is next to impossible. Therefore, the following warnings might be suggested:

> You have a right to know that no man, whether boyfriend or husband, may legitimately force you to abort a baby for which he does not wish to be responsible.
>
> You have the right to know that, if you decide on your own to have an abortion, you may experience unexpected moral guilt, either immediately or at some future time. That the body over which you have control is also associated with a conscience which responds to a higher moral standard over which you have no control.
>
> You have the right to know that a large number of women having abortions at early ages have lived to regret their decision, whether morally or psychologically, or sometimes even in the inability to have children in the future.
>
> You have the right to know that, if for any reason you do not feel that you can raise your baby with the love you would like to give it, there are many couples who would be thrilled to adopt the baby for themselves and to give your son or daughter the kind of life you would want your child to have. That if you *do* choose adoption, you may also have later feelings of guilt and regret, but typically on a scale far less than if you choose abortion.

If the post-abortion syndrome were only a matter of moral or psychological aftershocks personal to the mother, we might provide the "informed consent" suggested in these warnings, and decide that any further limitation on abortion is overly paternalistic. Women could choose to live with the consequences of their decision, no matter how difficult, no matter how shattering. However, it is what the post-abortion syndrome evidences about the morality of *abortion itself* that compels us to be paternalistic on behalf of the innocent unborn.

❧ Something that is morally neutral would not send so many women reeling with guilt and regret.

Whether or not any such warnings are ever given, the fact is that the guilt and post-abortion trauma associated with abortions of all kinds betray the argument that fetuses are nonpersons. Women seem to know intuitively that the decision to abort is like no other decision they will ever make. Label it as you will, they know that what they are terminating is human life.

I must say that this point alone has been the "swing vote" in my own evolving understanding of the abortion issue. In recent years I have come to see that, even wholly apart from arguments about abnormal *fetuses*, abortion cripples the *mothers*. And that simply would not happen if abortion were morally neutral. Something that is morally neutral would not send so many women reeling with guilt and regret.

The Eye of the Beholder

There is more than one story connected with the trauma accompanying the termination of a pregnancy. Lost in the concern about either post-abortion or pre-abortion trauma is the grief suffered by mothers who lose their babies through those "spontaneous abortions" which we call *miscarriages*. A friend's recent miscarriage was a terrible reminder of how differently the termination of a pregnancy can be viewed. I can still remember the excitement in Becky's voice when she first called to say that her pregnancy test had been positive. But suddenly, a long-awaited pregnancy had become a devastating disappointment.

What can be more telling than the contrast between a *spontaneous* abortion and a *chosen* abortion? With a miscarriage—perhaps as early as the eighth or ninth week—there is grief for loss of a *baby* whose anticipated birth was the cause of excited expectations. With an abortion—sometimes performed up to 12 or more weeks—there is "merely" the loss of an unwanted *fetus*.

Have you ever noticed that the only time those of us who are not in the medical profession refer to a *fetus* is when we talk about abortion? In every other case, we refer to a *baby*. We don't ask, "What are you going to name the fetus?" Nor do we console a woman who has just miscarried by saying, "I'm sorry you lost your fetus." In referring to pregnancy, we invariably understand that we are dealing with a little person developing in the womb. Only when it is subject to an abortion must a baby go incognito. Use of an assumed name? What have we got to hide?

John Leo suggests that "too many of us are dealing with this issue with a huge amount of denial. Sociologist Barbara Rothman, for instance, says that pregnancy 'takes its meaning from the woman in whose body the pregnancy is unfolding.' In other words, it's a baby if you want it, a clump of tissue if you don't. That is a bit of self-deception very common in feminist literature."[12]

As an example of that self-deception, consider Barbara Ehrenreich's recent claim, in the *New York Times*, that "a woman may think of her fetus as a person or as just cells depending on whether the pregnancy is wanted or not. This does not reflect moral confusion," she says by way of explanation, "but choice in action." (Would it be morally justifiable "choice in action" if a woman decided to kill an unwanted *husband*, claiming him to be a non-person?)

Ehrenreich then proceeds to let the *real* cat out of the bag: "Moreover, a woman may think of the fetus as a person and still find it necessary and morally responsible to have an abortion."[13]

Now we've got to the point of the argument! When will we ever wake up to the fact that "viability" and "personhood" are only diversionary skirmishes—that the real war is being fought over whether women can have abortions under any and all circumstances, *even if, by their own definition, it means having to kill innocent persons*?

Feminists Rhonda Copelon and Kathryn Kolbert tell us that "when pregnancy is finally viewed as a voluntary gift of life to another and not a woman's duty, the abortion debate will not turn on the question of when life begins. When women are accorded a right to be sexual, the sanctification of fetal innocence . . . will abate."[14]

Simply put, "viability" for feminists is the point at which a woman voluntarily wishes to bestow the status of life to her offspring. And with that definition we have approached the high altar of our generation's pro-choice religion. Sanctification of life when we wish to sanctify it becomes the ultimate expression of what happens when choice becomes God: Humankind is made in the image of humankind! And *de*humanized with the same ease.

The sad thing about "viability" is that, if such a line could be drawn, it would be a line based upon *dependence*: Because something is dependent, it is unworthy of protection. But drawing a line at that point runs counter to all our instincts. Normally when we see someone mistreated, our sense of outrage, our urge to protect, is inversely related to the person's ability to protect himself: The more *dependent* he or she is, the more protective we become. With "viability" as our guide, we act completely contrary to our normal sense of moral responsibility. Rather than appealing to our best instincts, "viability" brings out the very worst in us.

Can the simple variable of whether a child is *wanted* or *unwanted* really be a reasonable guideline for when human life begins? Can we so glibly say that, if a baby is not wanted, it simply doesn't exist? More than one woman has proceeded upon that assumption, only to face—perhaps after several years—the haunting realization that the clinically nebulous *fetus* she thought she had "terminated" was really a vibrantly healthy *baby* that she had killed.

In order for a right of choice to have any meaning, there must be "truth in advertising." Choices about abortion based on shadowy lines of "viability" which do not in fact exist are phantom choices—phantoms of conscience which will not cease to haunt us in a thousand nights of dark despair.

TEN

Defective Babies, Defective Choices

The history of man for the nine months preceding his birth would probably be far more interesting, and contain events of greater moment, than all the three score and ten years that follow it.

—Samuel Taylor Coleridge

ANYONE WHO HAS SEEN THE FILM *The Elephant Man* will never forget the moving portrayal of John Merrick, played so marvelously by John Hurt. It is the true story of a man in Victorian England who became known as the Elephant Man because of his terrible deformities. Merrick was discovered in a circus freak show by Dr. Frederick Treves, a surgeon at London Hospital. Dr. Treves, also a lecturer in anatomy, initially took a professional interest in Merrick's grotesquely enlarged skull, abnormal curvature of the spine, and the elephantlike fibrous growth which covered 90 percent of his body. Treves' professional interest soon developed into a warm, compassionate friendship with this very special individual.

As the film begins, Dr. Treves bargains with Merrick's freak-show keeper in order to have the privilege of examining Merrick at his clinic. Their conversation gives a flavor of how Merrick was objectified by all who came into contact with him: "I'd pay handsomely to see *it*," says Treves. "Are you the *owner*?" "Yes,

I'm the *owner*," responds Merrick's cruel keeper. Even one of Treves' fellow doctors shares this insensitivity when he learns that Treves has brought Merrick into the hospital for treatment: "The man's a complete idiot. He's an imbecile from birth." The chief hospital administrator agrees: "Don't waste your time. He doesn't belong here. This hospital doesn't accept incurables."

But to everyone's surprise, including Dr. Treves', Merrick reveals that he is highly intelligent, even literate. Although his physical deformities prevent clear speech, Merrick's mind is quick, and his disposition has the precious innocence of a lovely, inquisitive child. News of this special "elephant man" spreads throughout the whole of London, bringing requests from London's high society and theater luminaries for special introductions. Concerned that Merrick has once again become the object of a freak show, this time for socialites, Dr. Treves chooses a more private outlet for Merrick's social life. He invites Merrick to tea in his own home.

When Merrick is shown photographs of Treves' family, Merrick surprises Treves by asking, "Would you care to see my mother?" The movie never reveals his mother's whereabouts, nor the conditions under which she apparently abandoned him, but somehow Merrick has a small framed picture of her. "Your mother?" asks Treves with veiled excitement. "Yes . . . please." Even at first glance, her beauty is striking. "Oh, but she's . . . Mr. Merrick, she's *beautiful*." "Oh, yes . . . she had the face of an angel," Merrick responds proudly.

Merrick then reflects, with a certain sadness, "I must have been a great disappointment to her." Treves' wife hastens to reassure him, "No . . . no, Mr. Merrick. No son as loving as you could ever be a disappointment." But Merrick wonders wistfully aloud: "If only I could find her so she could see me with such lovely friends as I now have. Perhaps she could love me as I am. I've tried so hard to be good." At that Mrs. Treves floods into tears, and the camera fades to black.

But Merrick had yet to convince others that his life was worth living. At a hospital staff meeting where Merrick's resident status was to be decided, some of the doctors were hostile. "This creature has no business being here at all," says one, referring angrily to "these abominations of nature." "When will those rooms be vacated for use by better qualified, more deserving cases?" demands another. As if in response to their characterization of him as a worthless freak of nature (revealed in a later scene where he responds to an angry attacking mob), Merrick cries out: "I am not an elephant! I am not an animal! I am a *human being!*"

In time, Treves must confirm what Merrick suspects. "Can you cure me?" asks this gentle man calmly. "No," says Treves sorrowfully. "We can care for you, but we can't cure you." Resigned to his fate, and in a poignant close to their friendship, Merrick reassures a quavering physician and friend: "I am happy every hour of the day. My life is full because I know that I am loved."

Lessons from the Elephant Man

The Elephant Man gently but resoundingly rebukes a society which has come to accept the so-called eugenic abortions of deformed fetuses, and in some cases even the death of newborns found to be handicapped. Regarded as freaks fit only for a circus sideshow, these special unborn babies and newborn children too often encounter much of the same uncaring prejudice as that which faced John Merrick in Victorian times.

His is the story of how we so poorly misjudge the quality of human life—how we judge people by their packages, whether it's the color, nationality, or religion which happens to be stamped on the package. Or its sex, or bank account, or age. Or, God forbid, its physical perfection.

His is the story of how we make such indefensible moral choices. For it's not *how* we decide in individual cases whether a given life is "worth living," but it is *the very fact that we would make such a decision about people* which strips us of our own humanity.

Worse yet is the debauched use of "defective" fetuses to build an unconscionable case for abortion on demand, abortions for convenience, or, if one prefers, social abortion. As with the even rarer cases of pregnancies caused by rape and incest, abortion in the case of fetal abnormalities—representing only 1 percent of all abortions—is used to justify the other 99 percent of abortions in which there is no question of rape, incest, or fetal deformity. Even if abortion were morally justifiable in such exceptional cases, no similar logic is even remotely available to justify the typical pro-choice abortion.

The argument that women must have the right to choose an abortion because they might be faced with a deformed fetus is morally bankrupt for two reasons: First, because it argues from the tragic exception (eugenic abortion) to a non-tragic general practice (social abortion); second, because it wrongly assumes in the first place that the handicapped are not worthy of living.

Schizophrenia on the Disabled

Nowhere do you see our national schizophrenia more sharply focused than in the feminist classic, *Our Bodies, Ourselves*. In contrast to all the pro-choice talk about aborting defective fetusus, in Chapter 2 there is one poignant reminder after another that the handicapped are living, breathing, identifiable, people of intrinsic value. The caption beneath a heart-tugging picture of mother and child (the mother being disabled), reads, "This woman is post-polio and has no use of her arms and hands. She takes care of her daughter using her teeth and toes and love."[1] Had many physicians and couples followed current thinking about defective fetuses, such a wonderful example of maternal love would have been benignly aborted.

> ❧ Nothing is more of an object, of course, than the fetal, non-person "it" which is the subject of a "termination of pregnancy."

The pretentious talk about the suffering of the handicapped and their minimal quality of life—meant to justify eugenic abortions, and, by extension, social abortions—is beautifully undermined again in *Our Bodies, Ourselves*. Consider, for example, this insightful letter from a remarkable handicapped woman:

> There is something 'WRONG' with my body, so how can I possibly feel good about it or enjoy life in it? Simple answers are: *I have no choice* and *I want to*. The more complex answer is that there is nothing wrong with my body. It falls within the wide range of human experience and is therefore both natural and normal. I've been with this body all my life. I was born with it and I'll die with it. It's part of who I

am, and I'd be somebody else without this body just
the way it is.[2]

We must not forget that, in order to be born with that unique
body, this woman had to live for the complete term of pregnancy. Without her life having been allowed to develop in that
body, *she* would not *be.*

Says another disabled woman: "I have been lucky enough to
discover that I am still a whole and worthwhile person and feel
that all those dark years linked me profoundly to other women."[3]
A "whole and worthwhile person" is not how many pro-choice
advocates are characterizing the disabled in the battle for abortion. The right of choice must be maintained, we are told,
because the quality of life for the disabled, being below the level
of minimal acceptability, merits a humanitarian "termination."

What disabled women (and men) feel about how they are
treated may be the best commentary of all as to how society
regards their unborn "defective" brothers and sisters who are
aborted. This letter makes the connection:

> Having a disability made me very aware at an
> early age of the messages I was receiving from the
> larger society about how I was supposed to look and
> how you're supposed to be. Also, as the doctors
> poked and studied me endlessly, I learned more
> quickly than some non-disabled women that I'm
> seen as an object.[4]

Nothing is more of an object, of course, than the fetal, non-
person "it" which is the subject of a "termination of pregnancy"
(or, worse still, a tersely abbreviated "TOP"). The language of
devalued disability is the language of devalued abortion: "Many
of these [disabled] women are *silent and invisible*—many of us
choose to hide in order to avoid the pain of being stared at and
objectified, and the public, in fear, *does not acknowledge and accept
us.*"[5]

What is a disabled woman supposed to think when she
reads Chapter 2 of *Our Bodies, Ourselves,* where she is affirmed as
a woman of intrinsic value and human worth, then proceeds to
be told elsewhere that her mother should have had an unqualified right to kill her in the womb because she surely could not

have a "life worth living"? It's not only defective logic, which itself ought to be terminated, but it is also incredibly insensitive. What must disabled men and women think when they turn on their television and listen to a debate as to whether or not they have a right to exist!

The truth is that only the handicapped can tell us whether their lives are worth living. Those who have survived a society bent on eugenic abortions (selective breeding, really) tell us almost to the person that life *is* worth living. Thousands more have never been given the chance to speak.

Death for Deformity

A recent front-page article in London's *Sunday Times* appealed for women considering aborting their facially deformed babies to volunteer instead for the world's first "out-of-womb" surgery to correct the condition. "The new technique," explained *Times* medical correspondent Aileen Ballantyne, "involves pulling the head and neck of the fetus out of the womb to allow surgery, and then replacing the baby in the womb. It promises to correct cleft lips without scarring and with minimal disfiguration."

The appeal came after doctors in California successfully performed lifesaving lung surgery on a 24-week-old fetus by removing his left arm and chest from the womb, then putting him back. As in the California surgery, concerned parents were assured that, during the surgery, "The baby will be attached to the perfect heart and lung machine: its own mother."

Doctors stressed that "a developing fetus is a perfect patient, and the womb a perfect recovery area where wounds can heal rapidly, leaving little or no scarring. It is the developing fetus' extraordinary ability to recover and repair itself that makes the new concept of the 'fetus as patient' so attractive to surgeons."[6]

Fetus as *patient*? Can a non-person be a *patient*? Until now, tragically, many people have assumed that a fetus with abnormal features is a non-person, justifiably aborted. "Although cleft lips and palates can be partly remedied by surgery after birth," Ballantyne reports, "many couples opt to end such pregnancies once ultra-sound scans have identified the condition at 16-18 weeks." (Has it never occurred to us that a fetus sufficiently developed for us to identify cleft lips is a highly developed fetus indeed?)

The almost unbelievable result is that cleft lips and cleft palates—arguably the slightest of all forms of disfigurement or impediment as compared with other disabilities, and certainly not even remotely fatal—have now actually become a threat to a child's life! Says Anthony Rowsell, consultant plastic surgeon at Guy's Hospital in London, "We thought it would be 10 years before we were doing this operation—but so many people are now opting for a termination for this condition that for the baby it is effectively life-threatening."[7]

Even if one might feel strongly that abortion is indicated in severe cases of Down's syndrome, spina bifida, or anencephaly, how have we ever gotten to the point where we are willing to kill our own children for lack of cosmetic and functional perfection? Well worth noting are some of the many letters to the editor which were written in response to the *Times* article in which the specter of abortion in such cases was raised.

Susan Kitching, mother of five-year-old daughter Lucy (who was born with a severe unilateral cleft lip and palate), wrote:

> I was horrified to read that many couples now opt for abortion rather than risk having a baby with such a minor physical imperfection. My daughter is not some subnormal freak, but is perfect except in one minor physical detail—and she can, and does, lead a happy, fulfilled life. I cannot believe that even in adolescence, when she will be most sensitive about her appearance, she would prefer not to have been born rather than to face the so-called "trauma" of it all.
>
> What sort of society do we live in when a minor facial deformity, correctable by surgery, is viewed as so abnormal as to merit abortion?[8]

Perhaps it is too easy for us, even as an affected parent, to say that the handicapped (particularly in more serious cases) would always opt for life. But another letter allows at least one insider's view of lesser deformities. Siobhan Bowe thinks she is no more handicapped than her red-haired sister!

> I am a 17-year-old student who has a cleft lip but not a cleft palate. I had my first operation when I

was 11 weeks old, and my second when I was four, and I am due to have the final operation next year.

Having a cleft lip has in no way whatsoever made my life different from that of any other typical person of my age group. I am capable of doing absolutely anything an average person can do. I am not a social outcast because of my deformity, and neither my parents nor I have suffered any "psychological problems." I can honestly say that I have been subjected to no more ridicule than my younger sister who, to her misfortune, was born with red hair.

Why, then, do some parents prefer to kill their children rather than let them have such operations? There is no great trauma, and a cleft lip is not a serious disfiguring condition.

However, I write mainly for expectant mothers who know that their baby has a cleft lip and are considering termination. All I can say is: have your baby. If you do not, you will regret it for the rest of your life. With modern medical science as advanced as it is today, your baby will grow up to be a wonderful human being with a small facial scar who is capable of reaching for the moon and touching it. I should know: I'm living proof.[9]

Designer Babies

Siobhan's mention of her sister's "red-hair handicap" points the way to a scary 21st century, if the trend toward preselected babies continues. Ellen Goodman, associate editor and columnist for *The Boston Globe*, asks, "Can we 'just say no' to knowledge as prenatal testing shows us more?" She tells of sitting next to a woman who pats her rounded stomach and rolls her eyes to the ceiling, exclaiming, "Is she ever active today!" The "she" won't be born until several months later, but her mother already knows the baby's gender.

Like millions of expectant mothers over the past two decades who have had the benefit of amniocentesis and sonograms, this woman was pleased to know both the gender of her baby and the fact that it was healthy. "But what if she and her husband had regarded the sex of this child as a devastating disappointment?" asks Goodman. (Suppose, one might add, she were a Chinese, Indian, or Korean mother already with one daughter.) Goodman is concerned that soon there will be a simple blood test on pregnant women to determine the sex of the fetus. Doctors, of course, are delighted that science will then be able to screen gender-linked inherited diseases.

&. **We have *the test* in order to determine whether to paint the nursery pink or blue, or, in the alternative, whether to kill the child who, but for the test, would have slept in that nursery.**

Although even increasing numbers of pro-choice supporters are calling "sex selection" the most frivolous and sexist of motives for abortion, the option nevertheless is being exercised by some parents. Goodman notes with alarm that, although Americans have come to value genetic testing which leads to the diagnosis of diseases that cause pain, disability, and death, technology is rapidly becoming available to produce what she terms *designer babies*. "We may be able to identify the gene for height, hair color, eye color, perhaps even athletic ability or intelligence."

"There will always be parents" says Goodman, "who, out of ego or some perverse view of children as a perfect product, want to pick and choose genes according to a master plan. Should society encourage that, or even allow that? Must doctors perform tests and turn over information to patients to do with as they will?"[10]

A Life-or-Death Test

The problem, of course, is the prenatal *test*. Abortion naturally follows as a result of what is seen to be a benign, humanitarian *test*. Whether it be the sonogram, amniocentesis, or CVS (chorionic villus sampling, which will allow doctors to determine chromosomal anomalies and a number of other things within the first trimester)—it is *the test* that we all take for granted. Certainly doctors take *the test* for granted. It is ingrained in them as medical students. It's a given. If there is any way they can prevent the birth of handicapped infants, they are told they should do it. And it's *the test* that makes that possible.

Even we lawyers have gotten into the act. If a doctor is ever found guilty of encouraging parents to proceed toward having a child with Down's syndrome, then we make sure that the doctor is medically, legally, and financially liable for that child. Why? Because, as some courts have held, allowing a birth to occur that *could* have been eliminated, and by standards of practice *should* have been eliminated, is medical malpractice.

Therefore what becomes "standard practice" is counseling heavily balanced toward having the test, especially for mothers over the age of 35 (although, numerically, most Down's babies are born to women *under* 35). And what 40-year-old woman will not have the test if she is repeatedly told, both through the media and in the privacy of her own doctor's office, "You're a risk. There's almost one Down's syndrome birth in 20. Are you sure you don't want amnio?"

There can be no question about it—*the test* simply has to be the ultimate sad commentary on a pro-choice generation. We have *the test* in order to determine whether to paint the nursery pink or blue, or, in the alternative, whether to kill the child who, but for the test, would have slept in that nursery. Can that make any sense at all?

As one writer has suggested, "Eugenic abortion is a classic case of self-defeating logic. The natural concern of parents that a much-wanted child should be healthy has been translated into killing children who are not healthy. This is almost literally throwing the baby out with the bathwater."[11]

When death is the foregone conclusion for those fetuses who don't measure up, how can we possibly say that we have benefited from the test—apart from allaying the anxiety of expectant parents with *healthy* fetuses? For in the current climate of "health through death," the test does nothing to aid the health of children who might be handicapped. The solution to the problem has not been correction, but elimination. (The resources available for handicap research have declined in direct proportion to the increase in eugenic abortions.) If pro-life's characterization of *the test* and subsequent abortion is overly emotive, it is nevertheless accurate: What we have fostered is a search-and-destroy mentality.

Perhaps now, with such promising advances as "out-of-the-womb" surgery, the test can indicate when remedial surgery is necessary. But until such time as *corrective* technology catches up with *detection* technology, we are doing nothing more than forcing many parents into a decision either to abort or to be stigmatized for knowingly having brought a disabled person into existence.

That's the way with moral perversion, of course. You shift the blame on an innocent party to relieve yourself of your own guilt. In a pro-choice generation, there is "loving, caring humanitarian concern" in killing an unborn, handicapped child, and "unfeeling, misplaced duty" in bringing one into the world. Choice has become a lesser god whose moral standards permit good to be evil and evil to be good.

It would be easy enough to pontificate that, if prenatal testing is to survive as morally justifiable, it must be limited to use in detecting only those physical defects which are capable of correction—and that the alternative of abortion as a matter of course is morally unacceptable. Indeed, one might legitimately urge that, as compared with abortion itself in these instances, it is *the test* which ought to be made illegal. But putting the cat back into the bag is probably too much to ask. Dare to prohibit even mere *indiscriminate use* of the test and you will quickly find a lawsuit being filed on the basis of one's Constitutional "right to know," another contrived "right" discovered in the same judicial black hole as the so-called right to privacy.

Unfortunately, the "right to know" has brought about unspeakable tragedies for fetuses and mothers alike. On this score also, *Our Bodies, Ourselves* plays it straight. Two letters which are presented tell it like it is:

> I knew only positive results were reported by phone. The image of myself, alone, screaming into a white plastic telephone is indelible.[12]

> When I agreed to the amniocentesis I simply had not thought the implications through. It didn't occur to me the test could be positive. I had thirty-six hours to make a decision. I think I made the right

one, but I still keep reliving it, trying to justify the abortion to myself.[13]

These women are not alone. Millions of women are taking *the test* without thinking through the implications of an unexpected result. And when "the implications" lead to a previously unthinkable abortion, the decision haunts them relentlessly. Here too the authors of *Our Bodies, Ourselves* agree: "Research work [proves] the rather obvious fact that aborting a wanted baby is very different from aborting an unplanned one."[14]

No Denying the Pain

The issue of eugenic abortion is of course not so simple or neat in the doctor's office, where parents first learn that the healthy baby they expected is not to be. In years past, families did not discover the child's disability until he or she was born. Nor was their disappointment accompanied by a medical possibility of ending that life before birth. But now the options made available to the family—indeed, often *pressed* upon them—are soul-wrenching.

> ### ➴ Why not a society that offers the family of a disabled child real financial support, and round-the-clock assistance with care?

It's all well and good that those of us who have never been in their shoes can see a silver lining to the dark cloud of disability, but for the family, the dark cloud remains. The family of a spina bifida baby, for example, is often dependent upon hospital staff for many years. The mother, typically, is the one who devotes her life to the care and maintenance of this special child—a 24-hour-a-day task. And the family often suffers physically, financially, and emotionally in a variety of ways. Cited by many are the effects of added stress upon a marriage; the cost of keeping some children alive; the adverse impact on the lives of siblings; and so on.

In light of the obvious burden to the parents, we must ask ourselves how honest we are being when we argue for abortion on the basis of the *child's* suffering, if he or she is allowed to live. I'm afraid honesty would compel many parents to admit that it is *their own* hardship which they wish to avoid. And while no one could blame them for wanting to avoid that hardship, we are entitled to ask whether the killing of an unborn child can be justified fairly on that basis.

If there are parents of handicapped children who possibly say to themselves, "I wish my child had never been born," they are not alone. There are parents of dangerous criminals, drug addicts, and merely insolent or disrespectful children who would join in that chorus. But rarely will you ever hear the disabled themselves telling us that they wish they had never been born.

Family hardship simply cannot outweigh the sanctity of human life itself. Over and over I read, "Of course there is love for handicapped children, but also great hardship which none of us would want to take over ourselves. To refuse to help those who might be helped (that is, to refuse abortions), is contrary to religion and humanity." Despite the professed good intentions of such thinking, another response, and one in keeping with *true* religion, would be to offer *real* help. Today the offer is either *no child* (through abortion) or a handicapped child with little or no help. Why not a society that offers the family of a disabled child real financial support, and round-the-clock assistance with care? Perhaps more families would accept *that* kind of help.

But what, in the name of God, can be "religious" or "humanitarian" about killing unborn children? Can *any* parental hardship justify the killing of an innocent human being?

Aborted Life, Aborted Talent

There is a familiar story which bears repeating in a chapter such as this. The medical school professor tells his students, "I want your opinion about the termination of a pregnancy. The father had syphilis and the mother had tuberculosis. Of the four children born, the first was blind, the second died, the third was deaf and dumb, and the fourth had tuberculosis. What would you have done about the next pregnancy?" "I would have ended it," quickly answers one student. "Congratulations," responds the professor. "You have just killed Beethoven."[15]

I think immediately of another young man whose life would certainly not be "worth living" by many people's standards today. But, oh, what a contribution he has made in the field of literature! If I were to say he is an Irishman from Dublin, you might first think of Christy Brown, who suffered from cerebral palsy and whose book *My Left Foot* was turned into an outstanding film through the Oscar-winning performance of Daniel Day-Lewis. That would be a good guess and also a good example of what talent lies in the hands (and feet) of the disabled. However, I'm thinking of Christy's fellow Dubliner, Christopher Nolan, who won the Whitbread Book of the Year, Britain's most valuable literary prize.

Christopher is a young spastic poet who can neither speak, nor hear well, nor move himself, but he is able to type with a stick attached to his forehead. Doctors are amazed that he could learn any vocabulary at all, and even more amazed at how he seems to make up his own poetically expressive words. His book *Under the Eye of the Clock* is a thinly fictionalized autobiography of his childhood, making a triumphant and intelligent go of life. He used his Whitbread acceptance speech, given for him by his mother, to speak up for the handicapped and against abortion: "You all must realize that history is in the making. Tonight a crippled man is taking his place on the world literary stage."

In the unique style of his own writing, Christopher continued:

> Tonight is my night for laughing, for crying tears of joy. But wait, my brothers hobble after me hinting, "What about silent us? Can we too have a voice?" Tonight I am speaking for them.
>
> Tonight is the happiest night of my life. Imagine what I would have missed if the doctors had not revived me on that September day long ago. Can freedom now be denied to a handicapped man? Can "yessing" be so difficult that rather than give a baby a chance at life, man treads upon his brother and silences him before he can draw one breath of this world's fresh air?[16]

Accepting the Unacceptable; Loving the Unloved

Listening to Christopher, I can't seem to rid my mind of 'elephant man" John Merrick and those haunting words he shouted in the face of a belligerent mob threatening his life: "I am not an elephant! I am not an animal! I am a *human being!*" Surely he speaks on behalf of the deformed fetus as well: "I am not a freak! I am not a non-person! I am a *human being!*"

This wonderful man, this "freak" of nature, was one of the fortunate ones. Rejected by his mother, he had been adopted in love by others who cared. Yet still he was wistful: "Perhaps if I could find her . . . perhaps she could love me as I am."

Yes, John Merrick, she could indeed. And we as well. We must.

ELEVEN

Choice
On A Slippery Slope

The beginnings at first were merely a subtle shift in emphasis in the basic attitude of the physicians. It started with the acceptance of the attitude, basic in the euthanasia movement, that there is such a thing as a life not worthy to be lived.

—Dr. Leo Alexander
Consultant, Nuremberg Trials

ON APRIL 9, 1982, A BABY IDENTIFIED ONLY AS "Infant Doe" was born at the Bloomington, Indiana, Hospital. Living only one week, Infant Doe died at 10:30 P.M. on the night of April 15. Taken alone, his death would not have been terribly remarkable. Infants do die within a week of being born. What made Infant Doe's case different, however, was that an operation which could have been performed to correct a birth defect that closed off his esophagus and would not allow food to pass into his stomach was refused by the child's parents, in consultation with the medical team.

Coldhearted, you say? Unthinkable? Outrageous? There was one other important factor: The child also had Down's syndrome.

Given that additional factor, does it still appear that the decision of the parents was coldhearted, unthinkable, and outrageous? Undoubtedly it was an agonizing, lonely decision for them. Undoubtedly, too, it was as unthinkable to them as it

would be to any other parents facing such an unexpected tragedy after months of hopeful anticipation. Yet whether their
heart-rending decision was morally justifiable remains a legitimate question.

Even if one believes that abortion is morally permissible
before a defective fetus is actually born, a giant step must be
taken beyond that point in order to justify the taking of human
life *after* it is born. And, make no mistake about it, the parents'
refusal to authorize lifesaving treatment in this case was just as
much a *taking* of life as if they had starved their son to death. For
that is how he died. Nor can it be said that the death was
unintentional. But for the fact of his Down's syndrome (itself not
necessarily fatal), the boy would have undergone a fairly simple
operation on his esophagus and probably still be alive today.

When the legality of the parent's decision was questioned,
the Indiana Supreme Court voted three to one not to interfere.
That high court ruling is all the more remarkable when you
consider that courts all across the nation have regularly intervened *in loco parentis* in any number of cases where the parents'
religion (typically Christian Scientists or Jehovah's Witnesses)
forbade them from seeking medical assistance for their children.
Blood transfusions have been ordered time and again to save the
life of a threatened child.

What, then, was different in this case? The spotlight focuses
on the fact that the boy had Down's syndrome. Allowed to live,
he would have been a burden on the parents, the health-care
institutions, and society. Accordingly, the parents, the attend-
ing physicians, and the courts all agreed that his life was
expendable—*even after he had lived for over six days!* The issue was
no longer the *viability* of an abnormal fetus, but the *liability* of a
baby boy with Down's syndrome.

The Easy Leap from Abortion to Euthanasia

No one must minimize or dismiss lightly the grief experienced by the family of Infant Doe, nor the difficulties often
experienced by the families of other victims of Down's syndrome. Pat answers will not eliminate a depth of grief or daily
demands that most of us will never know. But individual hard
cases such as these always distort the larger picture. And in that
light we must marshal every ounce of our humanity to prevent a
slippery-slope view of choice which permits not only *prenatal*

killing, but also *neo*natal killing: infanticide—the killing of a baby *after* it is born. As perhaps best demonstrated in the case of Infant Doe, one can hardly escape being shocked by how far we have already moved down that dangerous slope.

Why Not Homicide?

As a former district attorney and currently a professor of criminal law, I cannot help but compare the case of Infant Doe with the law of homicide. From early common law, murder has been defined as the unlawful killing of one human being by another with malice aforethought. "Malice aforethought" is a special legal term signifying any person-endangering state of mind. One need not harbor even an ounce of hatred, spite, or ill will. Consequently, a person may be guilty of murder even if it is a so-called "mercy killing," as where he hastens the death of a loved one who is dying in excruciating pain.

As a practical matter, a jury might consider his good motive to be a mitigating circumstance and find him guilty of the lesser crime of manslaughter. However, whether murder or manslaughter, it is clearly a criminal homicide—the unlawful killing of one human being by another. Intriguingly, homicide statutes currently seem to be totally ignored in cases like Infant Doe, where, beyond any doubt, all the necessary legal elements for criminal homicide are satisfied.

From as early as the mid-1600's, there has never been any question that a fetus which is quickened, born alive, and lives for a brief interval of time is a "human being" for purposes of the law of homicide. Being alive for six days, as was Infant Doe, isn't even a close case. As for the requirement of a killing, court after court has held that parents have a special legal duty to care for their children. If a child dies because parents intentionally withhold lifesaving treatment, the parents are as guilty of killing the child as if they had done an affirmative act of violence.

The conscious decision of Infant Doe's parents to let him die evidenced unquestionably a criminal intent of the type encompassed by the term "malice aforethought," despite what they perceived as their good motives. Therefore, from the viewpoint of the law of criminal homicide, there is an open-and-shut case for manslaughter, if not murder. (Probably manslaughter, given the unusual circumstances themselves, plus the pressure typically applied by doctors, families, friends, and society at large.)

While I am not anxious to slap parents with criminal homicide charges in cases such as Infant Doe, we can hardly escape the inconsistency of our approach to the killing of newborn children. If a maniac were to burst into the neonatal ward of our local hospital and strangle to death a week-old infant, you can bet the community would be outraged if the district attorney refused to charge him with criminal homicide. The fact that Infant Doe's parents were not similarly charged can only be attributed to a difference in motives. Yet a good motive has never been held to be a legal defense to an unlawful homicide.

The plain fact is that a quiet, almost-unnoticed revolution has taken place. Among parents, doctors, hospital administrators, and courts, a philosophical consensus has been reached which is completely at odds with all prior assumptions of what is morally and legally acceptable. Now, under circumstances which may evoke our sympathy, parents can literally "get away with murder." Instead of channeling community sympathy through the jury's recognition of mitigating circumstances in a verdict of manslaughter, the new consensus turns a blind eye altogether.

Even if there are many people who would find that to be a welcome development, what we are witnessing is both an erosion in the rule of law and a deterioration in our respect for the value of human life. For what "good motive" will the next Infant Doe be allowed to die? How soon will it be before an Infant Doe is not simply left to die naturally, but is affirmatively put to death because "she" is not the "he" that the parents wanted?

Does that possibility seem stretched? Already, gender selection is taking place through legalized abortions. If no legal consequences attach to the homicide of newborns, then the day when Infant Doe may be killed because of gender can't be far away. Who would ever have guessed just 20 years ago that the parents of a Down's syndrome child in a Bloomington, Indiana, hospital—encouraged by medical staff—could with total legal impunity allow him to die when the means were available for him to live?

Turning Patients into Victims

Fortunately, we have not yet lost all sanity. Public outcry following the Infant Doe case resulted in the Child Abuse Amendment of 1984, which makes it a criminal offense *not* to treat certain infants—the only exception being where medical treatment would be futile or would simply prolong the death process. But even that law, unfortunately, does not solve all the problems. There is still the sticky question of when *that* standard is met in each case, and the more haunting issue of why the decision is to be made by a committee of doctors rather than the child's parents.

Presumably, the wishes of the parents will be considered as one of the most significant factors. However, there is a prevailing belief that parents in that situation are likely not to be in a good position to decide the child's, or even their own, best interests. More troubling still is the question of whether we have come to the point where social utilitarian theory pervades the committee room to such an extent that the crucial decision is affected by tight hospital budgets, staff availability, or, worse yet, personal bias against the handicapped.

Thomas Elkins, an obstetrician/gynecologist and professor at the University of Michigan, has given an insightful interview to *Christianity Today's* Harold Smith, covering many of the issues we have already discussed about neonatal euthanasia. Speaking as a Christian physician and a pro-life advocate, Elkins cautions against any superficial rhetoric which fails to appreciate that not all cases of neonatal deaths fit nicely within a convenient, articulable, black-and-white moralistic formula—not even for pro-life physicians. Perhaps *especially* not for pro-life physicians.

Although Elkins is professionally modest enough not to say so, part of the problem is that medical technology has moved into areas where angels fear to tread. We have gone from being surprised at what modern medicine can do, to expecting it, to demanding it! When five-month-old "preemies" are put on life-support systems, we tend to forget that, only a few years ago, there would not have been a chance in the world for the premature infant to survive. But because we now *assume* the use of life-support systems, we are thrown into a moral dilemma when such systems either are not used or are taken away when chances of survival seem impossible.

But artificial life-support is just what it says: *artificial*. If the line between denying artificial life-support and refusing a simple corrective operation is shadowy, it is nevertheless a vitally significant line. It is a line between being unable to save a baby that we would like to save if at all possible, and denying life to a baby who happens to come to us with an abnormality which doesn't meet our full expectations.

For Elkins and his wife, the issue is far from abstract. They are the parents of a child with Down's syndrome. Ginny is a constant reminder to them of both the difficulties and the special joys of having children who are "different" from the rest of us.

To Elkins, the idea of newborn as *patient* and fetus as *victim of abortion* is clearly a contradiction: "Once we have said positively that we want to support handicapped newborns, critically ill newborns, it's going to be very difficult to support a handicapped newborn at 25 weeks and yet say we can destroy it *in utero* one day or one week earlier with an abortion."[1]

The pro-choice argument that the fetus is not a person, and therefore is subject to abortion, becomes increasingly problematic in a society poised on the brink of being able to medically rescue all those former "non-persons." Any distinction between the week-old newborn baby, the soon-to-be-born infant in the womb, and the early gestating fetus is either sentimental or fanciful.

Pro-life Argument Turned Deadly

Incredible as it may appear, that all-too-obvious logic, though denied by most pro-choice advocates, is being accepted as true by other pro-choice advocates, but this time in support of infanticide. David Cannon's no-nonsense article on this shocking turn of events, *"Abortion and Infanticide: Is There a Difference?"*[2] parades a Who's Who list of today's intelligentsia who urge nothing less than utilitarian homicide. A few highlights will illustrate the brazenness of the thinking.

There is, first of all, Nobel laureate James Watson, one of the discoverers of the double helix structure of DNA, who seriously proposed in 1973 that infants should not be "declared alive until three days after birth," in order to allow parents the choice of disposing of their defective newborn!

Doctors Raymond Duff and A. G. M. Campbell give us reason to believe that someone is listening to Watson. In October 1973 they reported in the *New England Journal of Medicine* that more than 40 defective infants had been purposely allowed to die in the Yale-New Haven Hospital. Article after article confirms that this practice has occurred in hospitals throughout the nation and further abroad. And rest assured that it is *doctors* who are leading the way—*doctors* who have taken the Hippocratic oath to preserve life, yet who have encouraged parents to do the unthinkable.

"But isn't the idea of killing newborn babies completely out of step with the person on the street?" one legitimately might ask. Perhaps, but Nat Hentoff reported in the *Village Voice* that when he led a well-attended question-and-answer session at New York University Law School, a large majority of the women seemed to feel that they had a right to do away with their newborn. If any defects were missed by amniocentesis, these students felt they had a kind of '30-day return privilege' to dispose of the child.[3]

Of course, as David Cannon points out, "the idea of infanticide was not new, even for 'civilized society.' It was widely practiced in 19th-century France, and was not infrequent in England, as evidenced by adoption of the legal requirement that midwives swear anti-infanticide oaths."[4]

And was it not the ancient Spartans who prized physical strength and skill in combat so highly that any child appearing less than robust was thrown from a cliff on Mount Taygetus? In pre-Christian Rome, when a child was born, the child was laid at the father's feet. If the father lifted up the child, it meant he acknowledged it. If he turned away, the child was literally thrown out. Even Plato suggested that children of "inferior" persons and "any of the other sort who are born defective" should be disposed of by the guardians of the state.

What may be different in our generation—apart from the outright rejection of a Judeo-Christian value system—is a serious attempt even in an era of medical marvels to morally justify infanticide by elitist ideology.

In "The Rights and Wrongs of Abortion," for example, Professor Michael Tooley of Stanford University contended that there were no "morally relevant" biological differences between a fetus and a newborn, and thus any rational or consistent defense of abortion necessarily includes the defense of infanticide. He reasoned, relates Cannon, that to have a serious right to life, one must be a "person"—someone with the "concept of a self as a continuing subject of experiences and other mental states."[5] Given that sufficiently vague definition, a good case could be made that a child up to six months or a year old could be killed, and not just the newborn.

Look carefully at what is being said. In support of infanticide, these pro-abortion, think-tank intellectuals are conceding the very pro-life logic which is so vehemently rejected by pro-choice frontline regulars: that there is no definable difference between a newborn and a fetus in the womb.

Crossing Any Convenient Line

I once thought that we could all begin at a common starting point, on the delivery table, and all agree that we would be horrified if someone were to plunge a knife into a newborn baby as it lay there taking its first few precious breaths. I would then ask if we would not be equally horrified if someone were to plunge a sharp object into the womb and kill the baby just minutes before its natural birth. And back I would go in time to ask at which moment we would cease to be horrified. Seen in that light, we would always be presented with the fact that on some given day we are horrified that an unborn "child" is killed, but that on the very day before, we would permit the unborn "fetus" to be killed, seemingly with no moral compunction.

> &⁊ Blithely reject the sanctity of life and immediately you are thrust into bed with the proposition that not all human life is of equal worth. And then the door is wide open.

Yet now I realize how wide a gap has come between pro-choice and pro-life perspectives. To be sure, my characterization of plunging a knife into a newborn baby is still universally horrifying. It's "unscientific." But having hospital staff inject the baby with dihydrocodeine, a sensation-killing drug, so that it does not feed and therefore dies of starvation is well within the acceptable range of conscience for many pro-choice advocates who believe that not every life is worth living.

Given its potential for justifying the unthinkable, the importance of this pro-choice double-talk cannot be overstated. Cannon leads us still further, to Peter Singer, who wrote in the *New York Review of Books* in 1984:

The pro-life groups were right about one thing: the location of the baby inside or outside of the womb cannot make such a moral difference. We cannot coherently hold that it is all right to kill a fetus before birth, but as soon as the baby is born everything must be done to keep it alive. The solution, however, is not to accept the pro-life view that the fetus is a human being with the same moral status as yours or mine. The solution is the very opposite: to abandon the idea that all human life is of equal worth.[6]

Not all human life of equal worth? Is that what Peter Singer really meant to say? Cannon reminds us that "one of the main obstacles to fully legitimizing infanticide and feticide is the stubborn notion of human equality—the idea that all humans, regardless of physiological differences, have an equal claim on human rights.

"Peter Westen, professor of law at the University of Michigan, addressed this concern in a 1982 article, 'The Empty Idea of Equality,' in the *Harvard Law Review*. Criticizing the idea of equality, Mr. Westen asked whether some kinds of humans should be treated as 'persons' for purposes of the 'right to respect'—apparently his shorthand for right to life.

"In order to have this right, it is not enough to be human, as there is nothing intrinsic to humanhood—say, over animalhood—that entitles all its possessors to be treated equally. Instead, one must possess a certain 'trait that entitles anyone to be treated with respect.' Although he does not define this 'trait,' Mr. Westen concludes that deformed newborns and many unborn children are without it."[7]

If ever there were any doubt about it, this is clear proof of the unbreakable bond between those familiar words "created equally," from which all of our human rights are said to derive, and the sanctity of life. Blithely reject the sanctity of life and immediately you are thrust into bed with the proposition that not all human life is of equal worth. And then the door is wide open.

Back to a Fatal Future

All we have to do next is to decide which human life is less deserving of being saved—or, indeed, which human life is more deserving of being *taken*. First it is the unborn fetus, then the newborn handicapped, then the mentally ill, then the terminally ill, next homosexuals, and finally Jews. There's no need to protest that it couldn't possibly happen. It already has, with tragic results. Once the sanctity of life was rejected, the moral standard in Nazi Germany became a social and utilitarian standard: the welfare of the State.

Jewish pro-life advocate Dr. Bernard Nathanson is outspoken about what he terms "facile Nazi analogies" being made by his pro-life colleagues. "The Nazi experience was so utterly shattering that it defies any analogy, and it defiles the memory of the Holocaust to bring it into this discussion."[8] Apparently his primary concern is that "it is much less obvious to the society at large what we are doing in abortion than what Germany did regarding genocide."[9]

ð. We accept the divine injunction "You shall not kill" *except* where we can convince ourselves that there are those who are not fully human.

It's one thing, he suggests, to refuse to speak out when your Jewish next-door neighbors, and hundreds more like them in the community, are taken away, never to return. What's happening is too obvious to ignore. By contrast, one can be forgiven for not quickly or easily sorting out the issue of abortion, involving as it does an unseen victim who is killed by the decision of his own mother as opposed to some totalitarian regime, and within a familiar, even revered, framework of individual rights.

That may be why it has taken some of us a long time to wake up to the realities of abortion: We've been dealing with an unseen enemy within the sanitized walls of hospitals and clinics. How could the mass killing of human life be happening within institutions dedicated to the *saving* of human life! And all of it approved by the nation's highest court. Whoever would have thought it possible?

Dr. Nathanson is right, of course, to point out that "the German Nazis had strict *anti*-abortion policies—for 'Aryans.' "[10]

But certainly that did not make Hitler pro-life. (Remember that Romania's Ceausescu was not pro-life simply by being anti-abortion.) Jews, tragically, were *encouraged* to abort, as part of Hitler's racial-purity madness.

So the slippery slope from abortion to genocide may not be as straightforward in the German experience as is often implied. However, the point remains that, once regard for the sanctity of human life is demeaned through the eugenic abortion of *any* target group within a society—regardless of that society's particular overarching ideology—the climate is set for wider-reaching disrespect for life.

We head down the slippery slope when we decide that some groups of human beings ought to be denied the normal rights of humanity because they are *different*—whether by race, sex, age, or disability. Once separated from the human race, they become unprotected by the rules that apply to all other human beings. We accept the divine injunction "You shall not kill" *except* where we can convince ourselves that there are those who are not fully human. In Germany that ethic started in the 1920's with doctors and philosophers, then captured the imagination of politicians, then trickled down to many of Germany's ordinary citizens during Hitler's regime.

On the desk beside me is a picture of a German poster, produced by the Reichsnahrstand, showing a healthy Aryan man weighed down by a crossbar that he carries on his shoulder. Two inmates of a mental institution sit on either side of the crossbar, representing an obvious burden to the otherwise-strong German citizen. The caption reads, "You Are Sharing the Load!" The copy beneath the caption explains: "A genetically ill individual costs approximately 50,000 Reichsmarks by the age of sixty."

Compare that cost-effectiveness approach to life with a more recent example from Great Britain, where the Department of Health and Social Services justified prenatal screening in order to abort children likely to be affected by Down's syndrome and spina bifida: "The grossly handicapped spina bifida child and adult makes large demands on health and social services. It seems likely that, in general, *the cost of these demands will exceed the cost of a programme to detect the condition.*"[11] Why abort the disabled? Because it's *cheaper* than paying to take care of them! Are we ready to apply that logic to the elderly? Or AIDS patients?

It's the Hegelian principle—"only what is useful is good"—tragically applied to human life. Make no mistake about it, "the burden of maintaining the socially unfit," whether in a duped German generation or in our own pro-choice generation, is a doorway leading to indiscriminate death.

> **Having elevated personal rights to the high altar of a national religion, it becomes surprisingly easy to offer upon that altar even one's own off-spring as a sacrifice to the great god of Self.**

The German concentration camp doctor in the movie *Sophie's Choice* laments to another officer, "My father asked me what kind of medicine I practice here. What can I tell him? I do God's work. Yes, I do God's work. I decide who will live and who will die." How do we suppose the Creator of life must feel when his work is associated with the butchered, betrayed, and martyred children of the earth—whether in Nazi Germany, Stalinist Russia, or abortionist nations, East or West?

If, by and large today, American Jews remain generally favorable toward abortion despite the Holocaust (which Dr. Nathanson urges as proof that the Nazi argument is less than compelling), it may be for reasons which Dr. Nathanson has overlooked. Today's secular Jews, like today's secular "Christians" (and like many secular "Christians" in Nazi Germany), have lost a sense of the sacred. And with that loss, for far too many of them has come the further loss of an uncompromising commitment to the sanctity of human life in whatever form it may exist.

Not all Jews have lost a sense of the sacred, nor a respect for the sanctity of human life in whatever form. Jews who still adhere to the Mosaic law, and Messianic Jews, are almost without exception opposed to abortion. "How can you change *the Law*?" one pro-life Jew recently asked me. His reference to "the Law" was yet another reminder of how blithely we attempt to change human laws regarding abortion, when there is one Law we can never change.

Secularism doesn't do away with God; it simply substitutes its own lesser god. Having elevated personal rights to the high altar of a national religion, it becomes surprisingly easy to offer upon that altar even one's own offspring as a sacrifice to the great god of Self.

Little wonder, then, that the ancient Hebrews were strictly forbidden to sacrifice their children to the god Molech, as did their secular neighbors: "I will set my face against that man and I will cut him off from his people; for by giving his children to Molech, he has defiled my sanctuary and profaned my holy name."[12] The biblical injunction is also a warning to any who would turn a blind eye to the tragic fate of the children:

> If the people of the community close their eyes when that man gives one of his children to Molech and they fail to put him to death, I will set my face against that man and his family and will cut off from their people both him and all who follow him in prostituting themselves to Molech.[13]

If by any chance we've got the history of Nazi Germany in the 1940's all wrong, it doesn't lessen our responsibility to get it right regarding abortion in America in the 1990's. Shouldered with that compelling moral task, Dr. Nathanson and I, along with many others, join hands in common cause in the battle for the unborn.

How to Play God

Playing God is not just the brutal caricature of a concentration-camp mentality more easily associated with Nazi Germany. Dr. David Baum, neonatal physician and lecturer at Bristol University, speaking on behalf of pro-choice at a recent Oxford University debate, related his frank conversation with a delivery-room nurse in the "preemie" ward of a major hospital: "If the baby is under 1000 grams, we don't resuscitate. But if the baby is a *nice* baby, I sometimes put my hand on the scale."

Dr. Baum used this illustration to show that medical personnel are sensitive to the life they hold in their hands. But what do we suppose parents would feel if they found out that their own premature infant didn't look quite *nice* enough to evoke this sympathetic gesture? Are the scales on which life lies in the balance to be adjusted by personal judgments about *niceness*?

In her 1968 book *The Terrible Choice: The Abortion Dilemma*, Nobel Prize-winning author Pearl S. Buck (mother of a child retarded from phenylketonuria) tells why she would not have chosen an abortion had she been given an option:

> I fear the power of choice over life or death at human hands. I see no human being whom I could ever trust with such power—not myself or any other.
>
> We who are human beings cannot, for our own safety, be allowed to choose death, life being all we know. Beyond life lie only faith and surmise, but not knowledge. Where there is no knowledge except for life, a decision for death is not safe for the human race.[14]

Mother Teresa, in her 1979 Nobel Peace Prize acceptance speech, put the slippery slope in clear perspective: "If a mother can kill her own child, what is left but for me to kill you and you to kill me? There is nothing between."[15]

Of this, then, we must be absolutely certain: If any one innocent is declared unworthy to live, then *no* person has an absolute right to live. And without that absolute right, what we risk is a steady progression from extraordinary measures to preserve life, to ordinary measures, to no measures at all, to positive action to destroy unwanted human life.

Losing Sight of Personhood

To those who personally know the struggles of families with disabled members, the issue is wrongly framed in the first place. The issue is not whether every life is worth living, but whether we as a society are prepared to accept every life that God gives us and *make* it worth living. In fact, the issue for most parents of handicapped children is whether they are prepared to accept that *their own* lives may be much more worth living in the presence of those who come bundled in different packages than their own.

The testimony of many parents could be brought forward at this point. One father of an adopted girl with Down's syndrome reminds us that we may be overlooking a spiritual dimension in the care of the handicapped when we talk loosely about "humanitarian abortions":

> For us there is some (not great) hardship, but we can cope with this in exchange (perhaps selfishly) for the great love our daughter has brought us. Referring to handicapped children, the author Morris West said: "They will evoke the kindness that will keep you human. More! They will remind you every day that I (God) am who I am, that my ways are not yours..." We daily see our daughter evoking this kindness from her brothers and sisters and others.
>
> While medical science must progress, it must recognize the paradox that these children are *necessary* to us and that humanity will be the less without them. There is a spiritual dimension—which so often defies human logic—to the debate which we ignore at our peril. Perhaps we should reappraise our sanitized understanding of religion and humanity.[16]

The issue is not whether every life is worth living, but whether we as a society are prepared to accept every life that God gives us and *make* it worth living.

Our distorted view of "humanitarian relief" for potential parents of handicapped children through abortion and euthanasia tells the unborn and newborn, in effect, that they must meet *our* standards in order to be accepted. Hardly a *humanitarian* gesture! To be *humanitarian*, surely, is to accept life in whatever way we find it, and to do all we can as parents and a society to make that life a life worth living.

The surprise, however, is how the handicapped invariably turn around our own rejection of what they have to give. In a profound way, they rarely accept *us* the way they find us. They regard our own reluctance to accept them as unacceptable, and our own fear of loving them as a challenge to instill that love. To paraphrase familiar words, we have loved them because they first loved us.

Dr. Thomas Elkins speaks eloquently to that proposition:

> We look at our own child, Ginny, who has Down's syndrome, and see our own limitedness. She shows us love even when we, at first, were not totally accepting of her. These kids love us until we begin to love them back. And by loving them, we learn a whole new definition of love—something very akin to grace.
>
> In our country, we have been very much aware of physical attributes and their importance in being successful. But with a child like Ginny, we learn that love is deeper. It's love because of the personal qualities of that child and because of something of the spirit of God that's within that child—what we term personhood.[17]

The Disabled: Mirror to the Abled

I wonder if Dr. Elkins hasn't articulated for us the mystery surrounding the words of Jesus regarding the man born blind. You may recall that Jesus healed a man who was blind from birth. Instead of being grateful for the man's sight, the religious authorities were fearful of the power of anyone who could perform such a miracle. It threatened their own popular power base. So they asked Jesus what had caused the man to be born blind: "Was it because of the sins of his parents, or perhaps his own sins?" they sneered. But Jesus responded, "Neither this man nor his parents sinned, but this happened so that the work of God might be displayed in his life."[18]

Perhaps Jesus was referring only to this one man whom he healed as a demonstration of his divine power. Or it may be that, even now, Jesus is telling us something important with regard to how we ought to view those who are handicapped. Perhaps he is telling us that those for whom we feel pity and embarrassment are to be appreciated as reminders that *we* are the ones to be pitied. That *we* are the ones who ought to be embarrassed. That *we*, the beautiful people of the world, are the ones who are handicapped—the ones who are blind to life's true values; the ones who are unable to hear the cries of the defenseless; the ones who are spiritually twisted in our convoluted exercise of moral choice; and the ones falling headlong to our own destruction down the slippery slope of pro-choice logic.

TWELVE

Hard Cases
And Easy Outs

You want it, you take it, you pay the price.
—Bruce Springsteen in
"Prove It All Night"

SOME MONTHS AGO I ATTENDED a student-sponsored abortion debate at Oxford University's Union Society. Representing the pro-choice position were Dr. David Baum, Director of the Institute of Child Health at Bristol University, and Dr. Arthur Shaeffer, Director of the Centre for Professional and Applied Ethics, University of Manitoba. Speaking on behalf of pro-life were Ann Widdecombe, Conservative Member of Parliament for Maidstone, and Catherine Françoise, singer-actress and spokeswoman for The Society for the Protection of Unborn Children.

The setting in the Student Union's classic Debating Chamber graphically resembled the House of Parliament, with opposing advocates and their supporters seated across from each other, at times roaring approval and shouting out disagreement. Parliamentary debate in England is a far cry from the dreary formality of what we Americans tend to associate with "parliamentary rules."

I couldn't help noticing a number of peculiar twists to the evening's proceedings. For instance, who would have thought that the pro-choice side would have been represented by two men, and the pro-life side by two women? Then there was the pro-choice Dr. Baum who began his presentation by showing sympathy-grabbing slides (of a type normally associated with pro-life advocates) of families, disabled persons, and unborn babies, and then proceeded to take an unusually narrow pro-choice position, being rather classically anti-abortion except in rare cases of abnormal fetuses.

During the question time, there was a particularly exercised Catholic student who made a vehement speech against abortion, concluding her comments dramatically by pulling from her pocket a package of birth control pills and saying that she was making a personal choice about her reproductive capabilities by taking precautions against getting pregnant in the first place!

Finally there was Professor Shaeffer, citing a Canadian survey which concluded that women who supported pro-life were overwhelmingly uneducated and Catholic—oblivious to the fact that his two opponents on this night were not only Protestant but well-educated! Indeed, angrily noting the professor's chauvinist implications, Ms. Widdecombe herself quickly pointed out that she was an Oxford graduate and former participant in student debates in the same Chamber!

All in all, as you may guess from just these few snippets, the debate was a lively occasion. However, in the more formal first half you could hear a pin drop as the speakers' voices strained to reach the back of the hall without electronic amplification. For my money, it was during this time that the most significant argument of the night was made—by someone other than one of the participants.

Just as one of the speakers was making a crucial point, from out of nowhere came the totally unexpected whimper of a tiny baby. More wondrous than either crying or screaming, her faint little voice caught this audience of university students by surprise. At first there were curious glances, wondering what a baby was doing in the Debating Chamber. She became quiet again, and all eyes returned to the front of the room. Within a few moments, however, came a second whimper, this time evoking glances less curious than cutting.

We all know that look. It's the one people give when a baby cries during the wedding, or screams out during the graduation ceremony. It's the look that says, "Get rid of that baby! It's getting in our way!"

By now you surely must suspect where I'm headed with this illustration. As the baby's mother bolted for the door, already sensitive to glances she never saw, it occurred to me that the statement being made by many women having abortions (and sometimes by their partners as well) is very much the same: "Why did you have to bring that baby into my secure world at this point in time? It's ruining my life!"

At the end of the evening, the analogy proved to be even more appropriate than I had first thought. When I introduced myself to the child's parents, a pro-life rabbi and his wife, I learned that their lovely daughter's name was Chaya Mushka. "Chaya" is Hebrew for "life"! It was *life* that was interrupting the proceedings—*life* that had to be "gotten rid of."

The Kaleidoscope of Social Abortions

Human life is "gotten rid of" through abortions for a wide variety of reasons. Those that get all the press—"therapeutic" abortions to save the mother's life, "eugenic" abortions where there are abnormal fetuses, and rape and incest cases—comprise no more than 2 percent of all abortion cases. To be overly generous, make it 5 percent. What about the other 95 percent? By their very nature, the substantial majority of abortions, being "social" abortions, are difficult to categorize. Based upon social reasons, they meet a wide and often complex range of demands.

While we can never be statistically certain, it is possible anecdotally to know something of the various reasons which are given. Least surprising of all is the vast number of abortions chosen by *single* women—perhaps as many as 70 percent, including women who are widowed, divorced, or separated at the time. Even in this broad category there are a number of identifiable subcategories.

For instance, there is the very young teenager who knows she simply doesn't have the economic resources to maintain a child. Without either a job or the skills with which to acquire and keep a job, motherhood to her seems virtually impossible. Her reluctance to tell her parents (who likely could take over the financial support) is yet another sad commentary on the lack of trust and communication in many families.

Adoption might be an option, but abortion looks quicker and easier—particularly when the family's reaction *would* be hostile, and when "caring" pregnancy counselors strongly encourage abortion, as they almost always do.

Along with such economic considerations, or perhaps altogether separately, many younger girls in particular face a perceived reputation crisis. Even in a sexually liberated generation, pregnancy out of wedlock is still accompanied to some extent by social stigma: "If I keep the baby, even for adoption, everyone will know." "What will people at my church think of me?" "No one will want to marry me if I have a baby."

> ❧ The *bad* choices we make today may tempt us to make *horrendous* choices two months later.

For most younger girls, the fear begins at home: "How am I going to tell my parents?" "My parents will kill me if they find out." Or, quite the opposite, there actually may be selfless concern for the parents: "I can't hurt my mother and father this way. It would just kill them." (These are the words I have heard from more than one young woman whose parents are actively involved in Christian ministries. Although their decision can't be condoned morally, I certainly relate to their concern.)

Then there's the *pressured* abortion: "You're not seriously thinking of having it, are you?" demands the angry boyfriend. "Do you think we're going to stand by and let you ruin your life?" ask the shocked parents (perhaps more worried about what an "illegitimate" baby would do to *the family's* reputation). "You wouldn't want to ruin your chances for a good education," suggests the school counselor.

Younger girls probably could never appreciate the difference, but the perceived threat to their reputations is normally far less than that which is faced by single women well on their way to becoming professional women in the community. (After all, young girls "don't know any better.") More mature women are supposed to be just that—more mature, more careful, more circumspect.

And for the working woman, of course, there's no way to go off and live with the grandparents for nine months. There's simply no way around it for the young professional. Keeping the baby and giving it up for adoption would be front-page news at the office. And what would months away from work do to a budding career?

While marriage is always a possibility, 14- and 16-year-olds are hardly in a position to make that kind of commitment. And even the more mature woman is not likely to find marriage an option if there was not a strong love relationship to support the sexual relationship in the first place. In the absence of a pre-pregnancy commitment, "shotgun weddings" are notoriously unsuccessful.

This brings us squarely to the heart of the abortion problem: the sex-outside-of-marriage syndrome. A woman might say, quite unselfishly, "I don't want *this* man to be my child's father. I'll abort now and wait until I'm married to the *right* man." The obvious question is, Why is she having *sex* with a man she doesn't want to be the father of her children? And what goes for the goose goes for the gander: Why do *men* have sex with women they do not wish to marry and whose children they do not wish to father? Those of us who are single have some serious rethinking to do about the kind of sexual choices we have become accustomed to making. The *bad* choices we make today may tempt us to make *horrendous* choices two months later.

Unfortunately, even marriage does not automatically eliminate the problem. For married women the decision may be not to have *any more* children. Here again, the reasons may vary. It may be because of true economic hardship; or because of a conscious choice to give a better life to the children already born; or because of the strain of advanced age; or even because a woman just can't bear to face another round of dirty diapers and the intrusion into her now-freer lifestyle (and who could possibly blame her?).

If innocent human life were not in the picture, any one of these reasons would be sufficient to justify an abortion. Well, *almost* enough. There's still the nagging problem of post-abortion trauma (evidence itself that human life stubbornly insists on making itself known). Paint the worst scene you might imagine, and most women still have to weigh it against a lifetime of instant replays on the Guilt Channel. If pregnancy brings embarrassment, shame, and stigma, abortion brings remorse and moral recriminations from which few women can escape.

The Hurting Reality

Given the kinds of conflicts engendered by an unexpected child in one's life, it is no surprise that when the indicator in the home pregnancy test turns blue, it is anything but a joyous moment for many women. Denial, horror, fear, anger, and helplessness all crowd around, blurring disbelieving eyes with tears. In that split second of recognition, their whole world comes crashing down around them.

The parent-free weekend that led to the awkward moments of first intimacy is but a distant memory at such a moment. The smiling face across the dance floor before a night of wild carousing might not even come clearly to mind.

"Life" it may be, but it must be gotten rid of. Of course it must. What else is there to do? It will ruin *my* life!

Those first terror-filled thoughts were captured vividly by a student in my Law and Religion seminar last spring, in the descriptive opening to her term paper on the subject of abortion:

> The lights flashed and the music pulsated the entire building. Standing against the bar with Ping-Pong eyes, my brain was bubbling like my glass of champagne. The dark, smoky dance floor invited anyone and everyone, "free love its scheme." We all stood pulsating with the music in that vast sea of moving limbs. "Why am I here?" White teeth, broad smiles, long eyelashes, lovely hair, and a nice bubbly brain. Yes, this is the game that leads to big mistakes coupled with regret. Glances, moves, lips, and looks . . . yes, this is the ritual.
>
> Turning around slowly, so as not to disturb my already disturbed equilibrium, the walls tilted and the room spun and there he stood. Winking with my keen eye I screamed, "More wine for we are but swines with little time!" He smiled and walked toward me, set for the kill.
>
> And kill it was. No thoughts, no rationalization, for those had all drowned with my sweet wine.

Humanity at its finest animal state, beasts with one thing in mind, movement and empty touch. "There is no tomorrow!" whispered my incoherent, wine-filled brain. The rest is a fog of movements and sweat.

Now I stand before the mirror, clear-minded. "Tomorrow," and I'm sick in more than one way. Infested trash! My mind argues and tortures itself: "What have you done? You fool! All is wrecked! Damn you and your wine!"

What will I do? Splashing water on my face, wishing this was all a nightmare, I cry. Something is growing in me, infesting me, and wrecking my life. This is not happening! I've got to do something fast to get rid of this infested guilt. It's a simple procedure. It will hurt, but it won't hurt as bad as reality. I will escape this yet!

Ahhhhh!! What am I doing? I'm fixing a big mistake. Yes, that's it. I'm just fixing something. No one has to know.[1]

It will hurt, but not as bad as reality. That is the Hobson's choice of pro-choice. "How dare pregnancy ruin my life?" says she. "How can she do this to me?" says he. It will hurt, but not as bad as reality....

Pro-Choice, the Cult of Self

"Reality" for writer Kim C. Flodin was being "19, full of potential, my life and the things I wanted to do with it ahead of me. Surely those things would be much harder to accomplish if I was to be encumbered now with a baby. I whispered thanks for the *Roe v. Wade* ruling into my pillow every night while I waited for the appointment at the clinic."[2]

With rarely seen forthrightness, Flodin's self-assessment a decade later tells the story of pro-choice—at least *one* story, all too often repeated:

My abortions were thrust upon me by my carelessness and what almost seems to be anachronistic biological laws. People make bad decisions for which they should not have to pay with their whole lives, and no one can legislate biology.

I was pregnant, I carried two unborn children and I chose, for completely selfish reasons, to deny them life so that I could better my own. It may not sound catchy, but it's the only way I know how to say it. Now how the hell am I going to put all of that onto a poster? [3]

I don't know if it can fit onto a poster, but the bottom line for many women is clear: "I'm going to put my own happiness ahead of my children, even if it means having to kill them." If many abortions are done for ostensibly more compelling reasons, unfortunately in a large percentage of terminations, there are no compelling circumstances by any reasonable definition—only the elevation of self above all else.

❧ What else can one do but neatly sidestep the felony (killing human life), and plead guilty to the misdemeanor (selfishness)?

Without judging Ms. Flodin's own motives for being so forthright about the selfishness of her decision, it is altogether possible that a confession of selfishness (heard more and more these days from those who have had abortions) is but another way of evading the harsh reality of what a person actually has done. Confessing *selfishness* may be a convenient way to avoid having to confess the greater sin. When the unassailable pro-life arguments about the beginning of life finally sink in, what else can one do but neatly sidestep the felony (killing human life), and plead guilty to the misdemeanor (selfishness)?

If some find it disturbing that abortion should be characterized in such stark terms as "even if it means having to kill my children," it is significant to note that Ms. Flodin—pro-choice advocate that she is—did not shrink from recognizing the "son" that she had intentionally killed:

I believed it was a son. He romped through my dreams playing on the beach with a little red pail.

The waves toyed with his perfect feet and the breeze picked up his dark, wavy hair a bit. But however wonderful he might have been, once again the equation wasn't right. It just wasn't the right moment for me to become a mother.[4]

In a single word, Flodin has all but captured the essence of a pro-choice generation. The issue hardly matters, whether abortion, divorce, free sex, illegal drug use—the whole lot. That word is *equation*. "On one side [there was] this more-than-likely-blue-eyed baby and a lover who never knew, and on the other side [there was] me, Flodin admits."[5]

Equation. It's a word we all know, up close and personal. It's what the pro-choice movement is all about at the end of the twentieth century. Fill in the blank, whatever it might be, and on the other side is ME. Still, it's not quite as simple as that. In the pro-choice equation, ME is just a bit *more* equal than whatever happens to be on the other side of the equation. In fact, just enough more equal to rationalize getting rid of IT. Even if IT happens to be a husband or a wife. Or a son or daughter.

> ❧ **The stage has already been set with other convenient escape routes: bankruptcy, divorce, drugs, and suicide. Abortion is the consummate escape route.**

On the scales of an equation, divorcing a husband or wife takes some doing. Marriage has a way of making both parties close to equal weight. But an unborn baby put into an equation doesn't have a chance. Place an unborn baby and a woman on the scales, and the woman always wins. That's where the pro-abortion movement has a built-in advantage: Its most vocal members are women.

And among women, one of the most vocal is Gloria Steinem, who has cultivated the cult of Self to its maximum. Not only does she rationalize her own abortion, but she actually sees it as a positive experience of self-worth: "For me, seeking out an abortion had been the first time I stopped passively accepting whatever happened and took responsibility for my own life."[6] Of course that is not the issue. Is Ms. Steinem willing to take responsibility for destroying *another person's* life?

When we begin to weigh a woman's personal fulfillment against the life of an unborn fetus, we are back to square one: *When does human life begin?* (It always surfaces. It always *must*.) For if innocent human life is killed in an abortion, then the only morally justifiable grounds for terminating a pregnancy is to save the mother's life. Period. "Hardship pregnancies," though they evoke sympathy and demand society's support for thoughtful alternatives to abortion, cannot stand in the face of human life destroyed. Even more so, it should go without saying that *abortions of convenience* are all the difference between "understandable, but wrong" and "outrageous, without moral excuse."

Abortions of convenience are but escape routes from bad choices. But why should we be surprised that human life can be killed for nothing more than our own convenience? The stage has already been set with other convenient escape routes: bankruptcy, divorce, drugs, and suicide. Abortion is the consummate escape route, encompassing all the others: Encouraged by bankrupt moral rationalizations, we divorce parent from child, by means of life-killing chemicals, and end up mortifying our own souls.

What About Rape and Incest?

At the other end of the spectrum from abortions of convenience are those which occur in the wake of rape and incest. As a man, I realize that I don't know what it would be like either to be raped or to carry the baby of a rapist. Nor, for that matter, do most *women*, especially when it comes to experiencing pregnancy in rape cases. Practically, if I were forced to choose between a law permitting abortions only in rape cases and no law whatever against abortion, I would choose the former. (Such a law would stop 99.9 percent of all abortions.) And purely from an *emotional* standpoint, I would wish to support such an exception in any law prohibiting abortion.

However, difficult cases that they are, not even pregnancy by rape or incest can morally justify the killing of an innocent human life. The best proof of that is to consider how we would treat innocent life *out of the womb* in relationship to rape or incest.

Would we think it justifiable to take an *innocent* life to prevent the rape or incest in the first place? The answer to that question is obvious. As horrible as rape is, it cannot justify the killing of an innocent bystander in order to prevent it from happening.

And who is prepared to argue that we can kill an innocent child for the crime of his father? In a case of incest, the young girl is already being punished for the sins of her sexually abusive father. In such an instance, my heart desperately wants to convince my mind that the girl has paid a high enough price already. Why should she be forced to literally bear a greater burden? But I have no other way around the issue. If the fetus within her is a human being, as I believe it is, then the sanctity of life simply must prevail over all other considerations, no matter how seemingly unjust.

But if cold legalism is as unappealing to you as it is to me, there is still the victim of the incest to consider. Usually quite young, and at the mercy of a family that wants to hide what's going on behind closed doors, the girl herself may not be well-served by an abortion. In some cases, an abortion may actually assist in covering up the incest and prolonging the problem.

As for rape, virtually everyone agrees that, under normal circumstances, the *sanctity of life itself*, when innocent, must take precedence over even the *violent abuse* of human life. We see that most clearly when we consider the rapist himself: His victim cannot kill him with impunity the following day. Why, then, the innocent unborn child?

If the unborn fetus is in fact human life worthy of protection in every other case, there is nothing inherently different about an unborn fetus which happens to have resulted from a violent rape. That unborn child, too, is an innocent bystander.

Nor is the innocent unborn child the only one made to suffer. Contrary to what we might expect, post-abortion trauma in many rape cases appears to be no less pronounced than post-abortion trauma in non-rape cases. Rape followed by pregnancy followed by abortion leaves us with three victims: the woman who was traumatized initially by the rape; the unborn child who is traumatized by the abortion; and, for a second time, the woman who is traumatized by her *decision* to have an abortion.

Whatever else we might think of abortion in cases of rape, one thing is clear: The incidence of pregnancy from rape— where a woman has no control over her body—is minuscule compared with the astronomical number of non-rape pregnancies—where the woman *does* have control over her body. Therefore, the issue of abortion in rape cases has no bearing whatever on the legitimacy of social abortions in non-rape cases.

To the contrary, tolerating the killing of innocent human life under any circumstances renders us less able to be intolerant to the violation of a human life through forcible rape. Morality is a seamless garment. Pull one thread, and others soon begin to unravel. How can we protest violation of the *body* when we tolerate violation of the *soul*?

> ❧ **By providing abortion as an option, younger women in particular can be pressured into making a decision they would otherwise never have made.**

From the gut-wrenching cases of rape and incest, to the "hardship cases" where abortion is done under empathetic circumstances, to purely selfish "abortions of convenience," all the many reasons given for killing unborn children ultimately fail. It's *life* that is interfering with our lives. *Life* that is being "gotten rid of." *Human life* that we are killing in the name of difficult circumstances and bad timing.

Choice Where No Choice Exists

One of the most surprising statements you hear over and over again when you talk to women—especially younger girls—about abortion is: "I had no choice but to have an abortion." This letter, for example, tells how one young woman felt trapped into terminating her pregnancy:

> There were plans racing through my mind of where we would live, what we'd name it, what it would look like. . . . But, on his father's advice of "it'll ruin your life," he opted for an abortion. I was in shock, so I went along with him when he said

> that there was no way I could have it alone and that
> I'd be kicked out of the family.
>   Reality set in, and the choice was not mine.
> That's the heartache—the choice was not *mine*—it
> was his, my family's, society's.
>   It was his choice because he would have been
> the only financial support. It was my family's
> because of the rejection of me and the unborn. And
> it was society's because of the poverty cycle I would
> enter as a teenage mother.

What an interesting commentary on a *pro-choice* movement which virtually worships the right to choose! By providing abortion as an option, younger women in particular can be pressured into making a decision they would otherwise never have made. How was the girl who wrote this letter to know that her fears about being kicked out of the family were most likely unfounded? (I also get letters from mothers of young girls who have had abortions without telling them. Rather than "kicking their daughters out of the family," they are sad about the loss of grandchildren they never knew!)

As for the financial problems which were so feared, our young letter-writer had no clue how families often react—first in shock and rejection, but then in love and financial support. And the sad irony is pointed out in yet another letter—this one from the mother of a teenager who had become desperate, hostile, bitter, and heartbroken because of her decision. "What promised to be an answer to her problem only created a multitude of other problems," writes the concerned parent. "An unwanted child can create financial and social problems, but a self-terminated pregnancy causes emotional problems which themselves create financial and social problems."

I suppose there are many circumstances where a woman could be forgiven for thinking that she really has no other choice but to abort. Still, I wonder how many women have to face anything like "Sophie's Choice." In the film, Sophie (played so brilliantly by Meryl Streep) is in absolute horror when told by the concentration camp guard that she must give up one of her two children—one a boy, the other a girl. When Sophie reels at the thought of having to choose between her children, and protests that she simply can't, the officer cruelly insists: "You must make a choice."

Sophie's choked response is a bewildering, frantic "Don't make me choose! Don't make me choose!" "If you don't choose *one*, I will have to take them *both*," the officer responds coldly as he reaches toward them. Realizing that she has no choice but to choose, she thrusts her daughter into his arms, crying hysterically, "Take my little girl!"

I know that for many women "Sophie's Choice" must be the agony of thinking they have no choice but to choose abortion. But that is because, since 1973, abortion has been a legitimate *option*. If it were *not* an option, then for most women it would never be such a cruel decision. To be sure, there would be another difficult decision to be made as to whether to keep the baby for themselves or to give it up for adoption. But the agonizing decision about whether to *kill* their child would no longer be theirs to make.

If someone were to suggest that women would simply seek illegal abortions, the pre-*Roe v. Wade* experience indicates that most would *not*. Even allowing for the fact that we are now a society virtually addicted to abortion, it is still unlikely that a high percentage of women would resort to illegal means. Whatever might be the numbers of those who did, at least we would have given a stronger defense to younger women especially, who—whether pressured by boyfriends, parents, or "caring" counselors—now feel that they have no choice but to abort. The counselors in particular would be out of the picture.

It's the Baby That Has No Choice

If women feel trapped into having abortions—if they feel they really have no choice under the circumstances—the fact remains that they *do* have a choice. And, despite whatever pressures they feel (sometimes considerable), they are ultimately responsible for their choice. Proving that the final decision is theirs and theirs alone, it is *they* who pay the high price for their choice—not the parents, not the boyfriend, not the family-planning counselor. But whereas they ultimately *do* have a choice in the decision to abort, one thing is certain: The aborted baby does *not* have a choice.

Playing the role of Sally in the musical "Cabaret," (about a happy-go-lucky nightclub entertainer in pre-war Berlin), Liza Minnelli discovers that she is pregnant. Not knowing for certain who the father might be, her predictable response is "Obviously, I can't have it." However, upon reflection, she's not entirely sure the decision is so cut-and-dried. "Babies love you automatically, don't they?" she asks Brian, her friend and some-times lover. "They don't have much of a choice," Brian responds.

That thought seems to settle the matter for Sally. If babies love *you* automatically, how can you not love *them* automatically? Given that logic, having an abortion was out of the question. Or so we are led to believe. But only a couple of scenes later Brian learns that Sally has changed her mind and actually gone through with an abortion. Apparently Sally had a quick conver-sion to the creed of a pro-choice generation: "It hurts, but not as bad as reality." "On one side is a baby who loves you automat-ically, but on the other side is ME."

In a pro-choice generation, there is little regard for morality unless the morality has a direct link to some adverse result. Unless we believe that harm to ourselves results in the end, morality means nothing to us. Our pro-choice generation has convinced itself that children are harmlessly expendable, whether in a divorce or in an abortion. With divorce we rationalize by saying, "The kids are taking it real well." With abortion we rationalize by saying, "It would ruin my life." In each instance we find it amazingly easy to dismiss the terrible harm that is done to the children.

I wish you could have heard Chaya Muska's wondrous little whimper that night in Oxford. It would forever be a reminder that, whatever the unwelcomed interference in our lives, it is *life* that suffers in an abortion. It is *life* that we are "getting rid of"— *life* that has to die for our own selfish reasons.

Liza Minnelli, as Sally, was right. Babies *do* love us automat-ically. If only we'll let them.

THIRTEEN

The Hypocrisy Of Choice

YOU'VE PROBABLY SEEN IT in a copy of *Newsweek* or *Time*. It is a fetching photo of a young mother holding her smiling two-year-old son beside a peaceful lake. Beneath the photo is the headline, **"When I was fifteen, Planned Parenthood saved my life."** So begins a full-page ad from the Planned Parenthood Federation of America, which mirrors not only the happy contentment of motherhood beside a peaceful lake, but also the message of a pro-choice generation. The message? Joyful motherhood is achieved through abortion.

The copy beneath the headline opens with a testimonial from the mother in the photo, praising Planned Parenthood for "saving her life":

> I was never so scared.
>
> I was pregnant and afraid to tell anyone. A friend told me to go to Planned Parenthood. They were so wonderful. They talked to me about what I could

197

do. I knew I wasn't ready to be a mother. I wanted to tell my parents, but I didn't want to hurt them. Planned Parenthood helped me talk to them. I had an abortion.

Getting pregnant was the worst crisis of my life, but I know I made the right decision. I finished school, got married, and now I have two wonderful kids. I don't know what I would have done if abortion wasn't legal. My only choices were a back-alley abortion, trying to do it myself, or being a 15-year-old mother.

Planned Parenthood saved my life when I was fifteen. I got my future back.[1]

For over 70 years Planned Parenthood has had a reputation for being as American as motherhood, apple pie, and baseball. Well, at least apple pie and baseball. For despite the meticulously orchestrated public image, *motherhood* is the sworn enemy of Planned Parenthood. At the least, its very name tells us that motherhood is to be a planned reduction in the number of births that otherwise would normally occur.

Actually there is nothing shocking about that. A pro-choice generation can scarcely remember a time when family planning was *not* standard practice. Except for a relatively few couples today (mostly Catholic), family planning is a *given*. "How many children do you want to have?" schoolgirls ask each other at an early age. "We've decided not to have any more children," say the young couple who already have the model American family of 2.3 children. Deciding *whether* to have children, *when* to have them, or *how many* to have is what parenting is all about at the end of the twentieth century. Was it ever any other way?

If family planning—the *reduction* of motherhood through *prevention* of conception—were the sole aim of Planned Parenthood, it might merit its pristine reputation within the community. But today it is the *elimination* of motherhood through *abortion* which has become Planned Parenthood's primary stock in trade.

The Business of Abortion

By its own proud admission, Planned Parenthood is the world's oldest, largest, and best-organized provider of abortion and birth-control services.[2] Or as *Time* notes, Planned Parenthood is "the premier institution providing abortions around the country." With 170 affiliates, 21,000 volunteers and staff, over 800 clinics in the United States, and a multibillion-dollar international conglomerate with programs and activities in 120 nations around the world, Planned Parenthood is the unchallenged giant of a $500-million-a-year abortion industry in the United States alone,[3] and an estimated $10-billion-a-year industry worldwide.[4]

With all that money floating around, it goes almost without saying that it is not the privately funded organization it would have us to believe. In fact, you may be surprised to learn that money from your own pocket (totaling millions of tax dollars from all of us) annually goes to the support of Planned Parenthood's programs.

&. **Despite the meticulously orchestrated public image, *motherhood* is the sworn enemy of Planned Parenthood.**

George Grant, in his 1988 book *Grand Illusions: The Legacy of Planned Parenthood*, documents the unprecedented flow of public money to Planned Parenthood. Through the Title X appropriations of the Public Health Service Act ($142.5 million in 1987 divided among some 5000 health service providers), Planned Parenthood receives tens of millions of our tax dollars. In addition to Title X appropriations, Planned Parenthood receives additional millions of dollars from federal, state, and local measures that authorize public expenditures for "family planning" programs.

Although Planned Parenthood steadfastly insists that no federal money is used to fund abortions, this is nothing more than a gossamer distinction between the reception desk and the back room. Planned Parenthood's federally funded family-planning clinics serve as a funnel through which pregnant women are poured into medical clinics where the abortions are actually performed. If abortions suddenly ceased, Planned Parenthood would lose much of its reason to exist and most of its need for such vast amounts of public moneys.

Globally, the amount of public funding reaches astronomical proportions. George Grant reports, for instance, that—

> Internationally, various Planned Parenthood agencies have been able to skim the cream off of virtually every United States foreign aid package.... Additionally, Planned Parenthood gets a larger part of the untold billions in grants, contracts, and cooperative agreements of the United Nations Fund for Population Activities, the World Bank, and the Agency for International Development.[5]

Yet what is truly alarming is not just the vast amounts of money flowing with minimal accountability into a single multinational collective, but the end product of it all: the highly organized, carefully planned deaths of millions of unborn children.

Each year across the globe, Planned Parenthood is responsible, either institutionally or more indirectly through its highly respected influence, for the lion's share of the many millions of worldwide abortions. Typical of Planned Parenthood's attitude toward the global desecration of human life is the fact that China[6] has been cited by Planned Parenthood officials as a "model of efficiency,"[7] despite the nearly 100 million abortions, mandatory sterilizations, and coercive infanticides thus far performed.

⅍ Planned Parenthood "saved her life" (figuratively) by killing her child (literally).

Far from promoting joyful motherhood, Planned Parenthood promotes worldwide genocide. If "genocide" is thought to be overly emotive, what other term could we use to describe the deliberate, wholesale elimination of an unrepresented class? Granted, there is disagreement as to whether human life exists before birth. But if it does, Planned Parenthood has much to answer for. The phrase "crimes against humanity" certainly comes to mind.

Admittedly those are tough words, but how else will the horrific mission of Planned Parenthood be gotten across to a generation that is so caught up in the pro-choice mentality that not even the deaths of hundreds of millions of the world's children has so far penetrated so debased a philosophy?

"Saving the Mother's Life"

In light of what we know about the *real* Planned Parenthood Federation, the sympathy-grabbing ad presented at the beginning of the chapter warrants closer scrutiny. Even the headline "Planned Parenthood saved my life" is teeming with deadly contradiction. Rather than "saving" a life—which in the case of this perfectly healthy woman was but a figure of speech— what really happened in fact was the *taking* of a life. Put simply, Planned Parenthood "saved her life" (figuratively) by killing her child (literally).

"Planned Parenthood saved my life"—what an extraordinarily crass play on words! Virtually every piece of abortion legislation throughout the Western world permits termination of a pregnancy where the life of the mother is threatened. The principle is based upon the choice of evils between two possible victims, both of whom are innocent. In such a case, the life of the mother—with her already existing relationships, and possibly other children to care for—prevails over the nascent life of the unborn. So clear is the principle that virtually no pro-life advocate would dispute it. On this point, if on no other, pro-choice and pro-life advocates are in agreement.

Yet Planned Parenthood and other pro-choice advocates attempt to capitalize on this one obvious exception in order to justify abortion for any cause. And what a rare exception it is— perhaps no more than one-tenth of one percent of all abortions! Even when a mother's life is threatened, the baby can typically be delivered sufficiently early to avoid fatal consequences to either the child or the mother. (One recognized circumstance where that may not be possible is the tubal pregnancy. In that rare circumstance an abortion is indicated because such a pregnancy will only result in death for both mother and child.)[8]

Planned Parenthood itself has verified the rarity of cases in which "therapeutic" abortions are necessary in order to *truly* save the life of the mother. As far back as 1967, Dr. Alan F. Guttmacher, then president of Planned Parenthood World Population, wrote:

Today it is possible for almost any patient to be brought through pregnancy alive, unless she suffers from a fatal illness such as cancer or leukemia, and, if so, abortion would be unlikely to prolong, much less save, life.[9]

As Dr. Guttmacher points out, the true "therapeutic" abortion has become virtually extinct. Its only dubious purpose now is to provide an emotionally charged, if totally illogical, rationalization for abortion on demand.

No Alternative to Abortion?

Perhaps the most telling statement about Planned Parenthood's threat to motherhood is seen in the options given to the woman in the enticing ad. "I don't know what I would have done if abortion wasn't legal. My only choices were a back-alley abortion, trying to do it myself, or being a 15-year-old mother," reads the manipulative ad copy some 15 years beyond *Roe v. Wade* and any immediate specter of renewed back-alley abortions.

> &. Why all the pretentious moralizing about unwanted babies and child abuse, when adoption by parents eager to cherish their children is such a natural, loving alternative?

Did no one at Planned Parenthood counsel the young woman about the option of giving up the baby for adoption? Even if one happens to believe that adoption is an unloving act (more unloving than *killing* the child?), at the very least it ought to be an *option* seriously to be considered by any woman not wanting to keep her baby. The fact is, of course, that motherhood leading to adoption is *not* a favored option at the counseling desks of Planned Parenthood. The joy of motherhood, even for women desperately wanting to adopt, is simply not on the agenda. Tragically, Planned Parenthood's business is not adoption, but abortion. Not life, but death.

Planned Parenthood's Hidden Agenda

How can we possibly account for Planned Parenthood's blindness to the literal fact that, for every unwanted baby aborted, there is a family waiting to receive a child with open arms? Even if most WASP couples would consider adopting only WASP babies, we would still be able to save at least a third of all babies aborted. And even if the children of welfare mothers and drug addicts did not find as many open arms as other children, we would still be able to save at least one-fourth of all babies aborted.

Being as fair as possible with all the statistics, that is 250,000 children per year who could be saved outright! And given a concerted effort to change public attitudes, even the "less desirable" children could all be saved. So why the desperate rush to kill rather than to love? Why all the pretentious moralizing about unwanted babies and child abuse, when adoption by parents eager to cherish their children is such a natural, loving alternative? Why do we have publically funded programs designed to promote abortion rather than public-interest programs designed to promote adoption?

Putting aside the immediate temptation to speculate about abortion as big business, and about how millions of tax dollars might affect one's agenda, the truth is that Planned Parenthood's philosophical roots are deeply embedded in *population control*—sometimes humanitarian, sometimes frightfully sinister.

Selection of the Fittest

In 1922 Margaret Sanger, founder of Planned Parenthood, became convinced that social work on behalf of the poor was merely perpetuating what she called "the cruelty of charity." For Sanger, the better approach to poverty was elimination of the poor themselves—no, not by concentration camps and gas chambers, but by preventing their birth in the first place. It was Margaret Sanger who first coined the term "birth control."

But it is worth stepping back in time to see where Sanger's own roots lie. In the wake of the Civil War, it occurred to women who had worked in the abolitionist movement that there were parallels between the struggle for freedom of blacks and their own struggle for feminist emancipation. Their attention soon turned from abolition to the women's suffrage movement. By

1920 the feminists were successful in winning the right to vote for women.

One could be excused for seeing a parallel between the feminists' call for the "right to choose" at the ballot box at the turn of the century and the feminists' insistence on the contin- ued "right to choose" at the abortion clinic here at the end of the same century. However, as Marian Faux points out in her defini- tive book on the story behind *Roe v. Wade* (written sympathe- tically toward feminism, yet with admirable, objective candor), feminism itself has changed radically, sometimes ironically, in the passage of a century.

"The suffragists," says Faux, "had tied their cause to their roles as mothers. They argued that women would be better mothers, worthy of greater respect, if they could vote. It was essentially a conservative doctrine."[10] Feminism and mother- hood sharing the same bed? Who would have thought?

In that light, perhaps it would be worth exploring the "obvious reasons," as Faux puts it, why women's reproductive rights were not an issue in this first wave of feminism. Absence of "the pill" is probably *not* one of the "obvious reasons." Avail- able technology might later enhance the argument, but only some greater principle at stake would have marshaled feminist forces for another assault on behalf of women. And that assault simply did not come. Feminism lay dormant. Relative to repro- duction, women in the early 1900's were solidly in the camp of motherhood, with all that this might entail—the good, the bad, and the ugly.

Such debate as did take place pitted the socialists against the anarchists. Unlike the anarchists, the socialists were not inter- ested in women's rights, focusing instead on whether the working class would be better served by limiting its size. It was from this debate that the movement for birth control was spawned.[11]

A Surprising Pedigree

At this point enter Margaret Sanger. What Marian Faux tells us about Sanger, contraception, and family life is a revealing commentary on our present controversy:

> When Margaret Sanger rose from the radical
> ranks to ride the crest of the new movement and to

convert birth control...into a less radical, single-issue cause, she found herself at odds with the suffragists, who were politically conservative and feared that contraception, by any name, would destroy family life.[12]

Feminists opposed to contraception? It gives new meaning to the feminist anthem, "You've come a long way, baby!" Sanger herself had already gone a long way. She argued that charity programs for the poor were the "surest sign that our civilization has bred, is breeding, and is perpetuating constantly increasing numbers of defectives, delinquents, and dependents."[13] Vitriolically attacking social workers and churchmen who refused to appreciate the need to curb working-class fertility, Sanger called them "benign imbeciles, who encourage the defective and diseased elements of humanity in their reckless and irresponsible swarming and spawning."[14]

Not a terribly high view of either the underprivileged or those who have dedicated themselves to the bettering of others' lives! And also cruelly simplistic, if you think about it: The way to solve the problems of the underprivileged is to *eliminate* the underprivileged. What does that say for the *right of choice* of the underprivileged themselves? Do they have any say in the matter? Think about how they would react to Sanger's blithe solution to the problems of the underclass: "More children from the fit, less from the unfit; that is the chief issue of birth control."[15]

With that elitist view of population management, Sanger's humanitarian concerns turn ugly. "If we must have welfare," argued Sanger, "give it to the rich, not to the poor."[16] Her chilling call to "eliminate the stocks" that are detrimental "to the future of the race and the world"[17] is, unfortunately, more than just vaguely familiar.

Institutions often rise above their own founders, or indeed mellow through time. But still today, the work of the International Planned Parenthood Federation continues throughout the world to focus on sterilization and abortion as a means, not simply of family planning (voluntary), but of population control (involuntary). Certainly such action is hardly what you would expect from the kind of humanitarian organization that Planned Parenthood touts itself to be. The Sanger influence lives on: It's *elimination* which they seek, not *alleviation*.

Self-Defeating Programs

Sometimes we beat ourselves at our own game. Sometimes our best-intended actions come back to haunt us. I recall in the early 70's going into the local high schools in the eastern Oregon county where I was District Attorney, participating in the drug-education program. I don't think any of us involved in trying to stop the dangerous use of recreational drugs ever felt we were making any headway. With some of the kids—those who were already using drugs—it was much like a fumbling parent trying to tell a child about the facts of life: Sometimes the child knows more about it than the parent! (At least the mechanics of it.)

For the other kids, it was a school for scoundrels. What they didn't know about drugs we *taught* them. If some kids were put off drugs by what we described, others were intrigued. In retrospect, we have no doubt that drug education was as much a contributor to the problem as it was a solution. If we *informed*, we also created *options*. And the more vulnerable kids chose the wrong options.

Likewise, after two decades of sex education—a major part of Planned Parenthood's multimillion-dollar program—the verdict is in: Teenage pregnancies are up, teenage abortion is up, and sexually transmitted diseases among teenagers is up. "Safe sex" has been an abysmal, unqualified failure. Of course, the blame cannot be laid totally at the feet of Planned Parenthood or any other sex-education program. The fact is that adults as well as teenagers—all of us—live in a sex-saturated society. We live under a daily bombardment of sexual innuendo against which there is hardly any defense.

But couple that bombardment with sex-education programs which *assume* teenage sexual activity, and you soon get young students themselves assuming there is *supposed to be* sexual activity—or at the very least that sex is an acceptable option. We distribute condoms, teach how they are used, and then act surprised when teenagers have sex. When we further couple this naive approach to sex education with a public school system legally stripped of moral instruction, we then get all the *mechanics* of sex with little of its *values*. That's a coupling bound to produce illegitimate offspring, both physically and morally.

Remember the Planned Parenthood ad? "I knew I wasn't ready to be a mother," says the 15-year-old. True. (Although we tend to forget that there was a time when teenage marriages and motherhood were the rule rather than the exception, and it seemed to work at least as well as today's social chaos.) But if in fact a 15-year-old is not ready for motherhood, then she (as well as *he*) is not yet ready for *sex*. As we are constantly reminded by the statistics, sex and motherhood have an irrepressible way of going hand in hand.

The plain fact is that for all the good intentions behind sex education, young kids simply don't act responsibly with the information and technology with which they are supplied. Looking at how badly we *adults* mishandle it, it should not come as a shock that less mature teenagers simply aren't ready for making adult-like choices in a responsible manner.

It's frustrating enough when efforts at drug and sex education go awry. But frustration and disappointment turn to tragedy when we consider Planned Parenthood's deadly one-two punch. When its sex-education courses have revved up the troops and given them a false sense of security, and when (despite all the education) the birth-control pills and devices dispensed to them have failed, Planned Parenthood's solution to the problem is an unapologetic abortion: If it doesn't work, "fix it."

Tragically, for most teenage girls, abortion is the *ultimate* lesson in sex education. That's the moment when they *really* learn what sex is all about. And without unduly dredging up emotional horror stories (which indeed *could* be dredged up), you can bet it's a lesson they won't forget for the rest of their lives.

From Contraception to Abortion

It's easy to pass right over Planned Parenthood's twin programs of birth control and abortion without understanding what an odd pairing it has been historically. It should come as no surprise that the 1965 case of *Griswold v. Connecticut*, which challenged a 100-year-old Connecticut law prohibiting the distribution of birth-control devices, was instituted by the Planned Parenthood League of Connecticut. Executive director Estelle Griswold, along with Charles Lee Buxton, head of obstetrics and gynecology at Yale University, invited their own arrest (in order to set up a test case) by giving birth-control information and instruction to a married couple.[18]

Justice Douglas' opinion in *Griswold* opened the door for the first time to a revolutionary new Constitutional "right of privacy." Eventually, in *Roe v. Wade*, Justice Blackmun would walk through that door marked "private" in order to justify legalizing abortion. And once again Planned Parenthood would play a significant role, for not only did it submit an *amicus curiae* brief (one filed by a "friend of the court," someone other than a party to the action), but the woman who argued the plaintiff's case in *Roe* (Sarah Weddington) was active in both the National Organization for Women (NOW) and Planned Parenthood.[19]

However, between the *Griswold* case in 1965 and *Roe v. Wade* in 1973, Planned Parenthood made a rather dramatic about-face on the issue of abortion. (Remember, it was *contraception*, not abortion, that initially motivated Margaret Sanger and her Planned Parenthood dream.) In 1969 Virginia Whitehill, a volunteer for Planned Parenthood, could not even get her local Dallas chapter *interested* in the abortion issue—a fact which she attributed to their fear of jeopardizing the flow of public monies if they began lobbying for a political cause.[20]

"In fact," reports Marian Faux, "neither PP nor any other group involved in population control [such as Zero Population Growth] had ever shown much support of abortion rights for women. However logically aligned the interest of birth controllers and advocates of women's rights seemed to be, the interests and goals of the two groups were essentially incompatible."[21]

Faux's analysis on this point is invaluable:

> Feminists promoted individual choice. They believed women should control their own reproduction, including having whatever means were available to terminate an unwanted pregnancy.
>
> Where feminists wanted to redefine and reshape men's and women's roles, birth controllers firmly supported the nuclear family, which they saw as a key to maintaining stability. Putting control of reproduction in the hands of individual women was the last thing they wanted, since they advocated national and even worldwide controls on population growth. As a result, even though birth control and population activists supported the use of various forms of birth control, abortion was never one of them.[22]

Who should make the crucial decisions about reproduction: *individual women*, each having a right of choice, or government-backed *society*, mandating women's reproductive choices? As hard as it is to believe for a pro-choice generation, in 1969 Planned Parenthood was *for* population control (especially of the underclass) and *against* the individual woman's right of choice.

Even today outside the United States (where we have both a rights-conscious society and a stable, generally-affluent economic population) Planned Parenthood promotes socially mandated sterilization and other population-control programs in Third World countries—all of which makes a sham of the alarmist battle cry in our classic *Newsweek* ad. Referring to pro-life advocates, the ad warns, "They're trying to take away your right to decide for yourself."

If Planned Parenthood is concerned about anyone taking away women's right to decide, they might cast a more cautious glance at their pro-abortion ally, Molly Yard, president of the National Organization for Women (NOW). Implying that the government ought to take a more active role in limiting childbirths, Ms. Yard tells us, "We are going to have to face, as China has faced, the policy of controlling the size of families."[23]

As we know, according to the one-child policy in China, women pregnant with a second child face almost irresistible government pressure to have an abortion.

Adding irony to irony, the "fundamental human right" which they now so greatly fear being taken away is the right to have an *abortion*, which in 1969 was the second issue dividing feminists, who *favored* it, from Planned Parenthood supporters, who *rejected* it! Perhaps it had something to do with Planned Parenthood's statement in 1964 that "abortion kills the life of a baby, once it has begun."[24]

Of course, the talk today is all about "potential life" and "nonviable fetuses." "Baby? What baby?" Planned Parenthood now asks!

So great was the aversion to abortion in 1969 that when the Dallas Committee to Study Abortion searched around for logistical support, Planned Parenthood was among the many organizations which "were unwilling to take so public a stand as lending them a meeting place."[25] At that time, in fact, women's groups were in total disarray regarding reproduction rights:

Whitehill and several other women in the Dallas group thought that abortion was a useful tool in controlling population growth, but they firmly believed it should not be used on anything but a voluntary and individual basis. Their view put them at odds both with Planned Parenthood, the leading and most established population control group, which advocated sterilization but not abortion as part of its Third World population control program, and with feminists, who felt that poverty was not necessarily the cause of overpopulation and considered campaigns to sterilize women while denying them access to abortion highly discriminatory.[26]

In a matter of only two years, feminists had won the day. By 1971 Planned Parenthood of Dallas finally endorsed abortion reform.[27] Across the nation, Planned Parenthood chapters took up the rally cry. When Sarah Weddington and her colleague, Linda Coffee, needed assistance in writing the brief for *Roe v. Wade*, they were given access to Harriet Pilpel, Planned Parenthood's counsel in the *Griswold* case, who would write the amicus brief, and to Alan Guttmacher, head of Planned Parenthood.[28]

In whatever ways it happened, Planned Parenthood went from being opposed to abortion (because it was generally considered to be an immoral act!) to playing a major role in its legalization (on the basis of a right of choice, at least for *American* women), to becoming its major worldwide provider and champion.

Contraception or Deception?

In Third World countries even today, the emphasis in Planned Parenthood's program for "population control" is unquestionably on the word *control*. As in forced sterilizations. As in mandated policies resulting in abortion. Yet the *Newsweek* ad directed to Americans is all about abortion *rights*. "The President has urged the Supreme Court to take away our right to decide for ourselves," says the clip-out coupon, encouraging women to contribute to Planned Parenthood. "I'm writing him to tell him to respect every woman's personal privacy." Are we to believe that Planned Parenthood is preparing to distribute the same coupon among the sterilized women of Ethiopia and India? It's all as hypocritical as it is immoral.

And it's dishonest as well. Claims the ad, "There's an increasingly vocal, violent minority that wants to outlaw abortion for all women, regardless of circumstances. Even if her life or health is in danger." Heart-tugging stuff. Guaranteed to make pro-life advocates seem Draconian. But, as we have already pointed out, it is simply not true. It is only Planned Parenthood and a number of pro-choice advocates who trip over themselves in abusing what it means to "save a mother's life."

&. Certainly no one favors even one death from abortion, whether clinical, back-alley, or self-induced. But the figure of 10,000 deaths is a complete myth.

And the ad is manipulative as well. "When they don't get their way, they resort to threats..." says the ad, referring to pro-life advocates, hardly aware of the bold-faced words at the bottom of the page: **"Don't wait until women are dying again."** That veiled reference to the emotive specter of back-alley abortions could hardly be considered anything but emotionally threatening!

One of the most blatant examples of pro-choice distortion is found in an article appearing in *Ms.* magazine about what supposedly happened immediately following the author's abortion of a two-month-old fetus:

> Finally, after only 10 minutes, the abortion was over. The nurse rubbed my stomach as the doctor declared, "You're not pregnant anymore..." I felt relief. Still fighting off imaginary demons, I asked to see the large jar containing the by-products of my abortion. Fully expecting to see tissue, or even body parts, I was reassured to find only blood.[29]

Only blood? For a *two-month-old* fetus? You may wish to refresh your recollection of what an eight-week-old fetus looks like, as previously presented in the sketch.

Rusty Coathangers and Back-Alley Mayhem?

In all the abuse of statistics, polls, and medical information, no emotional threat has been more fraudulent—and persuasive—than the much-touted prospect of back-alley abortions should *Roe v. Wade* ever be overturned. Before abortion was legalized, so we are told in virtually all pro-choice literature, more than 10,000 women a year died from back-alley abortions. "Is that something we want to go back to?" we are asked rhetorically.

The pervasive public impact of the proverbial "rusty coathanger" was brought home to me recently when I was having lunch with a good friend and her ten-year-old daughter, Erin. While waiting for our meal to be served, my friend and I were having a lively discussion about abortion. Out of the blue, Erin, who had been idly playing with her napkin and silverware (or so I thought) suddenly chimed in: "Why do women have to die from rusty coathangers instead of having proper abortions?" I couldn't believe my ears! "What do you know about rusty coathangers?" I asked in disbelief. "*Everyone* knows about them," Erin shrugged, as if I were a fool for asking.

Certainly no one favors even one death from abortion, whether clinical, back-alley, or self-induced. But the figure of 10,000 deaths is a complete myth. It's not even simply an exaggerated estimate. The figure of 10,000 is nothing more than a calculated fabrication dreamed up for political purposes. Marian Faux's objective candor reveals how statistical exaggeration on the part of some pro-choice advocates was simply too effective to pass up:

> When I began to look into this aspect of abortion, several pro-choice reformers suggested that illegal abortion was not as dangerous as it had been depicted during the reform movement. Admittedly, an image of tens of thousands of women being maimed or killed each year by illegal abortions was so persuasive a piece of propaganda that the movement could be forgiven for its failure to double-

check the facts. The exaggeration was also a safe one. Since these were illegal activities, no records were kept, and the death and injury rate was an impossible statistic to pin down.[30]

Faux further reports that—

Birth control expert Linda Gordon has investigated the idea that the rate might not even have been as high as the eight thousand to ten thousand deaths that were attributed annually to illegal abortion. She concluded that abortions done after the mid-nineteenth century were not particularly unsafe or life-threatening, largely because women had stopped using abortifacients, toxic chemicals that affected the body's entire system, to terminate pregnancies.[31]

In a rare moment of inconsistency within her book, Marian Faux later contradicted this very information: "That eight to ten thousand women died each year from complications was the nation's least-discussed, if not best-kept, dirty little secret."[32] Proving her own earlier point, the back-alley argument is so compelling that it's almost impossible not to use.

Several physicians suggested yet another factor that may have reduced the dangers of illegal abortion:

As abortifacients fell into disuse, surgical abortions replaced them. The restrictive laws passed between 1860 and 1880 did not alleviate abortion so much as drive it underground. And if one stands by the accepted medical belief that the surgeon who does the greatest number of operations and is thus able to maintain and even hone his skills is the best qualified, then women have probably been better off in the hands of competent but "illegal" abortionists who did hundreds of the minor surgeries each week than with the family doctor who did one abortion a year.[33]

Without discounting the tragic deaths which *did* occur from back-alley abortions, the scene was never as black as it was painted—certainly nowhere near the 10,000 mark. And we have this upon the best of sources: Dr. Bernard Nathanson, former abortion reform activist and cofounder of the National Association for the Repeal of Abortion Laws, who personally presided over 60,000 abortions:

> How many deaths were we talking about when abortion was illegal? In N.A.R.A.L. we generally emphasized the drama of the individual case, not the mass statistics, but when we spoke of the latter it was always "5,000 to 10,000 deaths a year." I confess that I knew the figures were totally false, and I suppose the others did too if they stopped to think of it. But in the "morality" of our revolution, it was a *useful* figure, widely accepted, so why go out of our way to correct it with honest statistics?
>
> In 1967 . . . the federal government listed only 160 deaths from illegal abortion. In the last year before the Blackmun era began, 1972, the total was only 39 deaths. Christopher Tietze estimated 1,000 maternal deaths as the outside possibility in an average year before legalization; the actual total was probably closer to 500.[34]

Of course Dr. Nathanson reminds us that "in the old days" there were also a significant number of "walking wounded" who did not die but were infected by botched abortions.[35] Certainly the picture was ugly enough any way it was painted, but Dr. Nathanson goes on to make the point that, although the deaths of even 39 women is a matter of serious concern, it is altogether lopsided for society to consider only the deaths of from 39 to 500 women and ignore the more than *one million* unborn who are legally extinguished each year.[36]

From Back Alleys to Bedrooms

Far from fearing any wholesale slaughter that might follow in the wake of *Roe v. Wade* being overturned, many feminists are already preparing to take abortions out of the hands of a male-dominated medical profession altogether by learning how to perform safe abortions in the bedroom rather than in back-alley clinics. In a recent *Los Angeles Times* feature article, Ann Japenga and Elizabeth Venant report movement in this direction along several fronts:

> If *Roe v. Wade* is overturned or further compromised, a coalition of religious activists, midwives, feminist health-care workers, and others intends to take abortion underground.
>
> A Los Angeles mother of six, Carol Downer, is planning a January tour to 70 feminist centers across the country where she will teach women to perform abortions by using a kit made from ordinary items such as plastic tubing and canning jars.
>
> In Chicago, women are talking about reviving an illegal abortion service called "Jane" which performed 11,000 abortions in the years before the Supreme Court legalized the procedure.
>
> A Baltimore Quaker women's group is compiling a list of people willing to assist in an underground railroad that would transport women from states where abortion is restricted to states where it is more easily accessible.[37]

Charlotte Taft, director of the Routh Street Women's Clinic in Dallas "envisions home abortion techniques someday being taught as widely as CPR. The analogy to the lifesaving technique is not metaphorical, she said, adding, 'We know what happens with illegal abortions. Women die and lives are destroyed.'"[38]

I continue to be amazed at the shallowness of pro-choice arguments. On one hand, feminists argue that women die from back-alley abortions (as they indeed do in rare instances) but never once mention that the unborn child *always* dies. Will feminists never acknowledge the *other* human life which is always, inevitably, and inextricably involved in an abortion?

On the other hand, feminists forget all about having said "We know what happens with illegal abortions" when it comes to planning a new wave of illegal abortions. "While acknowledging that there are risks in taking abortion out of the medical arena, advocates of other alternatives say technological advances make an underground system safer now than it was in the days before *Roe v. Wade*."[39] So why all the threats and innuendos about back-alley abortions if the law is overturned?

In fact, in justifying a revival of the "Jane" movement, there is yet more evidence that illegal abortions never were the death-trap they are claimed to have been. Even under less medically-sophisticated conditions, "Jane members say their infection rate was about 3 percent, the same as that reported by physicians. They say *none* of their [11,000] clients died as a result of the illegally performed procedure."[40]

Therein lies the compounded fraud of emotional back-alley arguments: 1) They are made in order to justify the killing of millions of unborn children 2) on the basis of thousands of alleged maternal deaths which never occurred in the past and 3) on the further scant likelihood that they would ever significantly occur in the future in a world of revolutionized abortion technology.

Flaunting the Law

A final look at Planned Parenthood's ad shows just how morally bankrupt today's frenzied pro-choice campaign has become. In the ad, pro-life advocates are castigated for "attacking the Constitution," and are accused of resorting to illegal activities "when they don't get their way." It's difficult to see how Planned Parenthood can present such an argument with a straight face. As Japenga and Venant report in their article on the "Underground Army," "Independently, several groups came to the conclusion that they would help women obtain abortions *whether or not it was legal* and whether or not doctors were willing to perform the procedure."[41]

As ever, Planned Parenthood is at the forefront of undermining social values, this time calling for self-rule outside the bounds of law. "We're tired of men in federal and state government having control over women's bodies. We want to take control for ourselves," says Mary Ellen McNish, associate executive director of Planned Parenthood of Maryland, and an organizer of the Quaker underground railroad.[42] The hypocrisy gets especially nauseous when we consider Planned Parenthood's government-mandated sterilization programs in developing countries where womens' personal rights are conveniently expendable.

Here at home, if *Roe v. Wade* is ever overturned, and pro-choice advocates no longer "get their way," the message is already coming across loud and clear: "We'll do what we want, regardless!" Even if it means violating the law. Even if it means renouncing the Constitution (which, with a reversal of *Roe*, would be brought back into line with the fundamental right to life, guaranteed by the Constitution for all but the last two decades of our nation's history).

And what is Gloria Steinem's justification for breaking the law should *Roe* be overturned? "If the Supreme Court has created disrespect for the law by placing it too far outside public practice and belief, that's their problem."[43] Wait till your local gang member gets wind of *that* excuse for violating the law! And you can also rest assured that the Court will get the blame for any deaths which occur when women who take it into their own hands to disobey the law end up dying of illegal abortions!

So much for the rule of law. And so much for the pretentious nobility of the principle of pro-choice. By their own words, pro-choice advocates have announced to the whole world the true Magna Charta of the "pro-choice" generation: self-determination above all—even above the law, if necessary. "Pro-choice" is anything but the democratic principle it is claimed to be. It means nothing less than self-rule. *Moral* anarchy. *Social* anarchy. "We don't care what the law says; we will do as we please!"

FOURTEEN

Sacrificing Life For Lifestyle

The poorest countries in the world are those with legalized abortion.

—Mother Teresa in her
Nobel Peace Prize speech

BY THE TIME YOU FINISH READING THIS SENTENCE, 15 more people throughout the planet will have been born into this world—at a rate of three people per second. This year there will be between 90 million and 100 million more people in the world, roughly equivalent to the present combined population of the Philippines and South Korea. And this despite massive family-planning programs over the last several decades. Unless the trend is reversed, the global population, which now stands at 5.25 billion, could reach 14 billion by the next century, say some analysts.

Supposedly the Great Population Explosion threatens us once again. If you are old enough, undoubtedly you have heard it before. For more than half a century, Planned Parenthood and the Rockefeller Institute (to the tune of millions of dollars) have been inundating us with warnings of a population apocalypse. In the 60's and 70's, so we were told, everyone had to do his or her share in reducing the size of families, or else we would all be wiped out by overpopulation.

And we believed their population pitch, especially when the Pill opened the door for effective birth control in a way never before possible. With the Pill came more sex and fewer babies. With fewer babies came greater freedom, and with greater freedom came a different family lifestyle. Large working-class families were out; small affluent families were in. Contraception meant less quantity and more quality. It became a whole new way of living. No, a whole new way of *thinking*. It is that way of thinking that is the hallmark of a pro-choice generation: Above all things, *quality of life*.

As if the first assault were not sufficiently successful, we are now being hit with a second wave of media attention directed at overpopulation. Just as before, our attention is directed to what is happening in Africa and parts of southern Asia. There, according to Dr. Nafis Sadik, Executive Director of the United Nations Population Fund, "the biggest increases will happen in the poorest countries, those by definition least equipped to meet the needs of the new arrivals and invest in their future."[1]

Define "poor" in terms of "needs" and "investing in the future," as Dr. Sadik has done, and you have a liberal pro-choice generation here in America—with its fixation on quality of life—ready to eat out of your hands.

All we need at that point is for Lester Brown, president of the environmental group Worldwatch, to warn us that "the world faces famine unless families are limited to two children,"[2] and we're ready to bite. We don't even pause long enough to grasp the coercive implications of foreign governments intruding into their female citizens' rights to reproduction—an idea which is inimical to the pro-choice movement in our own country.

However, for domestic consumption it becomes a game of bait-and-switch. Once we are persuaded of the need to control population abroad—by whatever measures might be necessary—all of a sudden we have urged upon us a form of population control which we don't even need. This time it is not *contraception* in which we are urged to participate, but *abortion*—as if, without it, America would soon self-destruct from famines and starvation.

And the message comes from no less trusted a source than actress Katherine Hepburn. How could someone who brought tears to our eyes in *On Golden Pond* possibly mislead us? When she was honored in 1988 for her decades of work with Planned Parenthood, Ms. Hepburn noted a direct link between abortion and the problem of overpopulation. "Abortion is necessary," she said, unless women are going to be absolute slaves." Abortion is "the only practical way to handle a situation where the population would go mad otherwise. There are too many of us, anyway. It seems so obvious."[3]

What seems so obvious to Ms. Hepburn—that there are too many of us around—is not so obvious statistically. At least not here in America, where fertility has steadily decreased over the past two centuries and even now is below mere replacement level. It should also be noted that the poverty of many underdeveloped countries is more the product of backward economic systems (generally feudalistic or socialistic) rather than overpopulation. Witness the thriving (capitalistic) economies of Japan, Korea, Hong Kong, and Malasia.

&⁂ **By comparison with men and women around the world who face each day the cruel choice of which children will live and which will die, an abortion-on-demand society makes a cheap mockery of the "right to choose."**

If population is an issue in Third World countries, it is not a problem in Western industrial countries. One thing is certain: we know nothing of the kinds of decisions facing parents in famine-plagued parts of the world. In Ethiopia, for instance, families are having to decide who among them will survive and who will die. Reporting from Tigray Province, Mary Anne Fitzgerald records the death of one special little person:

> Yemani Gebre lost. Just seven months old, he was discovered tucked beneath his sick, exhausted mother's shawl, when she sought treatment for a starvation-related illness. Yemani's father had not

mentioned there was a baby dying from hunger. The recovery of his 35-year-old wife was more important, as she had six older children to look after.[4]

By comparison with men and women around the world who face each day the cruel choice of which children will live and which will die, an abortion-on-demand society makes a cheap mockery of the "right to choose." If anything, here in the Western World, the mythical "population explosion" is just a good excuse to do what we want to do anyway, for quite selfish reasons.

Despite all the propaganda, no one should be fooled as to why American couples in the 1990's are limiting the number of children born, using abortion if necessary. Certainly there is no national sense of some imminent population explosion in America that everyone is patriotically pitching in to avert. Instead, playing off the genuine poverty problems in developing countries, abortion here in the world's most affluent nation is pathetically rationalized on economic grounds. "But we can't _afford_ more children," say many modern parents—forgetting that they were raised in larger families when times were hard.

Whatever else might be happening in the Third World, a pro-choice generation in America is not concerned about over-population, but about quality of life. Not life itself, but _lifestyle_— even if lifestyle takes precedence over life itself.

Lessons About Quality from the Third World

Before we leave behind the problems of the Third World, we must not be misled by the tragic scenes of Ethiopia. Not all non-Western cultures with large families are to be pitied. In fact, in their eyes, it is _we_ who are to be pitied!

I was particularly touched a few months ago by a feature photo article in the London _Sunday Times Magazine_ by photographer Peter Turnley and journalist Brian Moynahan. Entitled "Domain of the Dispossessed," the article pictured some of the 15 million refugees of the world—Cambodians, Afghans, Mozambicans, Eritreans, and Palestinians—in tented or hutted camps near the troubles from which they fled.

Turnley, whose odyssey with his camera took him to all the major islands of the refugee archipelago, never saw fighting in a food line, never came across theft or hoarding. "Boredom, idleness and threatening depression are the chief enemies," writes Turnley, "not acquisitiveness. I was always being offered the little food they had, or a chair to sit on. It inspired me. Far from being 'cheap in the third world,' life is more precious to refugees."[5]

I wonder if we don't have much to learn about the "quality of life" from those whose lives we would describe as substandard. How, for example, does our society with its shallow materialism compare with what Turnley observed among the dispossessed?

> Their individual sense of basic dignity, of humanity, remains powerful: great attention is paid to personal hygiene and appearance, to clothes and adornment.
>
> In circumstances of, most often, total material loss—of country, home and possessions—family life assumes a fundamental importance: ties of kinship and friendship are keenly cherished.[6]

Can we in a materially blessed pro-choice generation say that family life for us assumes a *fundamental importance*? Is choosing to divorce those to whom we have made lifetime commitments—and the deaths of our unborn children—the "quality of life" we hold in such high esteem? Are death and divorce the supposed "good life" that smaller, more affluent families have brought us?

English author and social observer Malcolm Muggeridge recalls when he first became aware of the notion that too many children were being born. As a young boy he overheard his father and his friends talking about what was then referred to as the "Irish Question":

> As Socialists, they were in favor of the Irish being given self-government, but they shook their heads over the miserable conditions under which they lived, largely due, they considered, to their having too many children, encouraged thereto by reactionary priests to whom contraception was anathema. Thus, I was led to believe that the Irish were creating their own misery by inordinate procreation.

Later, I realized that attributing penury and undernourishment to excessive breeding was simply a device to evade responsibility for the poor and destitute.[7]

Updating his understanding of the plight of the poor decades later in southern India, Muggeridge laments, "They asked for food, and we gave them condoms."[8] But, as Muggeridge learned while visiting the people of India in their homes, the issue is not just about hunger and population. It's about quality of life:

> I got to know and like them, and visited some of their homes, where I was sure to be asked by their mothers how many children I had. When I told them I was unmarried and had none, they looked at me with the greatest sympathy.
>
> In the light of this experience of village India . . . I was not in the least surprised to learn that it was an experience in India that led Germaine Greer to alter her attitude toward alleged overpopulation, and bravely make a public announcement of the change.[9]

The poor are not necessarily impoverished. Sometimes it is the rich who are the poorest of all. Where most Americans have every modern convenience and personal luxury at their command, Africans, Indians, and Asians often have nothing but their children. Their children are their pride, their fulfillment, and even their "Social Security." By contrast, we in America are killing our children so that we can surround ourselves with careers and creature comforts which often leave us empty and unfulfilled.

Was it quality of life we were looking for? People from underdeveloped countries might point us to what Jesus taught about where we will *not* find it: "A man's life does not consist in the abundance of his possessions."[10] *Life* is where our energies ought to be directed. *Lifestyle* is fool's gold at the end of an illusive pro-choice rainbow.

Lessons from Mother Teresa

When you think of someone who epitomizes humanitarian concern, it is Mother Teresa, that frail woman of India who has become a woman of strength for the entire world. If anyone knows poverty and overpopulation up close and personal, it's Mother Teresa. Far from advocating sterilization or abortion in a society where there is abject poverty and overcrowding, a major part of her work is to rescue babies from abortion clinics.

On one occasion, two of her workers went to a Calcutta clinic where they found in a bucket eight children, still alive, who had been aborted. "They brought them to our House for Children," she said. "Three of them died after two days. One of them had been damaged so badly in her head that she is retarded. But the other four children were sent for adoption. They have brought so much joy to the lives of families who had no children."[11]

Of all the stories coming from her tireless work among the poor and diseased of India, I find this one to be among the most instructive to those of us in a pro-choice generation:

> We take care of nearly 93,000 lepers and we have been able to create rehabilitation centers for them. In every center, we make a home for the children because a child born of leprous parents is completely clean, completely healthy. So the mother has to give up the child to prevent the child from getting infected.
>
> It is very wonderful . . . very painful, to see the mother giving up the child even without kissing it. Tears roll down their faces but the love is much greater. This love is something we learn so much about from the poor people. I have never seen our people, the slum-dwellers, kill the child through abortion.[12]

The hard choices made by the disadvantaged throughout the world are more likely to be in favor of *life*, not death. No wonder, then, that Mother Teresa describes abortion as "a world evil." "It is the greatest threat to peace in the world today," she insists. "Once you have told a mother that she can kill her own child, what is there left for the rest of us?"[13]

It is here that the quality of life so revered by a pro-choice generation is betrayed. For in America, it is the *rich* who most favor abortions—not the poor. And it's mothers already having the most children who *least* abort. As a December 1989 *Los*

Angeles Times poll concluded, "Basically the higher people stand on the socioeconomic ladder, the more they support abortion."[14] This fact alone ought to put an end to the hypocritical argument from affluent upperclass liberals about the lack of public funding for abortions. Their question, "Why should rich women be able to get abortions when poor ethnic women can't?" has some interesting twists once you consider that most "poor ethnic women" don't *want* abortions.

For the underprivileged black community, pro-choice is not only a deceptive euphemism, but it also has a decidedly racist tone. While constituting 12 percent of the population, black women have 25 percent of all abortions. For every three black babies born, two are aborted. All of this in the face of polls showing overwhelming opposition to abortion among blacks. The pressure that "pro-choice" family-planning institutions put on black women to abort is hardly worthy of the label "pro-choice."

Despite this obvious targeting of the black community, it comes as no surprise that black liberal politicians, such as Jesse Jackson (formerly pro-life), now wave the politically advantageous flag of pro-choice. If Jackson and others were truly interested in the quality of life, they would push for abortion-directed public funds to be redirected to programs to help black women *enhance* their children rather than kill them.

In light of how we regard the value of life among the poor and racially oppressed underclass, Mother Teresa's words come as a stinging indictment: "The greatest disease in the world today is that of the spirit. People in the West are much poorer than those in many underdeveloped countries. People in the West suffer from a poverty of spirit. There are people who die from hunger. But hunger is not only for a piece of bread . . . there is hunger for the Word of God, hunger for love, hunger to be wanted. This is a very great disease, being unwanted."[15]

Poverty of spirit is the bane of an affluent pro-choice generation. We have not arrived; instead, we have lost our way.

Just how far we have lost our way is indicated in yet another biblical passage, about King Solomon, whose very name is synonymous with wisdom. You'll recall the story of the two prostitutes who came before Solomon upon a charge by one that the other had taken her newborn baby after accidentally killing her own. Hearing each woman testify that the other had taken the live baby for herself, Solomon ordered that the baby be cut in two, with each woman receiving half of its body.

When one of the women quickly offered to have the baby given to the other, while the other cried, "Cut him in two!" Solomon ordered that the baby be given to the woman with compassion. The willingness of the other woman to kill the child was all the evidence Solomon needed in order to know that she could not possibly be the mother.

When mothers can kill their own children—particularly with no more reason than to insure some "yuppie" notion about the quality of life—the world has gone mad! Our generation has greatly deceived itself about the meaning of human existence. We've focused in on personal freedom and things that money can buy while forgetting the value of the human spirit.

Whose Idea of Quality?

The pro-choice generation is, by and large, a generation without a sense of history. *Me* has no ties to *They* in other times and places. Therefore, we automatically assume that our values are the *only* or *best* values. For example, we forget (if we ever knew) that Depression families had six, eight, and sometimes ten or more children living in sparsely furnished houses, with no indoor plumbing.

I'm sure children in Depression families had all the problems typical of adolescents finding their way in the world, and certainly "the good old days" were not always as good as we like to remember. However, there can be no denying that Depression families made do with what little they had and found joy in the simple things of life. They had a quality of life that honored kinship and friendship. They knew the value of sacrifice and saving.

We're talking about our grandparents and, in some cases, our parents—people who often developed strong characters through the economic deprivation of those times. People who were people of faith: hardworking and honest; fulfilled people. People with a sense of values, who honored marriage commitments and weren't bothered if the soup had to be thinned out a bit to fill one more bowl at the table.

"For better or for worse, for richer or for poorer" were tested words in their day, and they passed the test. How is it that in an affluent society, where there is so little threat of "for poorer" ever happening, so many marriages fail the test? Has our pro-choice mentality given us too easy an option when we decide, for whatever reason, that "it just isn't working out"?

And what about the "unexpected pregnancies" that presented pre-Pill families with still more mouths to feed? As late as the 50's and 60's, relatively few women would have considered terminating unexpected pregnancies, even if it had been legal.

❧ How will we ever know what music, art, literature, or science we have snuffed out through abortions?

But in a pro-choice generation, an unexpected pregnancy almost begs an abortion. Yesterday's "unplanned" children are today's "unwanted" children. And "unwanted children" are prime targets of abortion. (More than half of all pregnancies each year are unintended. Half of the unintended pregnancies end in abortion.)[16] When "for better or for worse" can no longer sustain marriages, how surprising can it be that we are unwilling to accept the offspring of those marriages "for better or for worse"—whether perhaps abnormal or just "unscheduled"?

The Waste of Human Potential

In a pro-choice generation which sees itself as a human-potential generation, the *waste* of human potential is unfathomable. One out of every three babies conceived in America is aborted. If the natural mortality rate were 1 in 3, we wouldn't tolerate it. How will we ever know what music, art, literature, or science we have snuffed out through abortions? (Only a hardened cynic would suggest that we may also have snuffed out potential murderers, rapists, and Nazi dictators. No one comes out of the womb as a murderer, rapist, or twisted tyrant.)

We have already seen how easily we might have missed the inspired music of Beethoven. Have we also aborted prematurely the man who would have discovered a cure for cancer? Or the woman who would have discovered a lifesaving vaccine for AIDS?

I can't help but think of Jimmy Stewart in Frank Capra's timeless holiday classic, "It's a Wonderful Life." Stewart plays the part of George Bailey, a despondent family man who is saved from suicide by an elderly guardian angel (Angel 2nd Class, Clarence Oddbody) trying to earn his wings. When the savings-and-loan he inherited from his father meets with financial reversals despite his valiant efforts to rescue it, George Bailey begins to consider the unthinkable. "I'm worth more dead than alive," he laments.

He doesn't stop to think how he has managed to save scores of his fellow townspeople from having their homes taken away by his unscrupulous, Scrooge-like banking competitor. In panic and desperation, George finds himself at the river bridge, ready to end his life. That's when Clarence Oddbody enters the picture and teaches him some important lessons about how valuable his life has been to so many people. When George moans, "I guess it'd been better if I'd never been born at all," Oddbody grants him that wish! "You've got your wish. You've never been born. You don't exist," he curtly announces to his astonished friend.

George protests, asking, "If I wasn't born, who am I?" "You're nobody, you have no identity," says Oddbody matter-of-factly. "You've been given a great gift, George—a chance to see what the world would be like without you." Oddbody then takes George back through the town to see what it would be like in the absence of his many community-minded contributions. The town lacks any sense of decency or self-respect. People who George had helped in real life were social misfits without his influence.

"Strange, isn't it," Oddbody says to George after the time-capsule flashback. "Each man's life touches so many other lives, and when he isn't around, he leaves an awful hole, doesn't he? You see, George, you really had a wonderful life. Don't you see what a mistake it'd be to throw it away?"

At that point George realizes how much he wants to be back in the picture—to be with his family, to keep making a difference to the people in his community, to be *alive*. "I want to live!" cries George. "I want to live! I want to live! Please, God, let me live...."

Capra's touching and spirited tale has a happy ending. George returns to his home, to the clutching arms of his worried wife and children. Then, to his great surprise, his appreciative customers pour through the front door, bringing with them enough money to rescue the savings-and-loan. As everyone gathers around the Christmas tree and sings "Auld Lang Syne," you wipe away your tears and tell yourself that Oddbody was right: It truly *is* a wonderful life!

How will we ever know how many George Baileys we have aborted? Boys and girls, sons and daughters, who would have blessed our lives and grown up to contribute great things to our quality of life. I'll spare you the obvious melodramatic ending, "I want to live! I want to live! Please, God, let me live . . . " (as if from the silenced voices of aborted unborn children). But who can doubt that their deaths have left an awful hole in our society? Can we not see what a mistake it is to throw them away?

With them has died untold human potential. With them has died our own humanity. With them has died any pretense that "pro-choice" produces a wonderful life.

Abortion kills an unwanted child. The pro-choice philosophy is killing America's soul.

PART 3

❧

Resolving
Our National
Dilemma

FIFTEEN

Deciding Who Decides

Mad Hatter: "Where do you want to go?"
Alice: "I don't know."
Mad Hatter: "Then any direction will do."

—Lewis Carroll in
Alice in Wonderland

JUST WHEN YOU THINK that choice has become God, someone puts up a no-smoking sign. The pro-choice generation talks freely about pluralism, tolerance, and a person's "right to decide," but few generations have been more militantly intolerant. Disregard the no-smoking sign, for example, and you'll quickly learn that the pro-choice generation has given new meaning to the liberating words "free for all."

The "Sensitivity Police" seem to be everywhere. It's not just smoking that they're watching for, but drinking as well—at least drunkenness, at least on television. "Cheers," set in a Boston bar, would never make it to the air if proposed in the alcohol-and-drug-conscious 1990's. ("Cheers" got started in 1982.) Even so, we would be offended if Sam and his customers depicted drunkenness or used it for humor. We've come a long way from the days of Dean Martin impersonating a drunk.

But the Sensitivity Police have an odd-shaped jurisdiction: Just when smoking, drugs, and drunkenness are *out*, sex is *in*.

Or perhaps we could say that sex is *out*—out of the closet and onto our TV screens. Through the medium of television, America's living rooms are nightly hosts to homosexuality, incest, child abuse, rape, and sexually transmitted diseases. Programs such as "L.A. Law," "Hill Street Blues," "St. Elsewhere" and "thirtysomething" have conducted a frenzied race to see which of them could break the most sexual ground the fastest.

In commenting on "thirtysomething's" surprise showing of a gay couple together in bed, *Los Angeles Times* staff writer Diane Haithman points out the obvious incongruity of value judgments. Says Haithman, "While the gay relationship passed muster, the scene might not have aired had that same couple carelessly smoked a few packs of cigarettes or gotten drunk without identifying a designated driver."[1]

Pro-choice has a funny way of playing peekaboo: Now you see it, now you don't. We're pro-choice when it comes to homosexuality and abortion; we're anti-choice when it comes to child abuse, rape, smoking, and drunk driving.

Drunk driving you might figure. With drunk driving, there's a victim involved. That victim could be *us* next time. Smoking is a bit more problematic, since it's somewhat harder to prove conclusively that we get cancer from casual inhalation of other people's smoke. The smoking anathema is partly a matter of greater health consciousness and partly a matter of merely being offended. The more people who stop smoking for personal health reasons, the more people there are who simply do not like having smoke blown in their faces. We don't always need an identifiable victim before we call in the Sensitivity Police.

But where there *is* a victim, it's easier to draw the line. That's what prompts all the talk about so-called "victimless crimes." Over the years there have been campaigns for decriminalization of victimless crimes such as sodomy, prostitution, drugs, and gambling. After all, "they're only hurting themselves," we've been told naively. In the 60's we heard a call for decriminalizing the use of marijuana. In the 90's we are hearing renewed calls for legalizing *all* drugs. More and more people—including people in high places—are buying the idea that legalization is the only way to stop the violence associated with drugs. Apparently they are willing to trade one set of victims for another—a high price indeed for a pro-choice generation.

The high price of choice has also put us into a quandary regarding homosexuality. The gay lifestyle was nobody else's business until AIDS came along. Now the liberal heterosexual community is not so sure. Rightly or wrongly, heterosexuals blame homosexuals for the AIDS crisis and have begun to see that there are identifiable victims both within and without the gay community.

In San Francisco—by reputation the most sexually tolerant of American cities—voters recently rejected a law that would have permitted unmarried "domestic partners" to register their relationships at City Hall. In nearby Concord, voters repealed an AIDS-bias ordinance by 56 to 44 percent. Francie Wise, director of communicable disease control for Contra Costa County, lamented the vote, saying, "It's a hard lesson when fear and hate prevail, but I'm afraid that's the lesson we've learned."[2]

But it's not simply a case of toleration reaching its limit, or of latent homophobic hatred finally piercing the surface; it's a matter of coming face-to-face with shocking victims amid the rubble of moral chaos. We are not a people who appreciate abstract moralizing; morals are personal and morals are private. But show us a victim and you will get our attention—particularly if you and I might be that victim.

The problem is that the line we draw between "victimless crimes" and moral conduct involving identifiable victims has never been satisfactory. Are we really to believe, for example, that there are no victims in prostitution? Does one have to spell out the many ways in which the prostitutes themselves are victims of both the pimps and the men who objectify them for selfish sexual servicing? And are we to believe that there are no victims when a man gambles away the rent and grocery money needed by his family? A closer look behind the scenes will reveal how even legalized gambling feeds organized crime syndicates with their own stable of unmistakable victims.

No matter how shadowy the line, we continue to draw it at the point where recognizable victims are involved. It's all the more curious, then, that we should tolerate demands for abortion. If indeed it might be argued that drugs, homosexuality, and prostitution are victimless activities, and therefore off-limits to public censure, no similar argument can be made in favor of abortion. With drugs, homosexuality, and prostitution, a woman might plausibly make a case for having control over her own body. Perhaps society could tolerate a morality which adversely affects one's own self. But abortion is an altogether different story. With abortion, there is *always* a victim.

Clouding the Issue with Tolerance

"Who Decides?" is the latest question being asked by pro-choice advocates regarding abortion, as if the obvious and only answer is *women*. It's an interesting question, given the no-smoking signs, the threat of AIDS, and even the hearings into the Iran-Contra affair. When it comes to any number of activities in which individuals have made personal value choices, we are quite happy to say, *"We* decide!" Sometimes, as with smoking, it is less a matter of identifiable victims as it is a simple matter of having our "space" invaded.

> ❧ *Beauty* may be in the eye of the beholder, but *human existence* doesn't have that luxury.

"Cosmos" creator Carl Sagan asks the question that other pro-choice advocates also send our way: "Why should legislators have any right at all to tell women what to do with their bodies? To be deprived of reproductive freedom is demeaning. Women are fed up with being pushed around."[3] But Sagan knows where the crux of the issue lies. He is well aware of the limits of tolerance:

> And yet, by consensus, all of us think it proper that there be prohibitions against, and penalties exacted for, murder. It would be a flimsy defense if the murderer pleads that this is just between him and his victim and none of the government's business. If killing a fetus is truly killing a human being, is it not the *duty* of the state to prevent it? Indeed, one of the chief functions of government is to protect the weak from the strong.[4]

For Sagan, and for most of us, the issue is clear: If the fetus is a human being, it is a victim. And if it is a victim, the abortion debate is over. Whatever activity we might contemplate, the pro-choice philosophy loses all validity when someone else has to die.

That's why the abortion debate is not a matter of tolerance. That's why the question of "Who Decides" never gets to the real issue. That's why pro-choice, standing alone, cannot be the *right* choice. The debate over abortion will never cease until the issue of fetal personhood is decided once and for all. And by its very nature that issue cannot be resolved individually, as a personal decision. *Beauty* may be in the eye of the beholder, but *human existence* doesn't have that luxury.

So how are we going to resolve the issue? Through social dialogue and public referendum? Pro-choice advocates are panicked at the very thought! What else could possibly explain all the uproar in the wake of the *Webster* decision, in which the Supreme Court seemed to throw the issue of abortion control back into the hands of state legislatures? Dialogue and referendum take us beyond mere "choice" to *value judgments* about choice, where one's choices must undergo moral scrutiny: no more free rides; no more winning by default.

> **What better way to squelch at least 50 percent of the dialogue about abortion? With one stroke you simply disenfranchise the whole of the male population.**

In their hearts, pro-choice advocates know they can't win on the merits. That's why the debate is always couched in terms of "choice." And the tactic works! In a pro-choice generation, even people who are anti-abortion like to think of themselves as being pro-choice. After all, choice is the American way! Tolerance is our greatest virtue. Moral judgment is a private affair. Unless, that is, your moral judgment happens to be anti-choice in the matter of abortion. At that point pro-choice advocates smell judgmental smoke and immediately call the Sensitivity Police.

Disenfranchising Male Opponents to Abortion

If you happen to be a man, you are well aware by now that the Sensitivity Police have an automatic right to apprehend you for even daring to question what is unquestionably "a woman's issue." "How can a man possibly understand a woman's reproductive needs?" we are asked by women already angry about male dominance over their lives. What better way to squelch at least 50 percent of the dialogue about abortion? With one stroke you simply disenfranchise the whole of the male population.

However, that is where the obvious fallacy lies. Not all men are either anti-abortion or anti-choice. Many men are quite happy to be tolerant on the issue of abortion, to let a woman decide. In fact, it is amazing how tolerant men can be on the issue, especially when a woman in their life announces unexpectedly that she is pregnant!

❧ Out of the womb, child abuse is everybody's business. But inside the womb, it's "a woman's right to decide."

"Pro-choice advocates love to refer to their male supporters as "men of conscience." Apparently that means a man is entitled to an opinion on "a woman's issue" if he *agrees* that women should have a right to decide, but must keep quiet if he *disagrees*. What a convenient way to win a debate!

Of course, this approach is a no-win situation for today's liberated male. He is *expected* to have his consciousness raised on issues such as rape, "date-rape," sexual harassment, and child abuse. What woman of the 90's would respect a man who is aware of child abuse and does nothing about it? But if he happens to have his consciousness raised to the point of thinking that abortion is the *ultimate* child abuse, he is out-of-bounds even to make the suggestion. Out of the womb, child abuse is everybody's business. There can be no such thing as "choice" or tolerance. But inside the womb, it's "a woman's right to decide."

Carl Sagan and Ann Druyan point out that the line of demarcation is not that easily drawn:

> Does a woman's "innate right to control her own body" include the right to kill a near-term fetus who is, for all intents and purposes, identical to a newborn child?

We believe that many supporters of reproductive freedom are troubled at least occasionally by
this question. But they are reluctant to raise it
because it is the beginning of a slippery slope. If it is
impermissible to abort a pregnancy in the ninth
month, what about the eighth, seventh, sixth . . . ?
Once we acknowledge that the state can interfere at
any time in the pregnancy, doesn't it follow that the
state can interfere at all times?[5]

As for themselves, Sagan and Druyan would draw an arbitrary line only at the point where fetal thinking occurs, after
which the state could no longer act, but they have nevertheless
correctly identified the basic problem: Abortion is not "a
woman's issue" simply because the unborn baby is in the womb.
As a man, Carl Sagan is as entitled to make a judgment about
state interests in the unborn fetus as is his wife, Ann Druyan, a
woman. In resolving the national referendum over abortion,
feminists will have to do better than positioning Sensitivity
Police around the ballot box to prevent "No" votes from men
who happen to disagree. Moral issues cannot be resolved by
inverse sexism.

The Intolerance of Tolerance

In a recent issue of *The Atlantic*, I read with interest Neil
Postman's article "Learning by Story," in which he took issue
with E. D. Hirsch, Jr's., much-discussed list of 5000 names,
dates, aphorisms, and concepts that Hirsch believes a literate
person ought to know. By way of response, Postman also discussed Allan Bloom's *The Closing of the American Mind*, including
this observation:

His complaint is that most American professors
have lost their nerve. They have become moral rela-
tivists, which means that they are not capable of
providing their students with a clear understanding
of what is right thought and proper behavior.[6]

It should surprise no one that tolerance is more comfortable
with moral *relativity* than with moral *absolutes*. Hence you would

expect to find relative morality and social tolerance being taught in tandem in today's halls of higher education. (And from grade school up, for that matter.) But you might be greatly surprised to learn that the teaching of relative values and the virtue of tolerance has turned ugly on American campuses. Today's all-American tolerance, it seems, is liberal *intolerance* in disguise.

I mention Postman's article simply as a vehicle to underscore the point. On the same pages where he is quoting Professor Bloom's concern about the teaching of moral relativism in the nation's universities appears an ad for *Yellow Silk*, a "Journal of Erotic Arts." The ad promises "fiction, poetry, art, reminiscences, and reviews of material that celebrate the erotic in a way that manages to be both tasteful and juicy." But the kicker is a one-liner beneath the picture of a bare-breasted beauty lying in repose in a cool garden setting: "All persuasions; no brutality." *All* persuasions? But what if mine *is* brutality? Choice, unless it's the *wrong* choice? Tolerance except for the intolerable?

Certainly I'm not making a case here for brutality. The point is that, amid academia's praise for moral relativity, the advocates of pluralism and tolerance on America's campuses have arbitrarily decided what will be tolerated and what will not. Much like Hirsch's list, a checklist of toleration has been created to indicate what each of us must accept in order to maintain our credentials as a tolerant American. To the liberal mind, our choices must fall within the approved guidelines, or else those choices will not be tolerated.

What falls onto the list is very interesting in itself. If morals truly are relative, as the listmakers would have us believe, then *sensitivity* is all that's left. Morality is as capricious as it is arbitrary. It becomes trendy and manipulatable. In such a climate, sensitivity training replaces moral standards—and with a vengeance. Try speaking up for absolute moral standards and you'll quickly discover just how insensitive today's pro-choice generation can be.

The Language of Intolerance

Columnist George F. Will has been following the Sensitivity Police around on American campuses and has submitted this report:

Many schools have adopted stringent codes stipulating impermissible speech. Such codes often come in a package with mandatory "awareness" classes. These are inflicted by sensitivity tutors. Their task is to make students "aware" of officially approved thinking about race, "sexual preference" and other items of liberal orthodoxy. The proliferating rules proscribe speech that "slurs" or "stereotypes" or "stigmatizes" or "victimizes."[7]

The words drawing the attention of the Sensitivity Police are not just "nigger" and "honky." No one needs to be reminded that those words are off-limits. However, dare refer to homosexuals in the mildest of negative terms—even in humor (*especially* in humor?)—and the red lights begin to flash.

The pro-choice generation is not known for its sense of humor. Today's tolerance walks around with a singularly dour expression on its face. George Will notes that "the grim administrators of moral uplift at the University of Connecticut are empowered to punish students for 'inappropriately directed laughter.' "[8]

As for speech which "stereotypes" and "stigmatizes," once again it depends upon whose cage is being rattled at the time. If "queer" is definitely *out*, "homophobic"—pronounced with equal venom—is quite fashionably *in*. And when it comes to the abortion debate, nothing could be more stereotypical than dismissing all abortion opponents (including Catholics, Jews, and even atheists) as "fundamentalists," or even "pro-lifers," inevitably pronounced with an unmistakable tone of derision. The Sensitivity Police turn a deaf ear to the slurs of those who have put them on the payroll. Choice has civic approval, whatever it does; anti-choice, no matter how kindly spoken, is antisocial and un-American.

Today's assault against free expression on college campuses—by those who claim to cherish free speech and who demand it for themselves in the form of "academic freedom"—is nothing if not astounding. What it reflects is the extent to which self-proclaimed liberals are prepared to go in order to win moral debates by default. If they can ridicule others out of their true beliefs (by calling them "homophobic" or "fundamentalists"), then they have already won the battle.

Conspiracy of Silence

The most ironic aspect of the pro-choice generation is that it is anything but pro-choice. When one thinks of choice, one thinks of options, alternative points of view, and different sides. On a university campus, one thinks of academic inquiry, dialogue, and debate. But today there is only an eerie silence. If it happens at all, it happens with hushed tones, whispers, and furtive glances to monitor who might be listening. Sure, noisy pro-choice and pro-life rallies present us with a battle of the banners. But one would hardly mistake all that clamor for reasoned discussion of the issues. Where is that kind of dialogue taking place? How are we ever going to decide "Who Decides"?

"More than at any time in memory," observes George Will, "there are many subjects 'too sensitive' to talk about freely on campuses that are patrolled by prowling sensitivity-police.[9] From my experience as a law professor, I suggest that doesn't even take the presence of prowling sensitivity monitors. We now have a whole generation of students who have grown up on a steady diet of moral relativism, egalitarian values, and social tolerance. Rather than inculcating a sense of openness and civility, today's "value neutral" education has served to put a lid on legitimate, respectful, open discussion of "sensitive" subjects.

Professor Bloom has hit the nail on the head when he laments the closing of the American mind. Militant openness has resulted only in mandatory conformism. We know nothing but the party line, and will accept no substitutes. Not even any talk of them.

Today's campus, ringed with Sensitivity Police, is simply the most glaring indication of how tolerance has become intolerant. Normally no holds are barred in the ivory tower of academia. That there are now some subjects simply "too sensitive" to discuss, even in an academic setting, is a telling commentary on both the closed-mindedness of a pro-choice generation and the pro-choice strategy of victory by default. However, we should not think that the Sensitivity Police are restricted to the nation's campuses.

Journalist John Leo tells of a friend who recently ventured two opinions at a fashionable Manhattan dinner party: "1) That there are too many abortions in America, and 2) that abortion is a serious moral issue that is too often treated in a frivolous way." Leo vouches that his friend happens to be pro-choice, but notes that it was not enough to save him from his "reputation-wrecking gaffe." According to Leo, "Tongues wagged and gossip flew along phone lines. His own wife didn't speak to him for three days."

"What accounts for this astonishing and touchy orthodoxy?" ask Leo. Two factors, as he sees it:

> First, any urban gathering is bound to have one or two guests who have had abortions. When a male brings up qualms about abortion, these women are apt to think their abortion decisions are being second-guessed by someone who will never face the dilemma. Because of the reckless way the issue is treated these days, they may even think they are about to be accused of murder. Or the buried anguish they may feel about their abortions may well up and spill over as bitter argument. Men like my friend think they can keep the discussion safely abstract, but it never works. Beneath the orthodoxy there is too much unfocused conflict.[10]

It is John Leo's second factor that is perhaps more troublesome in the larger picture:

> Because journalists tend to accept liberal values, and because they generally agree with feminists, as I do, that male-dominated society has distorted women's lives, they tend to go along with feminist arguments, even in the highly debatable area of abortion. They tend to dispense with their objections.[11]

What Leo suggests here is not limited to journalists or college professors. Once the pro-choice philosophy of "live and let live" works its way into our mentality, and once we have a whole generation of people who have been weaned on the importance of women's rights, we tend to have an automatic response to the issue of abortion. Without stopping to ask whether there are any other compelling interests to consider, once we identify abortion as a matter of "women's rights," the pro-choice generation is already conditioned—Pavlovian-like—to support it.

In an age when discrimination is taboo, we haven't learned how to discriminate. In fact, as the opposite of discrimination, indiscriminateness has become a moral imperative.[12] Why then should we expect a pro-choice generation to sort out the difference between women's rights where no victim is involved, and women's rights where human life is in the balance?

As Johnny Carson says of comedic gags which stretch credibility to a breaking point, "If you buy the premise, you buy the bit." Even with credibility stretched far beyond the breaking point (since abortion involves an obvious victim), a liberated generation blithely says, "If it's a matter of women's rights, pro-choice on abortion simply *has* to be right, doesn't it?" Carson is at his funniest, of course, when the skit dies. When an unborn baby has to die because we slavishly adhere to social conditioning about women's rights, there's nothing funny about it. With human life at stake, it's time to rethink the premise.

Is Tolerance a Virtue?

All of us, I suppose, have taken it for granted that tolerance is a virtue. Certainly we would each hope that what we believe has the respect of other people, even if they happen to disagree with us. And few of us really want to be in the business of deciding what is acceptable behavior for everybody else. There is already enough unacceptable baggage to deal with in our own lives. But neither have we abandoned altogether being our brother's keeper. Just let the Ku Klux Klan resurrect lynching, or have some group of neo-Nazis talk about exterminating Jews again, and we will all throw down our pro-choice banners and become the most intolerant people you ever saw—and rightfully so. They could talk all day long about their "right to decide," but we wouldn't tolerate it.

Under those circumstances not one of us is going to say, "I'm personally against lynching and genocide, but I don't want to impose my values on others." When innocent life is at stake, we realize that we can no longer be pro-choice. At that point, pro-choice is license to kill.

In the battle over abortion, the question simply cannot be framed as one of tolerance. If an unborn baby is *not* a human life worthy of protection, then let a woman decide whether to have an abortion. On the other hand, if an unborn baby *is in fact* a human life worthy of protection, then a woman can have no choice. When innocent life is at stake, we have no choice but to protect it. To do otherwise would be to invoke the tyranny of tolerance.

In *The Rights of Man*, Thomas Paine reminds us that "toleration is not the *opposite* of intoleration, but is the *counterfeit* of it. Both are despotisms. The one assumes to itself the right of withholding liberty of conscience, and the other of granting it. The one is the pope, armed with fire and faggot, and the other is the pope selling or granting indulgences. The former is church and state, and the latter is church and traffic."[13] Pro-choice on the matter of abortion is not a virtue. It is not a matter of good-spirited, all-American tolerance. Pro-choice grants a liberty of conscience over life and death that none of us is entitled to exercise.

Saying no to pro-choice on the issue of abortion is not for the purpose of imposing our values on others. It is to keep others from imposing their values upon those who, because they are powerless to defend themselves, will never have a chance to choose their own values.

SIXTEEN

The Way Forward

A politician thinks of the next election; a statesman of the next generation.

—J. F. Clarke

ON JANUARY 22, 1973 IN THE CASE OF *ROE V. WADE*, the U. S. Supreme Court surprised the nation by striking down the abortion laws of most states and severely limiting the states' power to regulate abortion.[1]

To appreciate the significance of this ruling, it should be noted that from time immemorial until 1803 abortion had been a canon law crime under ecclesiastical (church) jurisdiction. Although some commentators are suspicious as to how an essentially religious law found its way into the English common law, the fact is that abortion *did* become recognized as part of the common law as early as 1644, as reflected in Coke's *Third Institute*. According to Coke (a respected legal commentator cited by early authorities), aborting the fetus of a woman "quick with child" was a misdemeanor offense.

However correct or incorrect Coke's analysis of existing law might have been in 1644, it is clear that subsequent legal authorities followed his lead. Sir Matthew Hale in his *History of the Pleas of the Crown* in 1736 confirmed abortion to be a misdemeanor at common law, as did Sir William Blackstone in his well-known *Commentaries* in 1765. The importance of this legal history is that American law was based substantially upon the English common law at the time our nation was founded. It is this law, for example, with which the writers of our Constitution would have been familiar.

Despite the well-established common law precedent making abortion a crime, there is little evidence of abortion prosecutions taking place throughout the 17th and 18th centuries, apparently owing to both a widespread moral consensus against the act and the lack of effective means to achieve an abortion. However, in the 19th century a spate of state statutes regulating and outlawing abortions began to replace the earlier common-law misdemeanor. During this period there was growing concern that new abortifacients threatened the lives of women seeking to terminate their pregnancies. It was these state statutes which *Roe v. Wade* struck down.

Far more important, and what must never be forgotten, is that the Court in *Roe v. Wade* blithely overturned centuries of precedent in which abortion had been considered both morally and legally unacceptable. Never before nor since has there been such sweeping disregard for fundamental morality in the halls of American justice.

Specifically, the Court held that in the *first* trimester of pregnancy a decision to abort must be left to the woman and the medical judgment of her physician. From that point up to the point of viability—basically the *second* trimester—the state may regulate the abortion procedure if restrictions are related to the health of the mother. Subsequent to viability—essentially the *third* trimester—"the State in promoting its interest in the potentiality of human life may, if it chooses, regulate, and even proscribe, abortion" except where it is necessary to preserve the mother's life or health.

By this decision, therefore, individual states were *permitted*, but not *required*, to regulate abortions in the second trimester and to forbid them in the third. If a given state decided neither to regulate nor to forbid abortions under the Court's guidelines, abortions in that state could be legal throughout the entire nine months of a pregnancy—up to the day a baby is born, if so desired by the mother. In a worst-case scenario, if a state were not to act in regulating abortion, nothing in the language of *Roe v. Wade* would prevent the killing of a near-term child even if a woman decides at the last minute that she simply doesn't want to experience the pain of giving birth.

By contrast with that seemingly stark possibility, virtually all states have in fact enacted *some* form of abortion regulation and have generally forbidden abortions in the third trimester, except where the mother's life would be threatened. An example of such state regulation is found in the widely disputed 1989 case of *Webster v. Reproductive Health Services*. In *Webster*, a bitterly divided Court held that a Missouri statute was Constitutional in requiring that, before performing an abortion on a woman 20 or more weeks pregnant, the physician must first determine whether the unborn is viable.

That "fine tuning" of *Roe v. Wade* was hardly the disaster that pro-choice advocates have bewailed ever since, nor the major victory that pro-life advocates have thought it to be. State regulation is still where the ballgame is to be won or lost. No new Constitutional ground was covered in *Webster*.

Time to Overturn Roe v. Wade?

So where do we go from here? Should *Roe v. Wade* be overturned? If so, how? The answer to the first question is clearly "Yes!" As it stands, *Roe v. Wade* gives Constitutional protection to abortion in individual states which might wish *not* to regulate or forbid it. Given that latitude, the laws of individual states do not go far enough in the protection of human life in the womb. Indeed, under *Roe v. Wade* they *cannot* protect life in the first trimester, and even under *Webster* they are fairly limited in protecting life in the second trimester.

From almost any perspective, the decision in *Roe v. Wade* is a judicial calamity. In "balancing the interests" (which, sadly, is the only alternative for judicial review once absolute moral values are rejected) the Court demonstrated a dreadful paucity of moral insight. Employing the language of "right of privacy," the Court elevated a woman's right of choice over the value of developing human life. Such a moral gaffe is all the more remarkable in light of the highly questionable Constitutional basis for the so-called "right of privacy" in the first place.

Certainly *Roe v. Wade* was not the first case to talk about a "right of privacy." This novel concept had been developed in the earlier case of *Griswold v. Connecticut*, which dealt with the use of contraceptives by married couples (a seemingly benign use of "right of privacy," given the high moral ground of marital relations). But even by the time of *Roe v. Wade*, the Court was still unsure where exactly the "right of privacy" was to be found in the Constitution. Note, for example, this implicit admission in the *Roe* decision:

> The right of privacy, whether it be founded in the Fourteenth Amendment's concept of personal liberty and restrictions upon state action, as we feel it is, or, as the District Court determined, in the Ninth Amendment's reservation of rights to the people, is broad enough to encompass a woman's decision whether or not to terminate her pregnancy.[2]

Unable to pinpoint just exactly where in the Constitution the so-called "right of privacy" was to be found, the Court nevertheless was certain that, wherever it might be located, it was "broad enough" to permit abortions! In this unprecedented fishing expedition, the Court was sure it had come back with a very big fish, despite the fact that no one could ever prove there had been such a fish of any size swimming around in the murky waters of Constitutional language.

But even if one were to allow such a judicial *fabrication*, one can hardly overlook the judicial *legislation* which followed on its heels. It would be one thing if the Court judicially legislated in a matter such as racial integration. Whatever opinion a person might have regarding court-ordered busing to achieve racial balance in public schools, there is at least a Constitutional foundation for such judicial action. Without any question, racial discrimination violates the Constitutional guarantee of equal protection.

By contrast, in *Roe v. Wade* the Court judicially legislated such novel concepts as "trimesters" and "viability" on the strength of an already-judicially-fabricated "right of privacy." As the country gentleman reputedly said, "If we had any ham, we could have ham and eggs, if we had any eggs!" Either fabrication without legislation, or legislation without fabrication, might possibly pass muster. But judicial fabrication bolstered by judicial legislation is simply asking too much.

Putting the Cat Back into the Bag

It is in this abuse of judicial power as a "Superlegislature" that *Roe v. Wade* is vulnerable to attack by the current Court. There is already precedent for the Court to turn its back on a prior decision, by acknowledging that it had no right to act as a "Superlegislature" in the first place—in other words, in a given case, that what was called a *judicial* decision was actually a *political* decision.[3] Significantly, that precedent came in an area of Constitutional law far more settled than the gossamerlike "right of privacy." Therefore one would hope that, at a minimum, the current Court would overturn *Roe v. Wade* on this precedent-laden judicial basis.

In this way the Court could deprive abortion of any supposed Constitutional justification and thereby give its approval to state legislation prohibiting abortion altogether (or perhaps with limited exceptions), as long as such legislation met a "rational basis" test. Without question, the protection of human life in the womb would stand as an eminently rational law, deserving at least the same level of protection as racial equality.

If it wished to do so, of course, the U. S. Supreme Court could take even more affirmative action in protecting human life in the womb, on the basis of the Fourteenth Amendment's equal-protection clause. Many states, such as California, now prohibit the unlawful killing of a fetus (interpreted to mean a "viable" fetus). The intent, of course, is to punish anyone other than the mother who intentionally kills such a viable, unborn fetus. An equal-protection argument could run in either of two directions: 1) protecting a viable fetus from being killed by its own mother, just as it is protected from an unlawful killing by anyone else; or 2) protecting *all* unborn fetuses—whether viable or not—just as *viable* fetuses are now protected by the laws of homicide.

The equal-protection arguments are straightforward: 1) If human life is worthy of protection from all third parties other than the mother, it is equally worthy of protection from its own mother; and 2) since any distinction between "viable" and "nonviable" fetuses is arbitrary, or at best inventively contrived (not to mention shifting with every advance in medical technology), no valid distinction can be made in the protection given to one type of fetus as opposed to the other. A more overarching equal-protection argument would hold that the protection of *newborn* infants from infanticide—a protection given by all states—must equally extend to *unborn* infants, without whom there would be no newborn infants.

The importance of the equal-protection approach is that unborn human life would be accorded *Constitutional* protection. The shoe would then be on the other foot: No longer could individual state legislatures *permit* abortions any more than they could choose to permit racial discrimination. No longer would lower courts have the liberty to elevate women's rights over the interests to be protected in unborn human life.

Under the current climate of national debate, however, this approach is probably more than one might reasonably expect from the Court. More likely is a return to the pre-*Roe v. Wade* stance in which states are permitted to regulate or prohibit abortion as they best see fit.

In the absence of any recognized Constitutional protection for the unborn, we will always and interminably be locked in an impasse between pro-choice and pro-life advocates from one state to the next. Legislative battles will be endless, and gubernatorial vetoes will be the subject of enterprising oddsmakers. Unborn babies in the womb will be kicked around forever as a political football. There is no escaping the dilemma: Pro-choice advocates *will* not relent, and pro-life advocates *cannot*.

Amending the Constitution

If the abortion controversy is ever to be put to rest, it most likely will have to come in the form of a Constitutional amendment—itself a political process with all the built-in difficulties already mentioned. The advantage of *this* political referendum, however, would be to settle the issue once and for all. Once for all *time*, and once for all *jurisdictions*. No more fads in point of view. No more bitter, unresolved civil war.

A Constitutional amendment would also have the advantage of clarifying the present Constitution. Any argument that the Constitution is too vaguely worded to encompass a right of protection for the unborn, or that "state action" must be shown before the power of the Court is invoked, would no longer pose a problem. The law would be clear, unequivocal, and fairly decided.

Who knows whether a Constitutional amendment to guarantee protection to unborn human life is possible at the present time? Although those who personally oppose abortion outnumber those who support it, today's pro-choice sentiment is at a fever pitch. Certainly no Constitutional amendment appearing to threaten a woman's right to decide would be viable until the issue of personal choice is clearly distinguished from the issue of abortion itself. So far, the pro-choice generation has lacked either the sophistication or the will to make that distinction.

So for the time being we may be left with skirmishes at the state level over the many sub-issues which seem to accompany the controversy: Whether minors seeking abortions should be required to notify one or perhaps both parents; whether there should be "waiting periods" or perhaps pre-abortion counseling; whether public funding ought to be available in support of abortions for those who cannot afford them. Like the first Civil War, our present conflict is set to last far beyond what anyone on either side would wish.

The Focus of Legislation

Looking down the road, when pro-life advocates consider prohibiting abortion through legislation, it is important for them to handle carefully the legal concept of murder for women who have abortions. As previously discussed, not all criminal homicides are automatically classified as murder. Given the anguished decision made by many women who choose to abort, the more appropriate classification for many cases might be manslaughter. Manslaughter denotes the presence of mitigating circumstances, consistent with the moral ambivalence which many women experience.

For women who have abortions coldly and calculatedly, it may be right to refer to abortion as murder. However, it is ultimately only God who can judge the moral severity with which women will be held accountable.

As a practical matter, when some pro-life advocates talk in terms of abortion being "murder," the public often assumes that pro-life legislation would jail women who have abortions (just like any other cold-blooded murderer) for 25 years to life. However, that notion plays into the hands of the pro-choice propaganda which suggests that under pro-life legislation women will be jailed as vicious criminals.

Historically, a woman seeking an abortion has not been the target of abortion statutes. Nor would she be the target under a

Roe v. Wade reversal. Just as in statutes prior to *Roe v. Wade*, the proper target is *the physician or other person who performs illegal abortions*. Cut off the availability of legal abortions, and for the most part abortions will cease. It is the same principle—already in place in several jurisdictions—in which statutes punish the *supplier* of illegal marijuana but not the *user*. No one is eager to throw women into jail for having illegal abortions. The idea is to *deter* them from having abortions in the first place.

> ঌ That we could even seriously consider the eventual possibility of over-the-counter death of unborn children is a mark of how far we have gone in a pro-choice generation.

If it should be argued that many women would then seek illegal abortions, the fact is that there is little the state could do in legal terms from that point forward in any case. Women who choose to go outside the law would be doing so at their own risk, both physically and morally. But at the very least the state would have ceased to be in complicity with the killing of unborn children. And that is a statement which *must* be made in whatever way it can be made. (Of course, the greater statement would be to support women in ways which will not make abortion the only apparent option.)

Death in a Pill

Unlike pre-*Roe v. Wade* abortion statutes, future legislation will have to reach beyond illegal abortionists to deal with new technology which promises to revolutionize the manner in which pregnancies are terminated. Perhaps no scientific development in our time has more potential for condemning our collective conscience than the new French-developed RU-486 abortion pill. What it achieves, of course, is nothing different from any other means of abortion: It terminates a pregnancy; it kills a newly conceived life. Yet what it potentially represents in the public mind is an outrageous statement about the legitimacy of "over-the-counter death."

For many feminists, the prospect of RU-486 (or some pill like it) being introduced into the United States signals a welcomed end to male-dominated medical abortions. As popularly perceived, RU-486 may be taken in the privacy of the home, economically and with relative ease. In truth, RU-486 is designed for supervised *clinical* use—not for unsupervised *in-home* use; and its threat to women's health has been criminally understated. Actually, many feminists are adamantly in agreement with that evaluation. The prospect of RU-486 has split feminists right down the middle.

The most damning evidence against RU-486 has finally surfaced—ironically at the very core of attempts to achieve population control and a better quality of life in China. Because of potential adverse side-effects from unsupervised use in rural areas of China, RU-486 has now been withdrawn from the most pro-abortion nation in the world.

Given that evidence, one can only wonder in amazement at how Planned Parenthood and NOW activists can steadfastly persist in their demand that the United States test RU-486 and begin the Food and Drug Administration approval process. How could the interests of women ever be engulfed in more abject confusion?

The real problem is that the debate over RU-486 is in the wrong venue. The principal reason the drug is running under a yellow caution flag in the United States is concern about safety and legal liability, not about the morality of its use. Even if RU-486 were certifiably safe for women, its widespread use would make a social statement almost beyond belief: that human life can be *taken* with the same ease as it can be *prevented*.

Since its introduction as a widely used contraceptive, "the Pill" has made its own statement about sexual freedom. If the Pill brought an enhanced quality of life for married women, it also played a significant role in creating a sexually promiscuous society. And it is not without its own share of blame for health risks to women. But whatever other adverse consequences it may have brought into play, the Pill *prevents* conception of new life rather than *killing* new life once it is conceived. By contrast, RU-486 is specifically designed to kill innocent human life. That we could even seriously consider the eventual possibility of over-the-counter death of unborn children is a mark of how far we have gone in a pro-choice generation.

Pornography used to be on the back shelf, if at all. Condoms used to be behind the counter. Now it's all up front with glossy covers and slick advertising. If some people have their way, we will see the day when abortions come packaged in plastic bottles with brand names like "Oops!" and "Second Chance." Abortion-by-vending-machine will make abortion-on-demand look absolutely antiquated! For many people any future abortion pill will be the ultimate guarantor of the selfish "good life."

Speaking at the 1989 American Medical Association conference for science writers, Dr. Etienne-Emile Baulieu, developer of RU-486, explained the *social* significance of an abortion pill. "In practical terms, choice is synonymous with freedom," said Dr. Baulieu. "Science cannot dictate how we believe," but it can increase people's choices and improve their quality of life.[4]

"Freedom," "choice," and "quality of life." With all that going for it, who could object to an "abortion pill"? However, what few people stop to consider is the natural progression of the pro-choice philosophy outlined by Dr. Baulieu. He stopped short of the full explanation, which is this: *Quality of life* in a pro-choice generation is synonymous with the *right to choose*; which is synonymous with *freedom*; which, in the case of RU-486, is synonymous with *freedom to kill*; which, because of the nature of the victim, is synonymous with *freedom to kill an innocent human being*.

Without question, RU-486 and its inevitable commercially produced successors must be thwarted by appropriate legislation. Pro-choice must not be allowed to accomplish through the back door what is forbidden through the front door. Death in a pill is no different from death at the end of a suction tube, unless by its ease of availability it becomes even more pernicious.

But Can Morality Be Legislated?

If there is any one statement about which everyone seems to be in agreement, it is that "morality can't be legislated." The idea is that one person's morality is as good as another's, so society is not at liberty to adopt moral standards through legislation. But if there is any one statement about which everyone seems to be overlooking the obvious, it is the same statement: that "morality can't be legislated." As Judge Robert H. Bork has put it, "Indeed . . . we legislate little else."[5]

Bork is also correct in pointing out that "if the statement that one man's moral judgment is as good as another's were taken seriously, it would be impossible to see how law on any subject could be permitted to exist. After all, one man's larceny is another's just distribution of goods."[6]

However, Bork freely admits that even he did not always appreciate that point. In the spirit of academic candor, Bork relates the story of a seminar on constitutional theory which he taught along with Alex Bickel. In the seminar, Bork says he took the position that it was "no business of society what conduct that did not harm another person took place out of sight." Bickel then posed a hypothetical:

> Suppose, he said, that on an offshore island there lived a man who raised puppies entirely for the pleasure of torturing them to death. The rest of us are not required to witness the torture, nor can we hear the screams of the animals. We just know what is taking place and we are appalled. Can it be that we have no right, constitutionally or morally, to enact legislation against such conduct and to enforce it against the sadist?

Bork says he cannot remember what answer he gave, but he now realizes that Bickel was right. "Morality, standing alone, is a sufficient rationale to support legislation."[7]

"There is no objection," Bork reminds us, "to segregation or even to slavery other than moral disapproval."[8] More pointedly, as recently as 1986 the Supreme Court upheld—at least as to homosexual sodomy—a Georgia statute making all sodomy criminal.[9] To that list I would add virtually all criminal laws, from "Thou shalt not kill" on down. Where do we think we got such laws? Simply out of a secular vacuum, or solely as a matter of social contract?

Perhaps no laws better illustrate the point that morality *can* be legislated than the so-called "statutory rape" laws, which criminally punish a man for having sexual relations with an "underaged female." The age limit itself has varied from 18 all the way down to 14, even in modern times. However, the law's thrust has always been the same: the protection of underaged women from male sexual aggression. It's a matter of morality—nothing less.

What's more, it is a matter of strict liability. We don't take any alleged ignorance as an excuse. Even in the last two decades of sexual liberation, only California has dared to give any defense at all to a man who claims to have been mistaken about the young woman's age. Other jurisdictions have specifically refused to follow California's lead.

Even more surprising is the fact that a man may be put in jail if convicted of "statutory rape," when for no other strict liability offense would so severe a punishment be allowed. Sexual liberation or no sexual liberation, Americans have a low tolerance for moral manipulation of the sexually naive.

ᴈ If *"religious* extremists" must not be allowed to impose their narrow beliefs, why should *secular* extremists?

Because "statutory rape" is rarely the subject of actual prosecution, it may speak to another aspect of legislating morality, to be discussed shortly. But make no doubt about it, morality *can* be legislated, and it *is* legislated. In fact, hardly any phrase is more familiar to lawyers than "the state's police power to regulate conduct adversely affecting the community's peace, health, safety, *morals*, and general welfare."

Should Morality Be Legislated?

However, simply because morality *can be* and is legislated does not necessarily mean that morality *should be* legislated. No one seriously proposes that all morality ought to be the subject of oppressive laws. Even if one could prove envy, greed, hatred, or misdirected lust, such immoral motives taken by themselves do not fall within the boundaries of man-made laws. (Nor would even outwardly-manifested immoral *acts* be worthy of the law's scrutiny in every case.)

When it comes to an issue like abortion, pro-choice advocates believe adamantly that there is no place for pro-life morality in legislative halls. Kate Michelman, executive director of the National Abortion Rights Action League (NARAL) has offered a letter presenting just that concept, in the hope that *Woman's Day, Family Circle, Good Housekeeping,* and *Ladies' Home*

Journal might publish the letter for their readers. When at the invitation of Helen Gurley Brown the editors of those magazines recently met with the editors of more politically-activist publications, such as *Ms.* and *Cosmopolitan*, the letter was presented as one which readers could send to state and federal legislators.

The letter says in part, "Religious extremists must not be allowed to impose their narrow beliefs on society as a whole; rather, each of us must be permitted to heed our own conscience and faith."[10] If *"religious* extremists" must not be allowed to impose their narrow beliefs, why should *secular* extremists? The belief that a woman should be able to kill her unborn child is just as much a moral belief as is the personal conviction that doing so is wrong. In such a case, one person's *immorality* is another's *morality*. In truth, it is the *pro-abortion* morality that has already been imposed upon a nation which—counting heads—is personally opposed to abortion.

❧ A woman may have a "right of privacy," but the killing of an innocent life is never a private matter.

Isn't it interesting how everyone wants to get in on the act? When the political fur was flying over animal rights in the recent Aspen, Colorado, referendum regarding a proposed ban on the sale of items made from animal skins, there was an odd sense of *déjà vu*. Almost predictably we had Mark Kirkland, president of the pro-fur lobby, saying, "The mayor's trying to legislate his morality." Kirkland argued that "freedom of choice" would be "legislated away" if the measure passed.[11] One can only wonder how this argument goes down with animal-rights activists, most of whom are pro-choice on the issue of abortion!

Once again, that is where pro-life activists have a leg up on animal-rights activists. Nothing could be more sacred—and thus more worthy of protective legislation—than human life. And at least some pro-choice advocates are honest enough to admit the obvious. Columnist Anna Quindlen, for example, is pro-choice all the way ("Today, on the issue of choice, it is time for us to choose it or lose it"), but she is keenly aware of the limitations to the "imposed morality" argument:

Those people who believe that abortion is murder are morally obligated to oppose it. To say that that is imposing religious beliefs on others is absurd. We have long ago agreed as a society that killing innocent people is the worst of our crimes.

The people who are convinced that abortion is the killing of a human being have no choice but to fight until they win.[12]

As always, it comes back to the question of whether the unborn fetus is human life. If it is not, then pro-lifers are unjustifiably imposing their judgments upon others. However, *if in fact* human life is at risk in an abortion, then society has every right to protect it through appropriate legislation. Indeed, it *must* do so.

Public Versus Private Morality

University of Michigan law professor Carl E. Schneider moves the issue of legislated morality closer to a resolution in observing, "It is hard to say to what extent the law should encourage people in their better impulses. Many of the law's attempts to do so—Prohibition comes to mind—have been moralistic in the narrowest sense and unsuccessful in the broadest sense."[13] Why was Prohibition such a notable failure? Because it attempted to impose a morality which only indirectly affected innocent third parties. If it is true that when you are intoxicated you might possibly kill someone (as in an auto accident), it is also true that you can be intoxicated *without* killing anyone. No one else need *necessarily* be involved.

In abortion, by contrast, there is *always* an innocent party affected. As opposed to intoxication, which is not in each case a direct threat to society, abortion cannot help but be a public offense in the strongest sense of the word. A woman may have a "right of privacy," but the killing of an innocent life is never a private matter. That is why it is fitting and proper to punish someone for the act of abortion, just as we find it altogether proper to punish those who, under the influence of intoxication, end up killing someone else. In the death of innocent human life, the killing always "goes public." At its heart and soul, killing human life is always a matter of morality—*public* morality.

There is another sense in which Professor Schneider's observation about Prohibition moves the argument along. It is altogether true that in the area of *private* morality—when it is *truly private*—the law is rarely the best vehicle for promoting one's personal conduct. Those who wish to drink will tend to do so regardless of any law prohibiting it. The same with those who wish to smoke marijuana or even, to some extent, to ignore the nationally mandated speed limit. In this sense, and in this sense alone, it is correct to say that "you can't legislate morality." If you could, we would all be moral robots. No amount of legislation can force any of us to do the right thing. No degree of harsh punishment can make us "good people."

> ❧ **Who says we can't legislate morality? Legislation itself has *become* our morality! Too often our *only* morality!**

In a particularly insightful article entitled "Justice Without Conscience Is Dead," James T. Burtchaell argues a case for even those laws which seem to fail, but which make an important statement of national conscience:

> The law will always fail if it is unsustained by the common conscience. But that is no reason for repealing the unsuccessful law, because the law has a further purpose: not to transform people, but to declare and disavow publicly what we commonly believe to be unfair or damaging. Laws are part of our public profession of justice. They are what we, as a people, are willing to promise out loud to one another.[14]

Burtchaell concludes with this thought-provoking observation: "You probably cannot tell the moral character of a people by reading their laws. But you can learn something about a people's character by observing what laws they lack."[15] What does it say about the moral character of the American people that they do not prohibit the killing of their own children?

The Role of Law in Fostering Morality

Morality is a response to various calls for us to act according to the highest good—whether those calls come from family upbringing, social traditions, religious instruction, or from the law itself. In the past, public morality was not a matter of "personal choice," but was woven into an intricate tapestry of our collective conscience, by which everyone was held personally accountable. Now that very tapestry is deteriorating at a rapid pace, and being pulled apart strand by strand by a pro-choice generation.

Look how each strand has been pulled away: Family upbringing has been shredded by broken homes; social traditions have been replaced by a value-neutral, "do-your-own-thing" philosophy; and religious instruction has dwindled into virtual oblivion, along with the shrinking influence of the liberal church. What is left but the law? Only the *law*!

At this point there ought to be red flags, bells, and whistles. In the wake of the demise of traditional sources of both public and private morality, the only moral source for a secular society is the *law*. For a pro-choice generation bereft of any transcendent point of reference, there is but one natural conclusion: If it's *legal*, it must be *moral*.

Who says we can't legislate morality? Legislation itself has *become* our morality! Too often our *only* morality!

How many of us, for instance, simply *assume* abortion is moral, particularly in what has become known as the first trimester, because the Supreme Court just happened to permit it during that time? Likewise, how many of us assume something is *wrong* with abortion in what has become known as the third trimester, because that is where the Supreme Court happened to draw the line? Can we say that our own view of abortion has not been colored by what the Court arbitrarily has deemed to be legal or illegal?

Shed the garment of transcendent morality, which causes us to ask what we *ought* to do, and we find ourselves standing morally naked, asking ourselves only what we can *get away with*. What does the *law* allow? As much as the law is shaped by the moral impulses of those who legislate, interpret, and administer it, the law is also the Great Shaper of society's morals.

Law—particularly judicial law—often runs before public opinion. At certain times it has been for the good. In the case of

Brown v. Board of Education, for example, it was the Supreme Court that boldly led the way to racial justice. It encouraged us in our *best* impulses at a time when as a nation we did not have the courage of our inner convictions. But sometimes, as in the case of *Roe v. Wade*, the Supreme Court permits our *worst* impulses to have free play. What could be more disastrous than a pro-choice Court leading a pro-choice generation wherever it wants to go?

In Search of Consensus

Something in me wants to agree with John Leo, who insists that "abortion may be a great evil, but it is folly to try jamming through a law. As Aquinas says, where there is no consensus, there is no law. And there is no consensus now either way."[16] But when law has become the very touchstone of morality, I wonder if we any longer have a choice but to attempt "the folly of jamming through a law."

Aquinas had the luxury of living in a time when a moral superstructure was deeply embedded throughout society, even apart from the law. In his day, under the heavy influence of the church, morality was hardly a matter of individual choice. Even where there was no consensus on a given issue, there was a crucial widespread consensus on the basic assumptions under-lying those issues. There may have been disagreement in detail and nuance, but the general framework was agreed upon. It was a theological framework into which all moral questions ulti-mately could be fit.

It is here that philosopher Alasdair MacIntyre contributes this keen observation:

> The most striking feature of contemporary moral utterance is that so much of it is used to express disagreements; and the most striking feature of the debates in which these disagreements are expressed is their interminable character . . . [T]hey appar-ently can find no terminus. There seems to be no rational way of securing moral agreement in our culture.[17]

MacIntyre is not saying that there is no such thing as capital "T" Truth in matters of morals, but only that we are not playing on the same field when we try to decide the outcome. We can't make any progress in our negotiations because some of us insist on sitting at round tables while others insist on square tables. It's not our *conclusions* that separate us, but our *premises*. We don't disagree about abortion as much as we disagree about the value of individual rights, and what "quality of life" is all about, and whether human life itself is accidental and therefore dispensable, or sacred and therefore inviolable.

In our generation there is no agreed-upon framework. *All* issues are up for grabs. Morality no longer has any broad-based theology upon which to rest its case. We are no longer a "Christian nation," not even a "Judeo-Christian culture." We are a prochoice generation: ad hoc, faddish, trendy, and self-directed. Therefore we are left either to political power struggles—to try "jamming through a law"—or to set our aim for the moral high ground, to claim it back from the secularist mindset, and to call a floundering nation back to its best impulses.

Leading, Not Pushing

Thomas J. Gumbleton is a Roman Catholic bishop in Detroit, Michigan, but carries well-earned liberal credentials as president of Pax Christi U.S.A., the National Catholic Peace Movement. For my money, when all is said and done, Gumbleton has elegantly shown us the way forward:

> As much as I wish that laws against abortion would solve all our problems, I do not believe they would. We need above all to change the hearts and minds of people. This is really the root of the whole problem. To some extent we have put so much effort into getting laws on the books that we have failed to persuade people of the basis for our moral stance.
>
> Changing hearts and minds is always the most difficult task; it is also the most essential. I would like us to spend a lot more time and effort on it. If we did, we might come to more agreement on the profound moral questions involved. Then the development of the legal structure would follow quite quickly.[18]

Unfortunately, changing hearts and minds is not always as simple as blocking a doorway and causing a teenage girl to decide at the last minute not to have an abortion. What is needed in the long run is a reasoned response to pro-choice that captures America's moral imagination. Some greater view of human life that calls people higher. Some appreciation of life in the womb that excites human compassion. Some challenge of conscience that will deny the urge to do that which is beneath our dignity.

Gumbleton's call for a moral revolution is seconded by Harvard Law School professor Mary Ann Glendon, who has scrutinized the Western world's abortion laws in her 1987 book, *Abortion and Divorce in Western Law*. Like Gumbleton, professor Glendon calls for "legal condemnation of abortion (even if it must be accompanied with exemptions from punishment in limited circumstances)" as an "essential first step toward repairing the damage the Supreme Court has done to our social fabric by lending its prestige to the position that abortion is 'private,' that it involves only a woman and her body, and that morality has no place in public discourse about life."[19]

But also like Gumbleton, Glendon recognizes that the larger battle will not be won at the statehouse. In her survey of other countries, Glendon discovered that there are sometimes major discrepancies between a country's laws and its abortion rate. Nor should we confuse the taking of the high moral ground with any particular religious perspective. Glendon notes, for example, that abortion is much more socially disapproved in both Northern Ireland and in the Republic of Ireland—by Protestants and Catholics alike—than in Catholic France or Protestant England.[20]

Comparisons like these put us on notice that a person doesn't have to buy into a particular religious faith—or a formal faith of any kind, for that matter—to be appealed to on the basis of his or her own sense of morality. Those who believe that human life is sacred because we are made in the image of God must also believe that in every human being there is a moral sense to which an appeal for human justice can be made—if made respectfully, calmly, knowledgeably, and with patience.

I find it interesting that both Gumbleton and Glendon isolate on what may be the most important factor of all in winning the hearts and minds of a pro-choice generation: proven concern for the women who are the current targets of America's abortion mania. Glendon, for example, favors systems of rewards and sanctions that "make abortion less attractive and motherhood less risky"—that is, medical care and adequate housing for women who otherwise would feel they have no choice but to have an abortion.[21]

Thomas Gumbleton stretches our horizons even further in lamenting how tragically we have prioritized our social concern:

> One tragic effect of the controversy is the waste of time and effort that ought to be devoted to social programs that would provide alternatives to abortion. We need to change structures that cut health-care and food programs, that force women and children to live in poverty. This is our common ground and our common work. Our groups, and all who value life, need to align our efforts with greater determination in these areas.[22]

For all of us, James Burtchaell makes the critical tie between caring social action and the winning of hearts and minds: "It is only when people's hearts and minds are touched and they undergo moral conversion that they can find the motivation to observe law. And the major force for moral conversion is usually the example and the appeal of a religious community."[23]

Rising to the Challenge

The greatest challenge we face is neither secularism nor the pro-choice philosophy. The greatest challenge we face is our own commitment to the cause of transcendent moral values and the welfare of our fellow human beings. Convincing rhetoric is the easier task; truth is on the side of human life and moral absolutes. The more difficult task is to lead a pro-choice generation to choose the good by what they see in *our own* choices.

Public morality is but an extension of private morality. The question that each of us must answer is: What kind of public morality would there be if everyone else's private morality were exactly like my own? Inquiring minds truly *do* want to know whether we practice in social concern what we preach so eloquently in condemnation.

If pro-life advocates are right to demand that the quality of life in the womb be recognized as of equal value with the quality of life outside of the womb, then pro-choice advocates are right to make the same demand in reverse. Pro-life must extend beyond the womb into every aspect of society. If each individual life is sacred, so is all of life. The only thing worse than single-issue politics is single-issue morality.

In the great battle for hearts and minds, a wistful pro-choice generation is watching. Have we given them reason to choose life? Have we given them reason to put the God of Creation before individual choice? Or indeed have we given them every reason to follow along blindly in the footsteps of another generation of whom it was said: "In those days Israel had no king; everyone did as he saw fit."[24]

There may be a place for banners and bumper stickers. There may be times when doors should be blocked. And surely there must come a time when *Roe v. Wade* is overturned, for abortion is the ultimate miscarriage of justice. But the victory will be achieved only when, as a chorus of one people joined together in pained conscience, America cries out in anguish at our greatest national sin. When that day comes, there will be no more need of laws, and the lion will lie down with the lamb. Not until then will we be at peace. Not until then will the battle over abortion have ended.

EPILOGUE

The eyes of God see all. Listen to me, Judah. There is absolutely nothing that escapes His sight.
—Sol
in *Crimes and Misdemeanors*

WHATEVER THE BATTLE, WHATEVER THE WAR, it is all too easy to lose sight of the individual casualties of the conflict. One by one—each with a face, each with a name—they lie wounded and in pain along every ridge and road. The pro-choice generation—so often scarred by self-inflicted wounds—is a generation of individuals in need of healing. From the young man dying of AIDS, to the children ignored by parents too busy divorcing each other to even notice, to the woman consumed with guilt for having killed the developing life within her own womb—we are a people with distorted vision, broken hearts, and confused minds in search of wholeness and restoration.

For more and more Americans, the battle over pro-choice thinking is not a distant philosophical skirmish but a personal inward struggle of the soul. And for one and a half million of America's children each year, pro-choice is not a battle of definitions or statistics but a cruel, violent sentence of death before they even draw their first breath.

Pro-choice is the Great Deceiver. It doesn't bring fulfillment, or happiness, or life. It bring only emptiness, pain, and death. How can we any longer ignore that pain? How can we any longer tolerate that death? How can we any longer choose *not* to decide?

It's no good taking comfort in the thought that *we* would not agree to an abortion when we are prepared nevertheless to let *others* choose to the contrary. Innocent human life isn't spared just because we refuse to be the executioner. Pro-life in heart and pro-choice in mind, is a convenient contradiction in which we have too long indulged. In what other circumstance would we dare refuse to come to the rescue of the defenseless?

If we are staunchly pro-life in our hearts, we must also be staunchly pro-life in our minds. If abortion is not right for *us*, for all the same reasons it is not right for *anyone*. It is not a matter of imposing our personal moral preferences upon others, but of calling them to a transcendent morality to which all of us have been called.

With life itself at stake, we must join together in calling for a national "consciousness raising"—not to a new understanding of parochial concerns giving rise to petty power struggles, acrid single-issue politics, and orchestrated causes in the promotion of selfish individualism, but to a new awareness of our own humanity. To a new awareness of the dynamics of pregnancy and to the inviolable value of human life. To perceive the unseen. To realize that what is being aborted is not simply nondescript fetal tissue, but active, developing human life in being. To appreciate our human nature. To understand that we are not simply evolutionary creatures, born of chance and destined to darkness at death, but created in the image of God and destined for glory!

Beyond simply "consciousness raising" we need a new national spirit dedicated to *"conscience-ness* raising"—a moral reawakening which calls us to accountability for freedom of choice. Which leads us to higher moral ground. Which demands that humanitarian concerns for the planet begin where the word *humanitarian* itself begins—with *human* life, both within the womb and without.

As suggested in this book, although abortion undoubtedly is the toughest battle of all, our cultural war is bigger than the issue of abortion alone. We are engaged in a great conflict over our most basic assumptions about life and about the source of our moral values. The war is between Self and Others—particularly the Great Other. It is a question of who will be God. Will individual *choice* become our God, or will the God of Creation be our God?

No longer do you and I have the luxury of avoiding the conflict. Our culture is being ravaged by a secularist philosophy of choice that threatens to destroy, not only babies in the womb, but our dignity as human beings. Without overstating the case in the least, moral choice is at risk. The very survival of our nation is at stake. And, with each passing minute—this *very* minute—another precious human life is in the balance.

For each of us, the moment has come. It's time to decide.

In Germany they came first for the Communists, and I didn't speak up because I wasn't a Communist. Then they came for the Jews, and I didn't speak up because I wasn't a Jew. Then they came for the trade unionists, and I didn't speak up because I wasn't a trade unionist. Then they came for the Catholics, and I didn't speak up because I was a Protestant. Then they came for me, and by that time no one was left to speak up.

—Martin Niemoller

Make Your Reading Count!

———————

After reading this book, you may want to pass it along to your representatives in Congress, or to other state and local political candidates. The issues confronting our pro-choice generation in the decade of the 90's are among the most important to ever face our nation. We believe that *When Choice Becomes God* presents the one message which America's policymakers most need to hear concerning these issues.

If you agree, why not share your personal copy with your elected officials? Along with the book, you may wish to enclose a brief personal note to express your concern regarding the direction we have chosen to take in a pro-choice generation. If elected officials sometimes seem distant and remote, rest assured that they listen carefully to both the ballot box and the mailbox.

———————

Notes

CHAPTER 1 — *CHOOSING THE UNTHINKABLE*
All quotations from Woody Allen, *Crimes and Misdemeanors* (Orion Pictures Corporation, 1989). Used by permission.

CHAPTER 2 — *THE BIRTH OF A PRO-CHOICE GENERATION*
1. Virginia Matthews, "Viewers Shun Satellite TV," in London *Daily Telegraph*, April 6, 1990.
2. Francis A. Schaeffer, *The Great Evangelical Disaster* (Westchester, IL: Crossway Books 1984) pp. 43ff.
3. Allan Bloom, *The Closing of the American Mind* (New York: Simon and Schuster 1987), p 30
4. Ibid., p. 56.
5. Robert N. Bellah, Richard Madsen, William M. Sullivan, Ann Swidler, and Steven M. Tipton *Habits of the Heart* (New York: Harper & Row, 1985), p. 65.
6. Ibid., p. 99.
7. Ibid., p. 101.
8. Ibid., pp. 122, 128.
9. Ibid., p. 129.
10. Bloom, *Closing*, p. 121.
11. Bellah, *Habits*, p. 130.
12. Ibid., p. 110.
13. Ibid.
14. Ibid.
15. Bloom, *Closing*, p. 119.
16. Ibid.
17. Ibid., p. 56.
18. Ibid., p. 57.
19. Ibid., p. 58.
20. Ibid., pp. 87-88.
21. Bellah, *Habits*, p. 108.
22. Bloom, *Closing* p. 86.
23. Ibid., p. 173.
24. Bellah, *Habits*, p. 75.
25. Ibid.

CHAPTER 3 — *ANY CHOICE BUT GOD*
1. Richard John Neuhaus, *The Naked Public Square* (Grand Rapids: William B. Eerdmans 2nd Edition, 1986), pp. 97 ff.
2. Ibid.

CHAPTER 4 — *SEPARATING CHURCH AND CHOICE*
1. United Press International, January 6, 1989.
2. *The New York Times*, December 10, 1989, Sec. 12JN, p.2; New Jersey Weekly Desk.
3. 1990 *Newsday*, Inc., Nassau and Suffolk Edition, January 7, 1990.
4. 1990 *New York Times*, Sec. 12NJ, p. 20, New Jersey Weekly Desk.
5. Bob Slosser, *Changing the Way America Thinks* (Dallas: Word Publishing, 1989), p. 192
6. Psalm 127:1.
7. Slosser, *Changing*, p. 45.
8. Barry M. Horstman (staff writer) in *Los Angeles Times*, December 3, 1989.
9. Horstman, *Los Angeles Times*, December 7, 1989.
10. Russell Chandler (religion editor) in *Los Angeles Times*, November 8, 1989.
11. Martin Schram in *Los Angeles Times*, November 24, 1989.
12. Ibid.
13. Arthur A. Lord in *Los Angeles Times*, December 13, 1989.
14. William F. Buckley, Jr., in *Los Angeles Times*, December 3, 1989.
15. *Los Angeles Times*, December 28, 1989, B2.
16. John K. Roth in *Los Angeles Times*, November 30, 1989.
17. Maria Newman (staff writer) in *Los Angeles Times*, December 5, 1989.
18. Dr. Bernard Nathanson, *Aborting America*, (Garden City, NY: Doubleday, 1979).
19. "Abortion Around the World," in *Christianity Today*, February 1990, p. 30.
20. Angela Lambert in the London *Independent*, February 7, 1990.
21. Robert Benne (professor of religion and director of the Center for Church and Society at Roanoke College) in *Los Angeles Times*, December 8, 1989.
22. Ibid.
23. Ibid.
24. Ibid.

CHAPTER 5 — *THROUGH THE EYES OF RADICAL FEMINISTS*
1. Kim C. Flodin, "Why I Don't March," in *Newsweek*, February 12, 1990, p. 8.
2. Gloria Steinem, "A Basic Human Right," in *Ms.*, August 1989, p. 39.
3. Ibid.
4. Andrea Dworkin, *Right Wing Women* (New York: Perigee, 1983).
5. *Harris v. McRae*, 448 U.S. 297 (1980).
6. Catherine A. MacKinnon, *Toward a Feminist Theory of the State* (Cambridge, MA: Harvard University Press, 1989), p. 184.
7. Ibid., p. 185.
8. Adrienne Rich, *Of Woman Born: Motherhood As Experience and Institution* (New York: Norton, 1976).
9. MacKinnon, *Feminist*, p. 150.
10. Ibid., p. 146.
11. *The New Our Bodies, Ourselves*, (London: Penguin Books, Second British edition, 1989).
12. Rhonda Copelon and Kathryn Kolbert, "Imperfect Justice," in *Ms.*, August 1989, p. 42.
13. MacKinnon, *Feminist*, p. 130.
14. Ibid., p. 140.
15. Thomas Paine, *The Rights of Man, Part I* (1791).
16. MacKinnon, *Feminist*, p. 186.
17. John Leo, "The Moral Complexity of Choice," in *U.S. News & World Report*, December 11, 1989, p. 64.
18. Ibid.

CHAPTER 6 — *WHALES, FURS AND HUMAN LIFE*
1. Public information piece distributed in Britain by Greenpeace Ltd., 31 Bridge Street, London EC4V 6DA, 1990.
2. "Atlanta Gets Tough," in *Christianity Today*, November 4, 1988, p. 35.
3. *The Reuter Library Report*, January 18, 1990.
4. Greenpeace.
5. *The New Our Bodies, Ourselves*, p. 333.
6. Shirley L. Radl, *Over Our Live Bodies* (Dallas: Steve Davis Publishing, 1989), p. 94.
7. Richard Winter, *Choose Life* (Basingstoke, England: Marshall Pickering, 1988), p. 36.
8. Shirley Radl, pp. 13 ff.
9. Genesis 1:24-30.
10. Deuteronomy 25:4.
11. Exodus 23:19.
12. Woody Allen, *Crimes and Misdemeanors*, 1989.
13. Ibid.
14. Ibid.
15. Carl Sagan and Ann Druyan, "Is It Possible to Be Pro-Life and Pro-Choice?" in *Parade*, Sunday, April 22, 1990, p. 4.
16. Ibid.

CHAPTER 7 — *CREATION, EVOLUTION AND THE RIGHT TO CHOOSE*
1. Stephen Jay Gould, *Wonderful Life* (Hutchinson Radius, 1989).
2. Thomas Paine, *The Age of Reason, Part First*.
3. Ibid.
4. Michael Hudson, in *Los Angeles Times*, November 8, 1989.
5. Paine, *Reason*.
6. Ibid.
7. Anselm Atkins, "Human Rights Are Cultural Artifacts," in *The Humanist*, March/April 1990 pp. 15 ff.
8. Ibid.
9. Ibid.
10. Paine, *Rights*.
11. Helena Curtis and N. Sue Barnes, *Biology* (New York: Worth Publishing, 1989), p. 951
12. Ibid.
13. Thomas Paine, *Common Sense*.
14. Paine, *Rights*.

CHAPTER 8 — *IF WOMBS HAD WINDOWS*
1. *Roe v. Wade*, 410 U.S. 113 (1973).
2. Jerome Lejeune in testimony to U.S. Congress, Senate Committee on the Judiciary *The Human Life Bill*, S-158, Ninety-Seventh Congress, First Session, 1983, Vol. 1, p. 8.
3. Sagan and Druyan, "Possible," p. 5.
4. Ibid.
5. Jo McGowan, "In India, They Abort Females," in *Newsweek*, February 13, 1989.
6. Ibid.
7. Mike Graham, "'Frankenstein' Debate Rages Round U.S. Baby," in the London *Sunday Times*, April 1, 1990.

8. William Sloane Coffin, "Life, Yes; But Is It Yet Human Life?", in *Los Angeles Times*, December 9, 1989.
9. Jocelyn Y. Stewart (staff writer) in *Los Angeles Times*, December 27, 1989, p. B1.
10. Gloria Steinem, "A Basic Human Right," in *Ms.*, August 1989, p. 40.
11. Stan Grossfield, "A Children's Hell," in *The Boston Globe*, December 24, 1989.
12. John F. Ankerberg, *The American Holocaust: Abortion in the 90's* (Chattanooga, Tennessee, Ankerberg Theological Research Institute, 1990).
13. Richard John Neuhaus, *The Naked Public Square* (Grand Rapids: William B. Eerdmans, 2nd Ed., 1986), p. 34.
14. Coffin, "Life, Yes."
15. Dr. Denis Cavanagh, inaugural address as professor of obstetrics and gynecology, University of Tasmania, 1972.
16. Harold Smith, "A Legacy of Life," in *Christianity Today*, January 18, 1985, p. 18.
17. Lennart Nilsson, "Drama of Life Before Birth," in *Life*, April 30, 1965.
18. Ibid.
19. Ibid.
20. Ibid.
21. Ibid.
22. Ibid.
23. Ibid.
24. Psalm 139:13-16.

CHAPTER 9 — *PHANTOM CHOICES*
1. UPI, June 25, 1981; *The Philadelphia Inquirer* as reported by David Cannon, "Abortion and Infanticide: Is There a Difference?" (The Heritage Foundation, *Policy Review*, Spring 1985), No. 32, pp. 12 ff.
2. Sagan, "Is It Possible?", p. 8.
3. Ibid.
4. Copelon, "Imperfect," p. 43.
5. Daphne Watkins, *The Practitioner*, Vol. 233, July 8, 1989, p. 990.
6. Ibid., p. 992.
7. Ibid. p. 990.
8. Robert Whymant, "Shrine of the Unborn Child," in the London *Sunday Times*, November 1982.
9. Leo, "Moral Complexity," p. 64.
10. Ibid.
11. Ibid.
12. Ibid.
13. Ibid.
14. Copelon, "Imperfect" p. 44.

CHAPTER 10 — *DEFECTIVE BABIES, DEFECTIVE CHOICES*
1. *The New Our Bodies, Ourselves*, p. 24.
2. Ibid, p. 25.
3. Ibid., p. 25.
4. Ibid., p. 24.
5. Ibid., p. 24.
6. Aileen Ballantyne (medical correspondent) in the London *Sunday Times*, February 4, 1990.
7. Ibid.
8. Susan Kitching in the London *Sunday Times*, February 11, 1990.
9. Siobhan Bowe in the London *Sunday Times*, February 11, 1990.
10. Ellen Goodman, "Designer Babies," in *The Boston Globe*, January 4, 1990, City Edition, Op-Ed p. 19.
11. G. Williams, "Eugenic Abortion and Attitudes to Disability," in SPUC Handicap Division Newsletter, 1989, p.18.
12. *The New Our Bodies, Ourselves*, p. 320.
13. Ibid., p. 319.
14. Ibid., p. 320.
15. Adapted from Charles E. Rice, *The Vanishing Right to Life* (Garden City, NY: Doubleday, 1969).
16. Philip Howard in the London, *Times*, January 20, 1988.

CHAPTER 11 — *CHOICE ON A SLIPPERY SLOPE*
1. Harold Smith, "A Legacy of Life," in *Christianity Today*, January 18, 1985, pp. 18 ff.
2. David Cannon (attorney adviser to Chairman of Federal Trade Commission), "Abortion and Infanticide: Is There a Difference?" in *Policy Review*, Spring 1985, No.32 (The Heritage Foundation), pp. 12ff.
3. Ibid.
4. Ibid.
5. Ibid.

6. Ibid.
7. Ibid.
8. Bernard N. Nathanson, *Aborting America* (Garden City, NY: Doubleday and Co., 1979), p. 183, (Life Cycle Books edition).
9. Ibid.
10. Ibid., p. 182.
11. Department of Health and Social Services, "Prevention and Health: Everybody's Business," HMSO, 1976 (italics added).
12. Leviticus 20:3.
13. Leviticus 20:4,5.
14. Pearl S. Buck, Foreword to *The Terrible Choice: The Abortion Dilemma* (New York: Bantam Books, 1968).
15. "Is Every Life Worth Living?", in *Christianity Today*, March 19, 1982.
16. Denis Homer in the London *Daily Telegraph*, February 14, 1990.
17. Smith, "Legacy."
18. John 9:3.

CHAPTER 12 — HARD CASES AND EASY OUTS
1. Terri West, "Abortion in the United States," paper for Law and Religion Seminar, Seaver College, Pepperdine University, London Program, Spring 1989.
2. Kim C. Flodin, "Why I Don't March," in *Newsweek*, February 12, 1990, p. 8.
3. Ibid.
4. Ibid.
5. Ibid.
6. Gloria Steinem, "A Basic Human Right," in *Ms.*, August 1989, p. 39.

CHAPTER 13 — THE HYPOCRISY OF CHOICE
1. Ad by Planned Parenthood Federation of America in *Newsweek*, December 11, 1989, p. 97.
2. "Celebrating Seventy Years of Service," in 1986 Annual Report of Planned Parenthood Federation of America, pp. 23,32.
3. Curt Young, *The Least of These* (Chicago: Moody Press, 1984), p. 30.
4. LeBeth Myers, *Women Around the Globe: International Status Report* (London: Guyon Social Resource Center, 1986), p. 137.
5. George Grant, *Grand Illusions: The Legacy of Planned Parenthood* (Brentwood, TN: Wolgemuth & Hyatt).
6. Remarks made at the Planned Parenthood-sponsored "Horizons in Reproductive Health Conference," Coronado, California, 1985. See Paul L. Bail's analysis in "Planned Parenthood Speakers Support Red Chinese Forced Abortion," in American Life Lobby *Issues*, June 1985.
7. See Stephen Mosher's *Broken Earth* (New York: Free Press, 1985. Also see Michael Weisskopf's Washington Post article titled "Abortion Policy Tears at China's Society" (January 7, 1985).
8. Paul B. Fowler, *Abortion—Toward an Evangelical Consensus* (Portland, OR: Multnomah Press, 1987), p. 170.
9. Alan F. Guttmacher, "Abortion—Yesterday, Today and Tomorrow," in *The Case for Legalized Abortion Now* (Berkeley, CA: Diablo Press, 1967).
10. Marian Faux, *Roe v. Wade* (New York: Macmillan Publishing, 1988), p. 26.
11. Ibid.
12. Ibid.
13. Margaret Sanger, *The Pivot of Civilization*: (New York: Brentano's Inc., 1922), p. 108.
14. Ibid., p. 115.
15. Margaret Sanger, "Birth Control," in *The Birth Control Review*, May 1919.
16. Sanger, *Pivot*, p. 96.
17. Ibid., pp. 116-17.
18. Faux, *Roe v. Wade*, pp. 69-70.
19. Ibid., p. 33.
20. Ibid., p. 104.
21. Ibid.
22. Ibid.
23. "Prochoice or No Choice?" in *Christianity Today*, November 4, 1988.
24. John T. Noonan, Jr., *A Private Choice: Abortion in America in the Seventies* (New York: Free Press, 1979), pp. 36 ff.
25. Faux, *Roe v. Wade*, p. 110-11.
26. Ibid., p. 121.
27. Ibid., p. 197-98.
28. Ibid., p. 217.
29. Sarah Mills, "Abortion Under Siege," in *Ms.*, August 1989, p.50.
30. Faux, *Roe v. Wade*, p. 87.
31. Ibid.
32. Ibid., pp. 106, 180.

33. Ibid., p. 88.
34. Nathanson, *Aborting*, p. 193.
35. Ibid.
36. Ibid.
37. Ann Japenga and Elizabeth Venant, "Underground Army," in *Los Angeles Times*, November 30, 1989.
38. Ibid.
39. Ibid.
40. Ibid. (emphasis added).
41. Ibid.
42. Ibid.
43. Steinem, "Basic," p. 41.

CHAPTER 14 — *SACRIFICING LIFE FOR LIFESTYLE*
1. Anton LaGuardia (foreign staff, in the London *Daily Telegraph*, February 15, 1990.
2. Ibid.
3. Slosser, *Changing*, p. 109.
4. Mary Anne Fitzgerald in the London *Sunday Times*, March 11, 1990.
5. Brian Moynahan, "Domain of the Dispossessed," in the London *Sunday Times Magazine*, February 18, 1990, p. 22.
6. Ibid.
7. Malcolm Muggeridge, "Life is Sacred," in *Human Concern*, No. 11, 1982, pp. 5-6.
8. Ibid.
9. Ibid.
10. Luke 12:15.
11. Mother Teresa, press conference, Dublin, Ireland, 1982.
12. Ibid.
13. Ibid.
14. George Skelton, "Bishop Called Out of Line in Killea Pro-Choice Case" (*Times* Poll), in *Los Angeles Times*, December 9, 1989.
15. Mother Teresa, press conference.
16. Marlene Cimons, (staff writer), "House Panel Accuses Koop of Ignoring Medical Evidence on Safety of Abortion," in *Los Angeles Times*, December 11, 1989.

CHAPTER 15 — *DECIDING WHO DECIDES*
1. Diane Haithman, "TV Taboos, Program Standards Change With Values," in *Los Angeles Times*, December 27, 1989.
2. Victor F. Zonana, "Gay Agenda Takes Beating—Even in San Francisco," in *Los Angeles Times*, November 9, 1989.
3. Carl Sagan and Ann Druyan, "Is It Possible To Be Pro-Life and Pro-Choice?" in *Parade Magazine*, April 22, 1989.
4. Ibid.
5. Ibid.
6. Neil Postman, "Learning by Story," in *The Atlantic*, December 1989, pp. 119 ff.
7. George F. Will, "U.S. Campuses Are Putting Sensitivity Police on Patrol," in *Los Angeles Times*, November 5, 1989.
8. Ibid.
9. Ibid.
10. John Leo, "The Moral Complexity of Choice," in *U.S. News & World Report*, December 11, 1989, p. 64.
11. Ibid.
12. Allan Bloom, *Closing*, p. 30.
13. Paine, *Rights*.

CHAPTER 16 — *THE WAY FORWARD*
1. *Roe v. Wade*, 410 U.S. 113 (1973).
2. *Roe v. Wade*, 410 U.S. at 153, 164-65.
3. See *West Coast Hotel Co. v. Parrish* (1937), 300 U.S. 379, and *Day-Brite Lighting, Inc. v. Missouri* (1952), 342 U.S.421.
4. Rita Rubin, "'Abortion Pill' Developer Claims Spotlight," in *Dallas Morning News*, October 4, 1989.
5. Robert H. Bork, *The Tempting of America* (New York: The Free Press, 1990), p.246.
6. Ibid., p. 249.
7. Ibid., p. 124.
8. Ibid., p. 122.
9. *Bowers v. Hardwick* (1986), 478 U.S. 186.
10. Cal Thomas, "Journalism Conspiracy?" in *Los Angeles Times Syndicate*, 1989.
11. Ron Harris, "The Fur Is Flying in Trend-Setting Aspen," in *Los Angeles Times*, December 25, 1989.

12. Anna Quindlen, "There's No Middle Ground to Abortion Rights Issue," in *The Register-Guard*, February 4, 1990.
13. Carl E. Schneider, "Rights Discourse and Neonatal Euthanasia," *California Law Review*, Vol. 76, January 1988, p.151.
14. James T. Burtchaell, "Justice Without Conscience Is Dead," *Christianity Today*, June 12, 1987, p. 26.
15. Ibid.
16. John Leo, "The Catholic Politics of Abortion," *U. S. News & World Report*, February, 19, 1990, p. 14.
17. Alasdair MacIntyre, *After Virtue* (Notre Dame, IN: University of Notre Dame Press, 2nd Ed., 1984), p. 6.
18. Thomas J. Gumbleton, "If All Life Is Sacred, So Is Each Life," in *Los Angeles Times*, December, 9, 1989.
19. Randy Frame, "Will Our Planet Be Prolife?" in *Christianity Today*, February 19, 1990, p. 32.
20. Ibid.
21. Ibid.
22. Gumbleton, "Life."
23. Burtchaell, "Justice," p. 26.
24. Judges 21:25.